4th International Workshop on Computational Terminology

(COMPUTERM 2014)

Held at COLING 2014

Dublin, Ireland
23 August 2014

ISBN: 978-1-63439-218-1

Printed from e-media with permission by:

Curran Associates, Inc.
57 Morehouse Lane
Red Hook, NY 12571

Some format issues inherent in the e-media version may also appear in this print version.

Printed by Curran Associates, Inc. (2014)

For permission requests, please contact the Association for Computational Linguistics at the address below.

Association for Computational Linguistics
209 N. Eighth Street
Stroudsburg, Pennsylvania 18360

Phone: 1-570-476-8006
Fax: 1-570-476-0860

acl@aclweb.org

Additional copies of this publication are available from:

Curran Associates, Inc.
57 Morehouse Lane
Red Hook, NY 12571 USA
Phone: 845-758-0400
Fax: 845-758-2634
Email: curran@proceedings.com
Web: www.proceedings.com

Introduction

Computational Terminology covers an increasingly important aspect in Natural Language Processing areas such as text mining, information retrieval, information extraction, summarisation, textual entailment, document management systems, question-answering systems, ontology building, etc. Terminological information is paramount for knowledge mining from texts for scientific discovery and competitive intelligence. Scientific needs in fast growing domains (such as biomedicine, chemistry and ecology) and the overwhelming amount of textual data published daily demand that terminology is acquired and managed systematically and automatically; while in well established domains (such as law, economy, banking and music) the demand is on fine-grained analyses of documents for knowledge description and acquisition. Moreover, capturing new concepts leads to the acquisition and management of new knowledge.

The aim of this fourth CompuTerm workshop is to bring together Natural Language Processing researchers to discuss recent advances in computational terminology and its impact in many NLP applications. The topics addressed in this workshop are wide ranging:

- term extraction, recognition and filtering, which is the core of the terminological activity that lays basis for other terminological topics and tasks;
- event recognition and extraction, that extends the notion of the terminological entity from terms meaning static units up to terms meaning procedural and dynamic processes;
- acquisition of semantic relations among terms, which is also an important research topic as the acquisition of semantic relationships between terms finds applications such as the population and update of existing knowledge bases, definition of domain specific templates in information extraction and disambiguation of terms;
- term variation management, that helps to deal with the dynamic nature of terms, their acquisition from heterogeneous sources, their integration, standardisation and representation for a large range of applications and resources, is also increasingly important, as one has to address this research problem when working with various controlled vocabularies, thesauri, ontologies and textual data. Term variation is also related to their paraphrases and reformulations, due to historical, regional, local or personal issues. Besides, the discovery of synonym terms or term clusters is equally beneficial to many NLP applications;
- definition acquisition, that covers important research and aims to provide precise and nonambiguous description of terminological entities. Such definitions may contain elements necessary for the formal description of terms and concepts within ontologies;
- consideration of the user expertise, that is becoming a new issue in the terminological activity, takes into account the fact that specialized domains contain notions and terms often nonunderstandable to non-experts or to laymen (such as patients within the medical area, or bank clients within banking and economy areas). This aspect, although related to specialized areas, provides direct link between specialized languages and general language;
- systematic terminology management and updating domain specific dictionaries and thesauri, that are important aspects for maintaining the existing terminological resources. These aspects become crucial because the amount of the existing terminological resources is constantly increasing and because their perennial and efficient use depends on their maintenance and updating, while their re-acquisition is costly and often non-reproducible;

- monolingual and multilingual resources, that open the possibility for developing cross-lingual and multi-lingual applications, requires specific corpora, methods and tools which design and evaluation are challenging issues;
- robustness and portability of methods, which allows to apply methods developed in one given context to other contexts (corpora, domains, languages, etc.) and to share the research expertise among them;
- social netwoks and modern media processing, that attracts an increasing number of researchers and that provides challenging material to be processed;
- utilization of terminologies in various NLP applications, as they are a necessary component of any NLP system dealing with domain-specific literature, is another novel and challenging research direction.

In the call for paper, we encouraged authors to submit their research work related to various aspects of computational terminology, ranging from term extraction in various languages (using verb co-occurrence, information theoretic approaches, machine learning, etc.), translation pairs extracting from bilingual corpora based on terminology, up to semantic oriented approaches and theoretical aspects of terminology. Besides, experiments on the evaluation of terminological methods and tools are also encouraged since they provide interesting and useful proof about the utility of terminological resources:

- direct evaluation may concern the efficiency of the terminological methods and tools to capture the terminological entities and relations, as well as various kinds of related information;
- indirect evaluation may concern the use of terminological resources in various NLP applications and the impact these resources have on the performance of the automatic systems. In this case, research and competition tracks (such as TREC, BioCreative, CLEF, CLEF-eHealth, I2B2, *SEM, and other shared tasks), provide particularly fruitful evaluation contexts and proved very successful in identifying key problems in terminology such as term variation and ambiguity.

The Computerm 2014 workshop received 14 submissions from 10 countries and 3 continents addressing issues on 12 languages. Further to a double-blind peer-review process, 6 papers were accepted for oral presentations and 7 as posters. The acceptance rate for oral presentations is 40% and the overall acceptance rate is 86.66%. We believe this workshop will be a nice place for fruitful research discussions, and the emergence of new research topics and collaborations. The objective of the combined oral and poster presentations is to strengthen this point.

Acknowledgments

First of all, we would like to thank the members of the program committee for the quality of their reviews. We are particularly grateful to Noemie Elhadad for accepting to give an invited talk. We are grateful to the COLING organizers, in particular Jennifer Foster, John Judge and Joachim Wagner for their help in the workshop organisation. And last but not the least, we would like to thank all the authors for the quality of their submission and their hard work. We also thank the participants to the Computerm 2014 workshop. Without all of them, this 4th workshop on Computational Terminology would not take place.

Workshop Organization

Organizers:

Patrick Drouin, Observatoire de linguistique Sens-Texte, Université de Montréal, Montréal, Canada
Natalia Grabar, CNRS UMR 8163 STL, Université Lille 1&3, Villeneuve d'Ascq, France
Thierry Hamon, LIMSI-CNRS, Orsay, France & Université Paris 13, Sorbonne Paris Cité, Villetaneuse, France
Kyo Kageura, Library and Information Science Laboratory, University of Tokyo, Tokyo, Japan

Program Committee:

Sophia Ananiadou, University of Manchester, National Centre for Text Mining, UK
Olivier Bodenreider, NLM, USA
Beatrice Daille, IRIN, France
Éric Gaussier, LIG, Université Joseph Fourier, France
Gregory Grefenstette, Clairvoyance Corp, France
Marie-Claude L'Homme, University of Montréal, Canada
Philippe Langlais, RALI, Canada
John McNaught, UMIST & National Centre for Text Mining, UK
Rogelio Nazar, Pontificia Universidad Católica de Valparaíso, Chile
Goran Nenadic, University of Manchester, UK
Jorge Vivaldi Palatresi, University Pompeu Fabra, Spain
Selja Seppälä, University at Buffalo, USA
Karin Verspoor, University of Melbourne, Australia
Pierre Zweigenbaum, LIMSI, France

Invited Speaker:

Noemie Elhadad, Department of Biomedical Informatics, Columbia University, USA

Table of Contents

Workshop Program

Saturday August 23, 2014

(8:45) Opening Remarks

(9:00) Session 1

9:00 *Generalising and Normalising Distributional Contexts to Reduce Data Sparsity: Application to Medical Corpora*
Amandine Périnet and Thierry Hamon

9:30 *Assigning Terms to Domains by Document Classification*
Robert Gaizauskas, Emma Barker, Monica Lestari Paramita and Ahmet Aker

10:00 *Identification of Bilingual Terms from Monolingual Documents for Statistical Machine Translation*
Mihael Arcan, Claudio Giuliano, Marco Turchi and Paul Buitelaar

10:30 by Coffee Break

(11:00) Invited Speaker: Noemie Elhadad

11:00 *Terminology Questions in Texts Authored by Patients*
Noémie Elhadad

12:30 by Lunch Break

(14:00) Session 2

14:00 *NPMI Driven Recognition of Nested Terms*
Malgorzata Marciniak and Agnieszka Mykowiecka

14:30 *Bilingual Termbank Creation via Log-Likelihood Comparison and Phrase-Based Statistical Machine Translation*
Rejwanul Haque, Sergio Penkale and Andy Way

15:00 *The ACL RD-TEC: A Dataset for Benchmarking Terminology Extraction and Classification in Computational Linguistics*
Behrang Q. Zadeh and Siegfried Handschuh

15:30 by Coffee Break

Saturday August 23, 2014 (continued)

(16:00) Poster Session

(17:00) Closing Session

Generalising and normalising distributional contexts to reduce data sparsity: application to medical corpora

Amandine Périnet
Université Paris 13, Sorbonne Paris Cité
Villetaneuse, France
amandine.perinet@edu.univ-paris13.fr

Thierry Hamon
LIMSI-CNRS, Orsay, France
Université Paris 13, Sorbonne Paris Cité
Villetaneuse, France
hamon@limsi.fr

Abstract

Vector space models implement the distributional hypothesis. They are based on the repetition of information occurring in the contexts of words to associate. However, these models suffer from a high number of dimensions and data sparsity in the matrix of contextual vectors. This is a major issue with specialised corpora that are of much smaller size and with much lower context frequencies. We tackle the problem of data sparsity on specialised texts and we propose a method that allows to make the matrix denser, by generalising and normalising distributional contexts. Generalisation gives better results with the Jaccard index, narrow sliding windows and relations of lexical inclusion. On the other hand, normalisation has no positive effect on the relation extraction, with any combination of distributional parameters.

1 Introduction

Distributional Analysis (DA) assumes that words occurring in a similar context tend to be semantically close (Harris, 1954; Firth, 1957). This hypothesis is usually applied through vector space models (VSM) where vectors represent the contextual information and distributional statistical data (Sahlgren, 2006). Each target word in a text is represented as a point defined according to its distributional properties in the text (Turney and Pantel, 2010; Lund and Burgess, 1996). Thus, the semantic similarity between two words is defined as a closeness in an n-dimension space, where each dimension corresponds to some potential shared contexts. The VSMs easily quantify the semantic similarity between two words by measuring the distance between the two corresponding vectors within this space, or the cosine of their angle. On the other hand, besides the high number of dimensions required (for example, Sahlgren (2006) uses VSMs with up to several millions of dimensions), VSMs also suffer from data sparseness within the matrix representing the vector space (Chatterjee and Mohan, 2008): many elements are equal to zero because only few contexts are associated to a target word. This disadvantage is partly due to word distribution in corpora: whatever the corpus size, most words have low frequencies and a very limited set of contexts compared to the number of words in the corpora. These last two elements make the similarity between two words hard to compute. Hence, methods based on the distributional hypothesis show better results when much information is available and especially with general corpora, usually of great size (Weeds and Weir, 2005; van der Plas, 2008). But the reduction of data sparseness is still an important aspect with general corpora. It is as well a major issue when working with specialised corpora. Indeed, these corpora are characterised by smaller sizes, and with frequencies and a number of different contexts especially lower. We focus here on this last point. We propose a rule-based method that aims at reducing context diversity by generalising contexts. The frequency of the obtained distributional contexts is then increased and, consequently, data sparseness and the dimensions of the vector space model are reduced. We present here a generalisation of the distributional contexts thanks to semantic relations acquired on corpora. The parameters of the distributional method are tuned to specialised corpora, especially in integrating those generalised contexts.

We first present a state of the art on data sparsity reduction within distributional methods. Then we describe the proposed context generalisation and normalisation method as well as the experiments

Proceedings of the 4th International Workshop on Computational Terminology, pages 1–10,
Dublin, Ireland, August 23 2014.

we performed to evaluate its impact on specialised corpora. Results are evaluated and analysed with precision, R-precision and MAP.

2 Related work

Reducing data sparsity is a main issue in distributional analysis. The existing methods aim at influencing the selection of useful contexts or at integrating semantic information to modify context distribution. Thus, contrary to the common usage, Broda et al. (2009) propose to weight contexts by first ranking contexts according to their frequency, and then take the rank into account to weight contexts. Other approaches rely on statistical language models to determine the most likely substitutes to represent contexts (Baskaya et al., 2013). These models assign probabilities to arbitrary sequences of words based on their co-occurrence frequencies in a training corpora (Yuret, 2012). These substitutes and their probabilities are then used to create word pairs to feed a co-occurrence model and to cluster the word list. The limit of such methods is their performance which depends on vocabulary size and requires an increasing amount of training data. Influence on contexts may also be done by incorporating additional semantic information: it has been shown that such information used to modify the standard distributional method can improve its performance (Tsatsaronis and Panagiotopoulou, 2009). This semantic information, in particular semantic relations, may be automatically computed or issued from an existing resource. Thus, with a bootstrap method, Zhitomirsky-Geffet and Dagan (2009) modify the context weights with the semantic neighbours proposed by a distributional similarity measure. Based on this latter work, Ferret (2013) addresses the problem of low frequency words. To better consider this information, a set of positive and negative examples are selected with an unsupervised classifier. A supervised classifier is then applied for re-ranking the semantic neighbours. The method allows to improve the quality of the similarity relation between nouns with low or mid frequency.

The sparseness problem may also be tackled from the algorithmic point of view by limiting the dimensions of the context matrix, especially by smoothing it in order to reduce the number of vector compounds (Turney and Pantel, 2010). Thus, Latent Semantic Analysis (LSA) (Landauer and Dumais, 1997; Padó and Lapata, 2007) implements a factorization method of matrices by Singular Value Decomposition (SVD). The original data in the context matrix is abstracted in independant linear components, that allow to reduce noise and to highlight the main elements. Besides reducing the computational cost, dimension reduction significantly improves precision in LSA applications. For instance, the use of the SVD to compute word similarity allows to obtain scores equivalent to human scores in a TOEFL test with multiple choice questions of synonymy (Landauer and Dumais, 1997). As for low frequency, the SVD is a way to counterbalance the lack of data (Vozalis and Margaritis, 2003). Also, some methods, as the non-negative matrix factorization (Lee and Seung, 1999), allow to better model word frequency. But, when it comes to the acquisition of semantic relations, performances do not seem better than the ones obtained with the LSA (Turney and Pantel, 2010; Utsumi, 2010). Furthermore, the dimension reduction makes easier to treat context vectors, but it does not solve the initial issue of building a huge co-occurence matrix. Random Indexing (RI) (Kanerva et al., 2000) may be considered as a solution to this problem, as it incrementally builds the context matrix according to an index vector of the target word randomly generated, as well as reducing the matrix dimension. RI and LSA have similar performance when identifying synonyms in a similar way than the TOEFL test (Karlgren and Sahlgren, 2001). Recently, the selection of the best contexts combined with a normalisation of their weights allows to improve the quality of a SVD reduced matrix (Polajnar and Clark, 2014). In the context of definition retrieval and phrase similarity computation, their impact depends on the compositional semantics operators used.

As above work, we aim at incorporating semantic information within distributional contexts, but by reducing the number of contexts and increasing their frequency. Contrary to SVD based methods that limit the contexts by removing information, here we both generalise and normalise contexts through the integration of additional semantic knowledge computed from our corpora.

3 Material

In this section, we present the corpus we use. We also describe the approaches used to acquire the semantic relations integrated in our method for context generalisation/normalisation.

Corpora To evaluate our approach, we use the Menelas corpus (Zweigenbaum, 1994). It consists in a medical text collection, in French, on the topic of coronary diseases. The corpus contains 84,839 words. It has been analysed through the Ogmios platform (Hamon et al., 2007). The linguistic analysis includes a morphosyntactic tagging and a lemmatisation of the corpus, with TreeTagger (Schmid, 1994), and a term extraction with YATEA (Aubin and Hamon, 2006). This last step allows to identify terminological entities (both single word units, for eg. *artery*, and complex terms (i.e. multi-word expressions), for eg. *coronary disease*, that denote the domain concepts).

Semantic relations acquisition Our generalisation and normalisation method of distributional contexts is based on semantic relations acquired from the entire corpus. We use several classical approches that allow to acquire semantic relations between terms. For context generalisation, we use lexico-syntactic patterns, lexical inclusion and terminological variation rules. Context normalisation is based on a rule-based synonymy acquisition.

- **Lexico-syntactic patterns (LSP)** We use the patterns defined by (Morin and Jacquemin, 2004) to detect 98 hypernymy relations between simple or complex terms, for instance: {`some |several etc.`} `SN: LIST` or {`other`}`? SN such as LIST`. The relations acquired with such patterns are usually relevant but the pattern coverage remains low.

- **Lexical Inclusion (LI)** This approach is based on the hypothesis that the lexical inclusion of a term (ex: *infarctus* in another (*infarctus du myocarde (myocardial infarction)* convey a hypernymy relation between those terms (Grabar and Zweigenbaum, 2003). We constrain the method by exploiting the term syntactic analysis provided by YATEA. We obtain 7,187 relations between the complex term and its head. This approach is known to acquire relations with high precision.

- **Terminological variation (TV)** Terminological variant acquisition method proposed by (Jacquemin, 2001) exploits morphosyntactic transformation rules, as the insertion or the permutation, (*chirurgie coronarienne (coronary surgery) / chirurgie de revascularisation coronarienne (Coronary revascularisation surgery)*) to identify semantic relations between terms.
  The terminological variation rules, essentially the insertion on our French corpus, allow to acquire 171 hypernymy relations.

- **Semantic compositionality (Syn)** For context normalisation, we use 168 synonymy relations acquired with the method defined in (Hamon et al., 1998). Based on the semantic compositionality principle, a synonymy relation is inferred between complex terms, if at least one of their component are synonyms (*infection de blessure (wound infection)* and *septicit de blessure (wound sepsis)*).

4 Distributional context generalisation and normalisation

A solution to the problem of data sparsity on specialised corpora or smaller size corpora consists in increasing the density of the context matrix by disregarding superficial variations of contexts that are not strongly statistically significant or that result from the noise of the distributional method. Thus, we generalise (conceptual abstraction) and normalise (abstraction of minor lexical variations) contexts using the semantic information extracted from our corpus. In that respect, we use semantic relations automatically acquired with standard methods on specialised corpora. After a brief description of the distributional analysis we performed on specialised corpora, we present the distributional context generalisation and normalisation.

4.1 Distributional method

We focus on the extraction of relations between nouns, tokens tagged as nouns by TreeTagger, and terms, specific terminological entities extracted during the linguistic analysis of the corpus by YATEA(see section 3). These semantic relations are crucial in specialised language. Nouns and terms are our targets. The distributional contexts of these targets correspond to adjectives, nouns, verbs and terms co-occurring with the target within a sliding window. A context is for us one element (a word or MWE), and it corresponds to one dimension in the vector space. For both targets and contexts, we consider the lemmas.

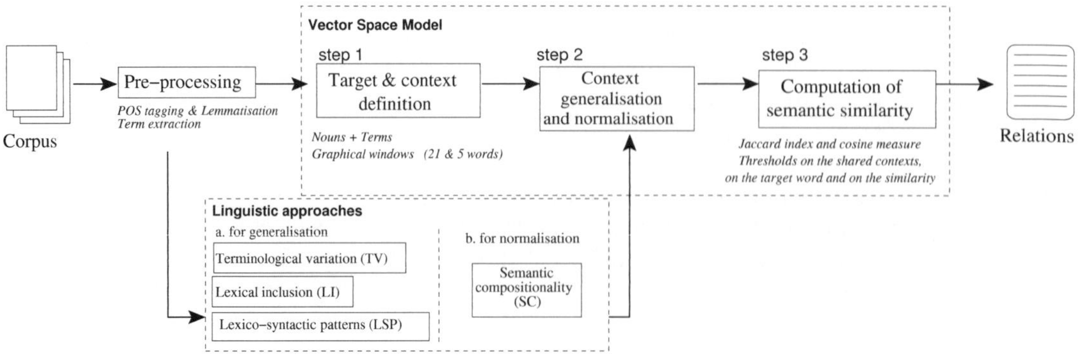

Figure 1: Process of distributional analysis

The overview of the distributional method is given in figure 1. The context generalisation and normalisation step takes place after the distributional context definition (see section 4.2). After extracting, generalising or normalising contexts, we compute a similarity score between each pair of target words, considering their shared contexts. We use the Jaccard index, recognised as suitable to specialised corpora (Grefenstette, 1994). The Jaccard index normalises the number of contexts shared by two words, w_m and w_n, by the total number of contexts of those two words, $ctxt(w)$. We also use the cosine of the context vector. In order to grant more or less importance to the information in contexts, we use these two measures combined with a weight function. With Jaccard, we use the relative frequency, that allows to consider the importance of a target, compared to the total number of contexts for the target. And with cosine we use Mutual Information (MI) (Fano, 1963). While these scores quantify the similarity between target words, it is necessary to apply thresholds to limit the proposed number of distributional relations and discard potentially noisy relations. We also intend to make the context matrix denser by applying thresholds on three distributional parameters: the number of shared contexts, the frequency of shared contexts and the frequency of target words. For each parameter, a threshold is automatically computed as the mean of the values taken by each parameter on the whole corpus. During the experiments (section 5), we test the impact of these thresholds on the results.

4.2 Rules of generalisation and normalisation of distributional contexts

Context generalisation and normalisation comes after the context definition step. It aims at reducing context sparsity and increasing the number of context occurrences. Generalisation and normalisation rules are separately applied and exploit additional semantic relations acquired on the corpus.

Rules of generalisation We generalise contexts with semantic relations automatically acquired from the corpus with hypernymy relations proposed by lexico-syntactic patterns and lexical inclusion (see section 3). While terminological variation approach does not propose semantically typed relations, the insertion rule is the only one used to acquire variants and it can be considered that the obtained relations are hypernymy relations. The hypernym and the hyponym are identified from the number of words present in each term: the shortest term then corresponds to the hypernym (*lésion significative (significant lesion)*), and the longest term is the hyponym (*lésion coronaire significative (significant coronary lesion)*).

We have then for each word $ctxt_i(w)$ in the context of the target word w three sets of hypernymy relations $\mathbb{H}_s(ctxt_i(w)) = \{H_1, \ldots, H_n\}$: $\mathbb{H}_{PLS}$, $\mathbb{H}_{IL}$ and $\mathbb{H}_{VT}$, with a hypernym set that may be empty. We define two substitution rules that allow to generalise contexts. Thus, for each word $ctxt_i(w)$ in the context of a target word w, we apply one of the following rules:

1. if $|\mathbb{H}_S(ctxt_i(w))| = 1$, then $ctxt_i(w) := H_1$, i.e. if the word in context corresponds to only one hypernym (H_1), acquired by one or several methods S, the word is replaced by this hypernym. For example, if lexical inclusion provides the relations *restriction / restriction du débit coronaire (restriction of coronary output), restriction du débit coronaire* is replaced by *restriction*.

2. if $|\mathbb{H}_S(ctxt_i(w))| > 1$, $ctxt_i(w) = \text{argmax}_{|H_i|}(\mathbb{H}_S(ctxt_i(w)))$, i.e. if context corresponds to several hypernyms acquired by one or several methods S, we take into consideration the hypernym frequency $|H_1|, \ldots, |H_n|$ in the corpus, and we select the hypernym with the highest frequency. For example, for the word *artère coronaire (coronary artery)* in context, the lexico-syntactic patterns provide the following hypernyms: *veine (vein), artère (artery)*, and *vaisseau (vessel)*, the one that is the most frequent is chosen and replaces *artère coronaire* in context.

4.2.1 Rules of normalisation

The normalisation rule aims at reducing semantic variation with automatically acquired synonymy relations. These relations are first organised in clusters of synonyms and a cluster representative is chosen: given the relations proposed by the acquisition method (section 3), the cluster representative corresponds to the most frequent word in the cluster. We have then for each target word $ctxt_i(w)$ in the context of the word w, a synonym cluster $\mathbb{S}_s(R) = \{S_1, \ldots, S_n, R\}$, with its representative R. We define one context normalisation rule applied for each word $ctxt_i(w)$ in the context of a word w to substitute the context word by the representative of the cluster it belongs: $if\ \exists R | ctxt_i(w) \in \mathbb{S}_S(R),\ then\ ctxt_i(w) := R$

5 Experiments and evaluation

5.1 Experiments

We performed several series of experiments on the Menelas corpus to evaluate the impact of both generalisation and normalisation rules on the quality of the acquired relations. Our baseline is the VSM without context substitution (VSMonly). First, we automatically compute the thresholds on the distributional parameters from the baseline (see section 4.1). The values of the thresholds are listed in table 1. We experiment two sliding window sizes ; a small window allows to detect classical types of relations (synonymy, meronymy, hypernymy, etc.) but increases the data sparseness problem. On the other hand, a large window provides more general relations, a contextual proximity.

Parameters	21 word window	5 word window
Similarity score	Jaccard: $sim > 0,000999$ Cosine: $sim > 0.9699$	Jaccard: $sim > 0,000999$ Cosine: $sim > 0.9699$
Number of contexts	2	1
Context frequency	3	2
Target frequency	3	3

Table 1: Definition of the threshold values on distributional parameters and on the similarity score according to the window width (21 and 5 words) and similarity measures (Jaccard index and Cosine)

We perform separately the experiments regarding generalisation and normalisation rules. With generalisation rules, in order to grasp the contribution of each linguistic method (see section 3), we define a set of experiments where context generalisation is performed using the hypernymy relations proposed individually by each method. The context generalisation rules $ctxt_i(w)$ are then applied separately using the sets $\mathbb{H}_{LSP}(ctxt_i(w))$ (VSM/LSP), $\mathbb{H}_{LI}(ctxt_i(w))$ (VSM/LI) and $\mathbb{H}_{TV}(ctxt_i(w))$ (VSM/TV). Then, sequentially, we apply generalisation rules by using the sets of hypernymy relations proposed by two linguistic approaches ($\mathbb{H}_{LSP}(ctxt_i(w))$ then $\mathbb{H}_{LI}(ctxt_i(w))$ – VSM/LSP+LI, $\mathbb{H}_{TV}(ctxt_i(w))$

then $\mathbb{H}_{LSP}(ctxt_i(w))$ – VSM/TV+LSP, etc.). All contexts are generalised following the relations proposed by one of the sets.Likewise, we combine the three sets of relations (for instance, $\mathbb{H}_{LSP}(ctxt_i(w))$ then $\mathbb{H}_{LI}(ctxt_i(w))$ then $\mathbb{H}_{TV}(ctxt_i(w))$ – VSM/LSP+LI+TV). By combining the hypernymy relation sources in several ways, we evaluate the complementarity of the approaches used for context generalisation. We also study the impact of the order of these methods in the generalisation sequence. All the hypernymy relations independently of the method used for their acquisition. We consider the set $H(ctxt_i(w)) = \mathbb{H}_{LSP}(ctxt_i(w)) \cup \mathbb{H}_{LI}(ctxt_i(w)) \cup \mathbb{H}_{TV}(ctxt_i(w))$ – VSM/ALL3. With context normalisation, we consider only one set of experiment, with normalisation of contexts (VSM/Syn).

All the experiments have been performed on both window sizes: 5 words ($\pm$ 2 words, centered on the target) and 21 words ($\pm$ 10 words, centered on the target). Indeed the window size influences the number and quality, but also the type of the relations acquired with distributional analysis. In general, a small window size (5 words) allows to have a highest number of relevant contexts for a given target word, but leads to more data sparsity than with a larger window (Rapp, 2003). Furthermore, the results obtained with small size windows are of greatest quality, especially for classical relations (synonymy, antonymy, hypernymy, meronymy, etc.), whereas larger windows are more adapted to the identification of domain specific relations (Sahlgren, 2006; Peirsman et al., 2008).

5.2 Evaluation

As usual to evaluate distributional methods, the obtained relations are considered as semantic neighbour sets associated to target words, and the quality of the neighbour sets is measured by comparing them to semantic relations issued from existing resources (Curran, 2004; Ferret, 2010). Thus, we compare the semantic relations acquired by our approach with the 1,735,419 relations in the French part of the UMLS metathesaurus[1]. The resource contains hypernyms, synonyms, co-hyponyms, meronyms and domain relations.

We used classical measures to evaluate the quality of our results: macro-precision (Sebastiani, 2002), the mean of the average precisions (MAP) (Buckley and Voorhees, 2005) and R-precision.

Macro-precision equally considers all target words whatever the number of semantic neighbours and provides a comprehensive quality of the results by computing the mean of the precision of each neighbour set. We consider one size of neighbour set for each target word: precision after examining 1 (P@1) semantic neighbour, the neighbour ranked first by its similarity score. Alternatively, we use R-precision that individually defines the size of the neighbour sets to examine as the number of correct neighbours expected for the corresponding target word (Buckley and Voorhees, 2005). To compute R-precision, we compare our results not to all the relations from the French part of UMLS, but to reference sets built from this resource, for each experiment. Thus, we have as many references as experiments. The mean of average precisions (MAP) is obtained taking in consideration the not interpolated precision of the semantic neighbours given their rank. It reflects the ranking quality and evaluates the relevance of the similarity measure used. Thus, the MAP favours the similarity measure that ranks all the correct semantic neighbours on top of the list. Reciprocally, adding noisy semantic neighbours at the end of the list does not discriminate against the method.

6 Results and discussion

In this section, we present and discuss the results we obtain, first with the 21 word window and then with the 5 word window. For both sizes, we present the number of relations acquired (*Acq. Rel*), the number of relations found in the UMLS resource (*Rel. UMLS*), and the results in terms of MAP, R-precision and precision to 1 (P@1). Before discussing our results, we briefly present some results of similar work.

Results in existing similar work In order to understand better our results, we first provide some results obtained in similar work. Keep in mind that these results are not obtained with the same corpus. Indeed, a major problem is that the comparisons with reference resources are often given for large copora and very frequent words (Curran and Moens, 2002), or for different tasks than our task. An effective comparison

[1] `http://www.nlm.nih.gov/research/umls/`

is then difficult. We first present results obtained on a similar task, but with general copora, and then results obtained on similar documents (i.e. specialised medical texts) but in a different tasks. Despite this limit, we can still quote for comparison the values obtained by Ferret (2011) for the evaluation of semantic neighbours extraction on English general copora (of 380 million words). The parameters of his VSM are a small sliding window of 3 words ($\pm$ 1 word centered on the target), the cosine measure and mutual information. In his work, Ferret (2011) considers three sets of target words according to their frequency. As in the Menelas corpus, the highest frequency of a target word is 270 and that only a few frequencies are above 100, we may consider the set of low frequency words, that occur less than 100 times. The highest values he obtains for those target words are a MAP of 0.03, a P@1 of 0.026 and an R-precision of 0.02. For more frequent words, occurring between 100 and 1,000 times, the values are higher: a MAP of 0.125, a P@1 of 0.209 and an R-precision of 0.104.

For a comparison with specialised texts, we can look at Moen et al. (2014)'s work on document similarity between care episodes in a retrieval system. The matrix is then a term-document matrix, and not a term-context one, and the task is different. We do not know exactly how the comparison is effective, but they obtain for their best system a MAP of 0.326 and a precision at 10 neighbours of 0.515.

	Acquired Rel.		Rel. in UMLS		MAP		R-precision		P@1	
	JACC	COS	JACC	COS	JACC	COS	JACC	COS	JACC	COS
VSMonly (baseline)	406	9,154	4	46	0.406	0.105	0.250	0.000	0.250	0.000
VSM/TV	472	5,322	8	24	0.280	0.149	0.143	0.053	0.143	0.053
VSM/LI	324	2,844	4	18	0.454	0.232	0.250	0.167	0.250	0.200
VSM/LSP	398	4,684	6	18	0.219	0.154	0.000	0.071	0.000	0.071
VSM/TV+LI	324	2,844	4	18	0.454	0.232	0.250	0.167	0.250	0.200
VSM/TV+LSP	398	4,678	6	18	0.219	0.149	0.000	0.071	0.000	0.071
VSM/LSP+LI	336	2,748	4	14	0.454	0.263	0.250	0.208	0.250	0.250
VSM/ALL3	336	2,982	4	16	0.414	0.259	0.250	0.192	0.250	0.231
VSM/Syn	474	5,282	8	24	0.280	0.157	0.143	0.053	0.143	0.053

Table 2: Results obtained with the Jaccard index and Cosine measure for a 21 word window

Large window For the large window, we present the results obtained with Jaccard and Cosine. We do not present all the generalisation sets because adding more relations (more methods) in the generalisation process does not change the results: once we generalise with two methods, the results get stable. We first observe a different behaviour according to the similarity measure in terms of relations acquired: Cosine allow to acquire many more relations than Jaccard, and as well more relations acquired with Cosine are found in the UMLS. However results are in general much better with Jaccard. Quite similar results are observed between both similarity measures when generalisation is perfomed with all three linguistic methods at a time (VSM/ALL3). Using the three methods at the same time for generalisation does not provide better results. Indeed, it even decreases the number of relations found in the UMLS. As for generalisation/normalisation, it allows to decrease the number of relations acquired by two when Cosine is used, that is good because the number of relations acquired with Cosine is extremely high, but it also divides the number of relations found in the UMLS by two.

When terminological variation is individually used, it always improves the quality of the results in terms of MAP, precision and R-precision for Cosine, whereas it always decreases the quality with Jaccard. The normalisation with synonyms with both similarity measures behaves similarly to generalisation with terminological variation: they both get the best recall.

With Jaccard, generalisation with lexical inclusion improves the MAP results, that means that the relations are better ranked. Lexical inclusion improves the results when used individually or within a combination. Lexico syntactic patterns with a large window have little (with Cosine) or negative impact on the results. Lexical inclusion allows to increase the MAP, R-precision and precision values when used after the lexico syntactic patterns with Cosine.

Finally, we can conclude that with a large window, the use of Jaccard and generalisation with lexical inclusion improves the quality of the relations acquired. But the recall is also really low. With Cosine, the recall is higher and generalisation with LI is also the best choice.

	Acquired Rel.		Rel. in UMLS		MAP		R-precision		P@1	
	JACC	COS	JACC	COS	JACC	COS	JACC	COS	JACC	COS
VSMonly (baseline)	1,882	16,178	6	60	0.502	0.118	0.333	0.054	0.333	0.048
VSM/TV	2,258	13,804	16	56	0.276	0.110	0.143	0.051	0.143	0.051
VSM/LI	976	6,172	2	38	0.536	0.132	0.500	0.067	0.500	0.067
VSM/LSP	2,112	12,656	16	50	0.187	0.106	0.071	0.057	0.071	0.057
VSM/TV+LI	976	6,172	2	38	0.536	0.132	0.500	0.067	0.500	0.067
VSM/TV+LSP	2,066	12,338	16	50	0.191	0.106	0.071	0.057	0.071	0.057
VSM/LSP+LI	934	5,996	4	38	0.378	0.135	0.250	0.067	0.250	0.067
VSM/ALL3	1,002	6,540	4	38	0.379	0.131	0.250	0.067	0.250	0.067
VSM/Syn	2,292	14,022	16	56	0.273	0.110	0.143	0.051	0.143	0.051

Table 3: Results obtained for a 5 word window– with thresholds on the distributional parameters

Narrow window With the 5 word window, the observations and results also differ according to the similarity measure used. The best results are also obtained with the Jaccard Index and the behaviour of both similarity measures is similar to the one observed with a large window: generalisation with lexical inclusion reduces by two the number of relations acquired but also the number of relations found in the UMLS. In order to better understand the behaviour of generalisation with lexical inclusion, and to improve the results in terms of recall without decreasing precision, manual evaluation is required. The results obtained with Cosine are lower than with a large window.

The choice of the similarity measure is a difficult choice and is linked to the other distributional parameters of the VSM. We can deduce that Jaccard with small corpora allows to get a better precision than Cosine, and obtains better results with a narrow window. Generalisation with lexical inclusion appears to be the best generalisation for both measures, and normalisation with synonymy relations does not improve the results.

But when LI is combined with relations acquired with lexico-syntactic patterns, its contribution decreases the results with the Jaccard index, and on the contrary improves the results with the Cosine. The order of the methods also matters and differs according to the similarity measure: with Jaccard, the generalisation with relations acquired with lexical inclusion before lexico-syntactic patterns has a lower precision than the inverse combination (i.e. VSM/LSP+LI).

7 Conclusion

In this paper, we address the reduction of data sparsity in matrices of context vectors used to implement the distributional analysis. We proposed to generalise and normalise the distributional contexts with synonymy and hypernymy relations acquired from our corpus. Words in contexts are considered as hyponyms and are replaced by hypernyms identified on the corpus, or are considered as members of a synonym set, and normalised with the cluster representative of this set. We performed some experiments on a French medical corpus combining several parameters. Even if the evaluation of distributional methods is difficult, we compare the results to the semantic relations proposed by the French UMLS. Several evaluation measures have been used to evaluate the impact of context generalisation and normalisation on distributional analysis. The analysis of the results show that when the size of the window that allow to produce distributional contexts is small and when the Jaccard index is used, it is better to generalise contexts with relations acquired with lexical inclusion. However, when the window is large, generalisation with lexical inclusion with the use of Jaccard index also improves the results. Normalisation seems to have no positive effect on relation extraction, with any combination of distributional parameters.

Beside a manual analysis of the relations and of the impact of the process of generalisation and normalisation on manipulated data, these results open several perspectives. The hypernymy relations we used have been separately exploited. But these relations could be considered as a sketch towards a taxonomy and we plan to adapt the context generalisation method in order to consider this network of relations acquired from corpora. Furthemore, all the relations acquired from corpora may be noisy. We plan to use other sources of relations as the ones contained in terminologies. It could then be possible to evaluate the impact of generalisation and of the relations when their terminological type is known. Finally, we plan to compare our method with two other dimension reduction methods, such as Random Indexing and LSA.

References

S. Aubin and T. Hamon. 2006. Improving term extraction with terminological resources. In *Advances in Natural Language Processing*, number 4139 in LNAI, pages 380–387. Springer.

O. Baskaya, E. Sert, V. Cirik, and D. Yuret. 2013. Ai-ku: Using substitute vectors and co-occurrence modeling for word sense induction and disambiguation. In *Proc. of SemEval - 2013*, pages 300–306, Atlanta, USA. ACL.

B. Broda, M. Piasecki, and S. Szpakowicz. 2009. Rank-based transformation in measuring semantic relatedness. In Yong Gao and Nathalie Japkowicz, editors, *Canadian Conference on AI*, volume 5549, pages 187–190. Springer.

C. Buckley and E. Voorhees. 2005. Retrieval system evaluation. In Ellen Voorhees and Donna Harman, editors, *TREC: Experiment and Evaluation in Information Retrieval*, chapter 3. MIT Press.

N. Chatterjee and S. Mohan. 2008. Discovering word senses from text using random indexing. In *Proc. of the 9th International Conference on Computational Linguistics and Intelligent Text Processing*, CICLing'08, pages 299–310, Berlin, Heidelberg. Springer-Verlag.

J.R. Curran and M. Moens. 2002. Improvements in automatic thesaurus extraction. In *Workshop on Unsupervised lexical acquisition*, volume 9, pages 59–66, Morristown, NJ, USA. Association for Computational Linguistics.

J. R. Curran. 2004. *From distributional to semantic similarity*. Ph.D. thesis, Institute for Communicating and Collaborative Systems School of Informatics University of Edinburgh.

R. Fano. 1963. *Transmission of Information: A Statistical Theory of Communications*. The MIT Press, Cambridge, MA.

O. Ferret. 2010. Similarit smantique et extraction de synonymes partir de corpus. In *TALN 2010*, Montral.

O. Ferret. 2011. Utiliser l'amorage pour améliorer une mesure de similarité sémantique. In Mathieu Lafourcade and Violaine Prince, editors, *TALN 2011*, volume 1, pages 155–160, Montpellier, France, juillet.

Olivier Ferret. 2013. Sélection non supervisée de relations sémantiques pour améliorer un thésaurus distributionnel. In *TALN 2013*, pages 48–61, Les Sables d'Olonne, France.

J.R. Firth. 1957. A synopsis of linguistic theory 1930-1955. *Studies in linguistic analysis*, pages 1–32.

N. Grabar and P. Zweigenbaum. 2003. Lexically-based terminology structuring. In *Terminology*, volume 10, pages 23–54.

G. Grefenstette. 1994. Corpus-derived first, second and third-order word affinities. In *Sixth Euralex International Congress*, pages 279–290.

T. Hamon, A. Nazarenko, and C. Gros. 1998. A step towards the detection of semantic variants of terms in technical documents. In *International Conference on Computational Linguistics (COLING-ACL'98)*, pages 498–504, Université de Montréal, Quebec, Canada.

T. Hamon, A. Nazarenko, T. Poibeau, S. Aubin, and J. Derivière. 2007. A robust linguistic platform for efficient and domain specific web content analysis. In *RIAO 2007*, Pittsburgh, USA.

Z. Harris. 1954. Distributional structure. *Word*, 10(23):146–162.

C. Jacquemin. 2001. *Spotting and discovering terms through natural language processing*. The MIT Press.

P. Kanerva, J. Kristofersson, and A. Holst. 2000. Random indexing of text samples for latent semantic analysis. In L.R. Gleitman and A.K. Josh, editors, *Proceedings of the 22nd Annual Conference of the Cognitive Science Society*, volume 1036, Erlbaum, New Jersey.

J. Karlgren and M. Sahlgren. 2001. From words to understanding. In *Proceedings of the 48th Annual Meeting of the Association for Computational Linguistics*, pages 294–308. Foundations of Real-World Intelligence.

T.K. Landauer and S.T. Dumais. 1997. A solution to plato's problem: The latent semantic analysis theory of acquisition, induction, and representation of knowledge. *Psychological Review; Psychological Review*, 104(2):211.

D.D. Lee and H.S. Seung. 1999. Learning the parts of objects by nonnegative matrix factorization. *Nature*, 401:788–791.

K. Lund and C. Burgess. 1996. Producing high-dimensional semantic spaces from lexical co-occurrence. *Behavior Research Methods, Instrumentation, and Computers*, 28:203–208.

H. Moen, E. Marsi, F. Ginter, L.-M. Murtola, T. Salakoski, and S. Salanterä. 2014. Care episode retrieval. In *Proc. of the 5th International Workshop on Health Text Mining and Information Analysis (Louhi)*, pages 116–124, Gothenburg, Sweden. ACL.

E. Morin and C. Jacquemin. 2004. Automatic Acquisition and Expansion of Hypernym Links. *Computers and the Humanities*, 38(4):363–396.

S. Padó and M. Lapata. 2007. Dependency-based construction of semantic space models. *Comput. Linguist.*, 33(2):161–199.

Y. Peirsman, H. Kris, and G. Dirk. 2008. Size matters. tight and loose context definitions in english word space models. In *ESSLLI Workshop on Distributional Lexical Semantics*, Hamburg, Germany.

T. Polajnar and S. Clark. 2014. Improving distributional semantic vectors through context selection and normalisation. In *Proceedings of EACL 2014*. To appear.

R. Rapp. 2003. Word sense discovery based on sense descriptor dissimilarity. In *MT Summit'2003*, pages 315–322.

M. Sahlgren. 2006. *The Word-Space Model: Using Distributional Analysis to Represent Syntagmatic and Paradigmatic Relations between Words in High-Dimensional Vector Spaces*. Ph.D. thesis, Stockholm Univ., Sweden.

H. Schmid. 1994. Probabilistic part-of-speech tagging using decision trees. In *New Methods in Language Processing*, pages 44–49, Manchester, UK.

F. Sebastiani. 2002. Machine learning in automated text categorization. *ACM Comput. Surv.*, 34(1):1–47.

G. Tsatsaronis and V. Panagiotopoulou. 2009. A generalized vector space model for text retrieval based on semantic relatedness. In *EACL 2009*, pages 70–78, Stroudsburg, PA, USA. Association for Computational Linguistics.

P.D. Turney and P. Pantel. 2010. From frequency to meaning: Vector space models of semantics. *Journal of artificial intelligence research*, 37:141–188.

A. Utsumi. 2010. Evaluating the performance of nonnegative matrix factorization for constructing semantic spaces: Comparison to latent semantic analysis. In *Proceedings of SMC*, pages 2893–2900. IEEE.

L. van der Plas. 2008. *Automatic lexico-semantic acquisition for question answering*. Thèse de doctorat, University of Groningen, Groningen.

E. Vozalis and K. G. Margaritis. 2003. Analysis of recommender systems' algorithms. In *The 6th Hellenic European Conference on Computer Mathematics & its Applications (HERCMA), Athens, Greece*.

J. Weeds and D. Weir. 2005. Co-occurrence retrieval: A flexible framework for lexical distributional similarity. *Comput. Linguist.*, 31(4):439–475.

D. Yuret. 2012. Fastsubs: An efficient and exact procedure for finding the most likely lexical substitutes based on an n-gram language model. *IEEE Signal Process. Lett.*, 19(11):725–728.

M. Zhitomirsky-Geffet and I. Dagan. 2009. Bootstrapping distributional feature vector quality. *Comput. Linguist.*, 35(3):435–461.

P. Zweigenbaum. 1994. Menelas: an access system for medical records using natural language. *Computer Methods and Programs in Biomedicine*, 45.

Assigning Terms to Domains by Document Classification

Robert Gaizauskas, Emma Barker, Monica Lestari Paramita and Ahmet Aker
Department of Computer Science, University of Sheffield, United Kingdom
{r.gaizauskas,e.barker,m.paramita,ahmet.aker}@sheffield.ac.uk

Abstract

In this paper we investigate a number of questions relating to the identification of the domain of a term by domain classification of the document in which the term occurs. We propose and evaluate a straightforward method for domain classification of documents in 24 languages that exploits a multilingual thesaurus and Wikipedia. We investigate and provide quantitative results about the extent to which humans agree about the domain classification of documents and terms also the extent to which terms are likely to "inherit" the domain of their parent document.

1 Introduction

In an increasingly interconnected world, characterised by high international mobility and globalised trade patterns, communication across languages is ever more important. The demand for translation services has never been higher and there is constant pressure for technological solutions, e.g., in the form of machine translation (MT) and computer-assisted translation (CAT), to increase translation throughput and lower costs. One requirement of these technologies is bilingual lexical resources, i.e. dictionaries, particularly in specialist subject areas or domains, such as biomedicine, information techology, or aerospace. While in theory statistical MT approaches need only parallel corpora to train their translation models, there is never enough parallel material in technical areas or for minority languages to support high quality technical translation, so specialist bilingual terminological resources are very important. Similarly, human translators using CAT systems need support in the form of bilingual terminological resources in specialist areas about which they may know very little.

The EU FP-7 TaaS project has created a cloud-based terminological service, which makes available bilingual terminological resources for all EU languages. These resources include both existing terminological resources and resources derived automatically from parallel and comparable corpora available on the web. Additionally, the service's user community is able manually to supplement or correct these resources. Like many other terminology resources (e.g. IATE[1], Eurotermbank[2]), terms in TaaS have *domains* associated with them. This is done for a number of reasons: (1) *Computational Feasiblity*: While in theory a translator faced with a translation task could provide the set of documents to be translated to a system that dynamically assembled a bespoke terminological resource specific to this task, this is not computationally feasible, at least not in a time-frame a user is likely to accept. Much more feasible is to collect bilingual terminology off-line and store it within a term repository with an associated domain or domains. Then, an on-line user, having identified the domain of the document(s) to be translated, searches for terms within that domain or may have terms from the domain into which his documents are automatically classified made available to him. (2) *Sense Disambiguation*: Term expressions, or their translations, may have multiple senses, but these are likely to be in different domains. By restricting the domain when looking up terms, sense confusions are less likely to occur. (3) *User Preference*: Our

[1] http://iate.europa.eu
[2] http://www.eurotermbank.com

Proceedings of the 4th International Workshop on Computational Terminology, pages 11–21,
Dublin, Ireland, August 23 2014.

discussions with technical translators show they are used to and comfortable with the notion of domains and prefer terminological resources structured by domain.

Assuming, therefore, that term resources are to be structured into domains, the question arises as to how this is to be done automatically for automatically acquired terms. While the notion of domain is inherent in most definitions of "term"[3], most term extraction systems identify terms using grammatical patterns and/or statistical occurrence information applied to and gathered from corpora deemed to be either in-domain or general/multi-domain. I.e. such tools do not have any inherent notion of domain, but instead rely on the external provision of documents pre-selected by domain to determine the domain of the extracted terms. But how valid is this procedure?

In this paper we explore several questions related to the assignment of terms to domains. These questions were addressed within the evaluation of that component of the TaaS platform which automatically creates bilingual term resources (the Bilingual Term Extraction System, aka BiTES). Specifically:

1. How well can a simple vector space classifier built from a multilingual thesaurus automatically classify documents into domains prior to assigning these domains to the terms within the documents?

2. To what extent do humans agree about the assignment of terms to domains?

3. How accurate is the assumption that terms can be assigned to the domains of the documents in which they are found?

The rest of the paper is structured as follows. Section 2 gives a brief overview of the BiTES system as a whole and the domain classification component in somewhat more detail. In section 3 we describe the evaluation of those parts of BiTES relevant to the questions above, detailing the evaluation tasks, participants and data used and as well as the results of the evaluation. Section 4 provides analysis and discussion of results. Section 5 discusses related work. We conclude in Section 6.

2 System Components

2.1 BiTES overview

The Bilingual Term Extraction System (BiTES) uses different workflows, each comprising a set of tools run in sequence, to collect bilingual term pairs. Each new bilingual term pair found by BiTES is fed into a database for later retrieval. The workflows consist of four different types of tools:

1. tools for collecting Web resources, such as parallel and comparable corpora from which the bilingual terms are extracted;

2. tools for performing document classification into pre-defined categories or domains;

3. tools for extracting terms from or tagging terms in monolingual documents collected from the Web;

4. tools for bilingual alignment of tagged terms in parallel or comparable document pairs collected from the Web.

Each workflow can be run in an offline and periodic manner and starts with document collection from the Web followed by document classification. The output of the document classifier is passed to the monolingual term extractor. Term-tagged document pairs are fed to the bilingual term alignment processor to extract bilingual terms. The main goal of BiTES within the TaaS platform is to automatically collect large numbers of bilingual term pairs off-line that are then stored in a database for later retrieval by users. This database of automatically collected terms is consulted when other pre-existing, and presumed higher quality, manually gathered terminological resources, such as, EuroTermBank or IATE, which are also available in the TaaS platform, do not contain translations for terms the user seeks.

[3] For example Bessé et al. (1997) define term as "a lexical unit consisting of one or more than one word which represents a concept inside a domain"; ISO 1087-1:2000 defines term as "verbal designation of a general concept in a specific subject field".

In this section we detail only the domain classification component of BiTES as it is the component that has the most direct implications for the research questions addressed in the paper and as the underlying methods and performance of the other tools used in BiTES have been reported elsewhere (Aker et al., 2012; Pinnis et al., 2012; Su and Babych, 2012; Skadiņa et al., 2012; Aker et al., 2013; Aker et al., 2014b; Aker et al., 2014a).

2.2 Domain Classification

2.2.1 Domain classification scheme

Despite the existence of various domain classification schemes, the TaaS project has created its own domain classification for several reasons. First, the TaaS platform requires a suitable classification system which is easy to use, yet provides broad coverage of the topics that are of greatest interest to users working in terminology management and machine translation. The project conducted a user study to identify the set of required domains. Various classification systems were considered, including the Dewey Decimal Classification (DDC) and Universal Decimal Classification (UDC). These schemes, however, are too complicated to be used by terminologists (the latter uses 10 level-1 domains and more than 60,000 level-2 domains) yet still did not sufficiently cover relevant subject fields identified by our users, such as IT, medicine and mechanical engineering. The Internal Classification for Standards (ICS) scheme was considered next, as it covers technical subject fields, but it was lacking with respect to legal and humanities domains. Intially, therefore, the TaaS project decided to adopt the domain structuring used in the EuroVoc thesaurus, which includes a broad range of domains. However, with 21 level-1 domains and 127 level-2 domains, it too is quite complex and focuses more on European Union domains than the industry-related domains identified in our user study. Therefore, various modifications to the EuroVoc domain scheme were performed to merge and delete various domains so as to increase the scheme's suitability for the project and also improve its practicality and ease of use. This resulted in what we here refer to as the TaaS domain classification scheme, which contains 11 level-1 domains and 66 level-2 domains[4]. A mapping from EuroVoc level-1 and -2 domains to TaaS level-1 and -2 domains was manually established.

2.2.2 Document classifier

Many approaches to document classification have been proposed in the literature – see Agarwal et al. (2014) for a survey. Our domain classifier uses the well-explored vector space approach. For each language, each domain is represented by one vector and each document to be classified by another vector. The cosine similarity measure (Salton and Lesk, 1968) is calculated between the vector representation of the input document and the vector representation of a domain and serves as a measure of the extent to which the document belongs to that domain. The highest scoring domain may be chosen if hard classification is required, or a vector of scores, one per domain, may be returned, if soft classification is needed. The advantage of this approach in our setting is that we can exploit an existing multilingual, domain-structured thesaurus to build our domain vector to deliver domain classifiers for 11 domains in 24 languages, without the need for collecting training data.

To create a vector representation for an input document, the document is first pre-processed and stop words and punctuation are removed from it. The TaaS project covers 23 of the 24 official EU languages[5] as well as Russian. For each of these languages we took the entire dump of Wikipedia and weighted each word in the articles using $tf * idf$ (Manning et al., 2008). Any word whose idf is below a predefined threshold is used as a stop word. Using this method we collected stop word lists for all 24 languages. To identify punctuation we used simple rules covering the major punctuation symbols. After filtering out stop words and punctuation, the remaining words in the input document are stemmed. We adopted Lucene stemmers for all languages for which these resources are available in and implemented new stemmers for Latvian, Lithuanian and Estonian. Finally, term frequency counts for the stems in the input document are gathered, idf scores are taken from the Wikipedia dump and $tf * idf$ weights are computed and stored to create the vector representation of the input document.

[4]A full specification of the scheme is available at: `https://demo.taas-project.eu/domains`.

[5]The omitted language is Irish, for which insufficient data was available for training our tools.

To create domain vectors we did the following: (1) For each domain and language, we manually downloaded the relevant EuroVoc term file from the EuroVoc website[6]. (2) We used the EuroVoc-to-TaaS mapping described in Section 2.2.1 above to map all terms belonging to a specific EuroVoc domain (level-1 or -2) to the corresponding TaaS domain (level-1 or -2). (3) For each TaaS domain (in each language) we built a domain-specific vector from the set of newly derived TaaS terms in the domain. Since our vector elements correspond to single words, we convert any multi-word term in the domain into multiple single word representations. To do this we process each multi-word by splitting it on whitespace, removing any words that are stop words and finally stemming the remaining words. For any single word terms we simply take their stems. Finally, all the word stems so derived are stored in a vector. We use simple term frequency, measured across the bag of stemmed words derived from all terms in the domain, as a weight for each stem. In the experiment below we report results only for classification into the 11 level-1 TaaS domains – see Table1.

Level-1 Domain	Level-2 Domain
Agriculture and foodstuff	Agriculture, forestry, fisheries, foodstuff, beverages and tobacco, and food technology.
Arts	Plastic arts, music, literature, and dance.
Economics	Business administration, national economics, finance and accounting, trade, marketing and public relations, and insurance.
Energy	Energy policy, coal and mining, oil and gas, nuclear energy, and wind, water and solar energy.
Environment	Climate, and environmental protection.
Industries and technology	Information and communication technology, chemical industry, iron, steel and other metal industries, mechanical engineering, electronics and electrical engineering, building and public works, wood industry, leather and textile industries, transportation and aeronautics, and tourism.
Law	Civil law, criminal law, commercial law, public law, and international law and human rights.
Medicine and pharmacy	Anatomy, ophthalmology, dentistry, otolaryngology, paediatrics, surgery, alternative treatment methods, gynaecology, veterinary medicine, pharmacy, cosmetic, and medical engineering.
Natural sciences	Astronomy, biology, chemistry, geology, geography, mathematics and physics.
Politics and administration	Administration, politics, international relations and defence, and European Union.
Social sciences	Education, history, communication and media, social affairs, culture and religion, linguistics, and sports.

Table 1: TaaS Domains

3 Evaluation

To evaluate the BiTES system we devised a set of four human assessment tasks focussed on different aspects of the system. These tasks were designed to assess the domain classifier, the extent to which terms found in a document judged to be in a given domain were in the domain of their document, the accuracy of the boundaries of extracted terms in context and the accuracy of system proposed bilingual term alignments. In this paper we focus on the first two of these tasks only. As noted above the TaaS project addressed 24 languages in total. Evaluation of all these languages and language pairs was clearly impossible. We chose to focus on six languages – English (EN), German (DE), Spanish (ES), Czech (CS), Lithuanian (LT) and Latvian (LV) – and five language pairs EN-DE, EN-ES, EN-CS, EN-LT and EN-LV. This gave us exemplars from the Germanic, Romance, Slavic and Baltic language groups.

3.1 Human assessment tasks

3.1.1 Domain classification assessment

In the domain classification assessment task we present participants with a document and the TaaS set of domain classes (see Table 1), and ask them to select the TaaS level-1 domain that in their judgement best represents the document. We provide a brief set of guidelines to help them carry out this task.

[6]http://eurovoc.europa.eu

We encourage participants to select a primary domain wherever possible – i.e. a single domain that best represents the document. But we allow them to select multiple domains from the list provided, if they believe the text spans more than one domain and they are unable to decide upon a primary domain. If they do opt to select multiple domains we ask them to keep the number of selected domains to a minimum. For example, the Wikipedia article entitled "Hydraulic Fracturing" [7] discusses a wide range of topics, including the process of hydraulic fracturing and its impacts in the geological, environmental, economic and political spheres. For this document, which we use in our guidelines for the task, we recommend assessors choose "Energy" as a primary domain and possibly also "Industries and Technology", since these two domains best represent the overall document content, which is chiefly concerned with what is described as a "mechanical" process in the "industrial sector of mining", the products being natural gas and oil. But we would limit our selection to these two.

The aim is for participants to select domains from the list we provide. However, in the event that they are unable to do so, we provide an option "none of the above", which they may select and then provide a domain of their own. In the guidelines we ask them to spend some time reviewing potential domain candidates, and combinations of candidates, before opting to provide an as yet unspecified domain. I.e. they should only select the option "none of the above" if they have genuinely exhausted all the possibilities using one or more domains from our list.

3.1.2 Term in domain assessment

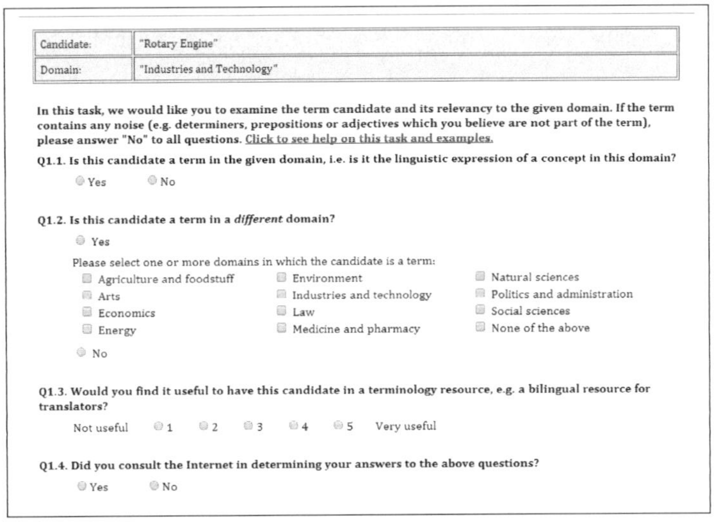

Figure 1: Judging a Term Candidate in a Domain

This is the first of two tasks assessing the (monolingual) extraction of terms. It assesses whether an automatically extracted term candidate is a term in a proposed, automatically determined, domain. Assuming the candidate is a term, a subsequent task assesses whether the boundaries of the term candidate, when taken in their original document context, are correct.

In this task (see Figure 1) we present assessors with a term candidate and a domain and then ask them to judge if the candidate is a term in the given domain or if it is a term in a different domain. If they judge the term to be in a different domain we ask them to specify the alternate domain(s). In this question the candidate and the domain category are assessed together but we do not provide any specific context, such as the source sentence or source document. As with the previous task we provide a brief set of guidelines to help assessors carry out the task.

We ask assessors to base their judgement on the entire candidate string. If the string contains a term but also contains, additional words that are not part of the term then they should answer "no". For

[7] Aka "fracking", see `http://en.wikipedia.org/wiki/Hydraulic_fracturing`

example, consider the candidate "excessive fuel emissions" and the domain "Industries and Technology". Although most people would agree that "fuel emissions" is a term, Q1.1 and Q1.2 should be answered "no" in this case since the candidate also contains noise, i.e. the word "excessive". Superfluous articles, determiners and other closed class words are also considered "noise" in this context.

We encourage assessors to search the Internet, as translators and terminologists might do, to help determine whether the entire candidate is indeed a term in the given domain. Web searches can provide examples of real world uses of a candidate in different domains. We also allow assessors to consult existing terminological or dictionary resources, online or otherwise, during the evaluation task. However, participants are encouraged not to assume that such resources are complete or entirely correct and advised that such resources be used with some consideration and caution.

Finally, if assessors have answered "yes" to one of Q1.1 or Q1.2, they will also be asked to indicate the utility of the term candidate in Q1.3, however this aspect of the assessment is not of interest here and will not be discussed further.

3.2 Participants

We recruited experienced translators to participate in the evaluation tasks. For English and for each language pair, three assessors carried out each of the evaluation tasks. In total our study involved 17 assessors – one assessor took part in DE only, EN-DE and EN only tasks. All assessors had an excellent background in translation in a wide variety of domains, with an average of 8.5 years translation experience in the relevant language pairs. All assessors who evaluated the English, Lithuanian and Latvian data were native speakers. For each of the remaining languages (Czech, German and Spanish), 2 were native speakers whilst 1 was a fluent speaker with over 54 years, 15 years and 12 years experience (respectively) in using these languages as a second language.

3.3 Data

3.3.1 Domain classification

For the domain classification task, we selected a set of documents to be evaluated using the following approach. First, we gathered all articles from the August 2013 Wikipedia dump in each of the assesment languages and extracted the main text paragraphs, i.e. tables, images, infoboxes and URLs were filtered out. The number of articles ranged from 50,000 (for Latvian) to 4,000,000 (for English). We then ran our domain classifier over each document in this dataset and assigned to each document the top domain proposed by the classifier, i.e. the domain with the highest score according to our vector space approach (Section 2.2.2). During processing we filtered out documents whose top domain scores were below a previously set minimum threshold and those whose document length was below a minimum length. Finally, for each domain D, we sorted the documents classified into D based on their scores, divided this sequence into 10 equal-size bins and selected one document from each bin. Since we were classifying documents into one of the 11 level-1 TaaS domains, this resulted in 110 documents for each language[8].

3.3.2 Term extraction

For the term in domain assessment task, we narrowed the task to focus on two domains only – "Industries and Technology" and "Politics and Administration" – since we could not hope to assess sufficient terms in all domains in all languages. We extracted terms from all documents contained in the top bin of the domain classifier, i.e. the 10% of documents in the domain with the highest similarity score to the domain vector, using TWSC as the term extractor tool (Pinnis et al., 2012). Next, we selected 200 terms from both domains, choosing terms of different word lengths: 50 of length 1, 70 of length 2, 50 of length 3 and 30 of length 4. This distribution was chosen in order to approximate roughly the distribution of term lengths one might expect in the data[9]. This process was repeated for each of our six languages.

[8]The Latvian set contains a slightly smaller set (i.e. 106 documents) due to a fewer number of documents found in one of the domains (i.e. 6 documents in the "Energy" domains).

[9]This distribution was chosen after analysing term lengths in the EuroVoc thesaurus and in the term extractor results, which indicated that terms length 2 are the most common, followed by terms length 1 and 3, and terms length 4 are found to be the least common. We boosted slightly the numbers of length 4 terms in our test to try to eliminate very small number effects.

3.4 Results

3.4.1 Domain classification assessment

A total of 656 documents (in 6 languages) were assessed and on average 1.2 domains were selected for each document. Regarding human-human agreement, at least 2 assessors fully agreed on their domain selections (including cases where more than one domain was selected) on 78% of the cases. When considering cases where at least 2 assessors agreed on at least one domain, agreement increases to 98%.

Regarding human-system agreement, since 3 assessors participated in each assessment, we produced two types of human judgments: *majority* (i.e. any domains selected by at least two assessors) and *union* (i.e. any domains selected by at least one assessor). We computed the agreements between the classifier and both the majority and the union human judgments. Results averaged over all domains and languages show the system's proposed top domain agreed with the majority human judgment in 45% of cases and with the union of human judgments in 58% of cases. Broken down by language, agreement with the majority judgment ranged from a low of 35% (EN) to a high of over 53% (DE) while agreement with the union of judgments ranged from a low of 48% (EN) to a high of over 64% (CS). By domain, agreement with majority judgment ranged from just over 12% (Agriculture and foodstuff) to 88% (Medicine and pharmacy) while agreement with the union of judgments ranged from 23% (Agriculture and foodstuff) to over 91% (Social sciences).

Recall (Section 3.3.1) that our test data includes documents from different similarity score bins. This enables us to analyse the agreement between the assessors and the classifier in more detail. In general we see a monotonically increasing agreement with both the majority judgement and union of judgments as we move from the lowest to highest scoring bin. The highest agreement is achieved in bin 10 which represents the 10% of documents "most confidently" classified to a given domain, i.e. those documents with the highest similarity score to the domain vector. Just under 80% of these documents (77.27%) are included in the union of assessors data and 63% are included in the majority. I.e. for approximately 77% of the documents most confidently classified to a domain by our classifier, at least one in three humans will agree with the domain classification and for about 63% the majority of humans will agree.

3.4.2 Term in domain assessment

Term length	Total	Term in the given domain	Term in a different domain
All length	457	88%	12%
1	144	88%	12%
2	182	87%	13%
3	84	92%	8%
4	47	91%	9%

Table 2: Terms with different term length

Languages	Total	Term in the given domain	Term in a different domain
All languages	457	88%	12%
CS	103	86%	14%
DE	79	82%	18%
EN	80	88%	13%
ES	54	80%	20%
LT	47	98%	2%
LV	94	97%	3%

Table 3: Terms of different languages

A total of 1,200 candidate terms in 6 languages were assessed by 3 assessors and the majority judgments (i.e. cases where at least two assessors agree) show that 38% terms were assessed to be candidate terms in the given domain, 5% terms were assessed to be candidate terms in a different domain, and the rest (57%) were deemed not to be terms.

This indicates that out of all candidate terms which were identified to be correct terms (43% of the data), 88% were assessed to be in the same domain as the documents they were extracted from. Further analysis showed that the 57% of candidates judged not to be terms could be further broken down into 33% which contain an overlap with a term, i.e. term boundaries were incorrectly identified, and 24% which neither are nor overlap with a term.

Of the 43% candidate terms that were judged to be terms, we examined the variation in extent to which they were judged to be terms in the given domain across term lengths and across languages. These figures are shown in Tables 2 and 3. We also examined variation in the extent to which these terms were judged to be terms in the given domain across the two domains we were investigating: in "Industries and

Technology" 92% of the terms were judged to be in the given domain and 8% in another domain, while for "Politics and Administration" these figures were 85% and 15% respectively.

For the 43% of the term candidates that were identified as correct terms (457 terms), all three assessors agreed about the domain of the term, i.e. they either accepted the domain proposed by the system for the term or they agreed on an alternative(s), in 45% of the cases. In 54% of the cases there was not universal agreement but at least two assessors agreed on at least one domain they assigned to the term. Only in 1% of the cases was there no overlap in judgment about term domain.

4 Analysis and Discussion

Let us now return to the research questions we raised in Section 1. Our first question was: *How well can a simple vector space classifier built from a multilingual thesaurus automatically classify documents into domains prior to assigning these domains to the terms within the documents?* First, we have to view system performance in the context of human performance. Results in the last section show that 2 out of 3 humans agree 78% of the time on exact assignment of (possibly multiple) domains to documents and 98% of the time if only one of the domains they assign to a document need to match. Over all languages and domains our classifier achieves only 45% agreement with the majority judgment and 58% with the union of judgments. However, if we restrict ourselves to the highest confidence domain assigments, then the picture is much better: 63% agreement with the majority judgment and 77% with the union of judgments. This restriction reduces the number of documents from which terms could be mined from if accurate domain classification is important – but so long as there are lots of documents to mine terms from this may not be important. Furthermore note that our classifier could easily be used to select multiple domains, perhaps, e.g., when the differences in scores between highest scoring domains is small. This would make the comparison with the human figures fairer (now the system can only propose one domain per document while the humans can propose several) and could only result in higher system figures relative to human ones. We conclude that the vector space classifier utilizing domain representations derived from a pre-existing multingual thesaurus has much to recommend: it is simple, it needs no training data, it is straightforwardly applicable to multiple (24 in our case) different languages and its performance is adequate if it is suitably constrained.

Our second question was: *To what extent do humans agree about the assignment of terms to domains?* Our results show that in less than half the cases do all three human assessors agree with the assignment of a term to a particular domain. However, in 99% of the cases at least two of three assessors concur on at least one domain to which the term belongs. This suggests that using overlap with two of three human assessors is a good approach to measuring automatic domain assignment to terms.

Our third question was: *How accurate is the assumption that terms can be assigned to the domains of the documents in which they are found?* Tables 2 and 3 show that on average 88% of terms are judged to be in the domain of the document in which they are found. Furthermore there is relatively little variation in this figure – it ranges from a low of 80% (ES) to a high of 98% (LT) and a low of 87% for terms of length 2 to a high of 92% for terms of length 3. This suggests that assigning domains to terms based on the domain of the document the term is found in is a relatively safe thing to do, but is by no means perfect: just over 10% of terms will have their domains incorrectly assigned by making this assumption.

5 Related Work

There has been extensive work on the development of automated techniques to extract terminology from document collections. Such term extraction approaches can be grouped into three categories based on the information used to extract terms: approaches using purely linguistic information, approaches using purely statistical information and those using combinations of both. An analysis of different approaches is given by Pazienza et al. (2005). For the most part, however, such approaches make the assumption that domain-specific, and perhaps also non-domain-specific, collections of texts are available. Justeson and Katz (1995), for example, assume that term frequency of a limited sort of noun phrases in domain-specific texts is sufficicent to indicate termhood. Others such as Chung (2003) and Drouin (2004) look at statistical contrasts between domain-specific and general comparison or reference corpus. See also

(Kim et al., 2009; Marciniak and Mykowiecka, 2013; Kilgariff, 2014). By contrast our approach does not presuppose the existence of documents pre-classified by domain (though we could benefit from this). Rather our approach starts by classifying a document into a domain and then extracting terms from it and assigning them the domain of the document.

Utsuro et al. (2006) and Kida et al. (2007) extract terms from web-documents. The domain specification of a term is determined in two stage approach. In the first stage for a term under inspection web-documents which mention the term are collected. Then these documents are divided into two sets: domain relevant and domain-irrelevant documents. A document whose content similarity to a domain specific corpora is above a predefined threshold is regarded as relevant. Any other document is regarded as irrelevant. In the second stage a ratio of times the term occurs in the relevant and the irrelevant set is computed. This ratio is used to determine whether the extracted term belongs to the domain in hand or not. Again, a domain-specific corpus is assumed for this approach to proceed.

Benedictis et al. (2013) use bootstrapping to collect domain specific terms. They start with some manually selected domain specific seed terms, perform web-search to obtain documents, extract further terms and re-start the process with the new terms. The documents returned by the search engine are assumed to belong to the domain in hand and so are the extracted terms. By contrast our approach does not require manually selected terms, but instead uses an existing domain structured multingual thesaurus.

6 Conclusion

In this paper we have investigated a number of questions relating to the identification of the domain of a term by domain classification of the document in which the term occurs. We proposed and evaluated a straightforward method for domain classification of documents in 24 languages which uses a multilingual thesaurus to construct "domain vectors". We investigated the extent to which humans agree about the domain classification of documents and terms. And, we investigated the extent to which terms are likely to "inherit" the domain of their parent document. Our results show that the domain classification method has significant merit, that humans generally, but by no means universally, agree about domain classification of documents and terms, and again that terms are generally, but certainly not universally, likely to be of the same domain as the document in which they occur.

7 Acknowledgments

The authors would like to acknowledge funding from the European Union FP-7 programme for the TaaS project, grant number: 296312. We would also like to thank the human assessors without whose careful work the results reported here would not have been obtained. Finally we thank our project partners in the TaaS project for user studies with translators and terminologists, contributions to the TaaS system, and development of the TaaS domain classication scheme and the EuroVoc-to-TaaS mapping.

References

Basant Agarwal and Namita Mittal. 2014. Text classification using machine learning methods-a survey. In *Proceedings of the Second International Conference on Soft Computing for Problem Solving (SocProS 2012), December 28-30, 2012*, pages 701–709. Springer.

Ahmet Aker, Evangelos Kanoulas, and Robert J Gaizauskas. 2012. A light way to collect comparable corpora from the web. In *Proceedings of Eighth International Conference on Language Resources and Evalution (LREC)*, pages 15–20.

Ahmet Aker, Monica Paramita, and Robert Gaizauskas. 2013. Extracting bilingual terminologies from comparable corpora. In *Proceedings of the 51st Annual Meeting of the Association for Computational Linguistics (ACL 2013)*.

Ahmet Aker, Monica Paramita, Emma Barker, and Robert Gaizauskas. 2014a. Bootstraping Term Extractors for Multiple Languages. In *Proceedings of the International Conference on Language Resources and Evaluation (LREC)*.

Ahmet Aker, Monica Paramita, Mārcis Pinnis, and Robert Gaizauskas. 2014b. Bilingual dictionaries for all EU languages. In *Proceedings of the International Conference on Language Resources and Evaluation (LREC)*.

Teresa Mihwa Chung. 2003. A corpus comparison approach for terminology extraction. *Terminology*, 9(2).

Flavio De Benedictis, Stefano Faralli, Roberto Navigli, et al. 2013. Glossboot: Bootstrapping multilingual domain glossaries from the web. In *Proceedings of the 51st Annual Meeting of the Association for Computational Linguistics*, pages 528–538.

Bruno de Bessé, Blaise Nkwenti-Azeh, and Juan C. Sager. 1997. Glossary of terms used in terminology. *Terminology. International Journal of Theoretical and Applied Issues in Specialized Communication*, 4:117–156(39).

Patrick Drouin. 2004. Detection of domain specific terminology using corpora comparison. In *Proceedings of the Fourth International Conference on Language Resources and Evaluation (LREC2004)*.

John S. Justeson and Slava M. Katz. 1995. Technical terminology: Some linguistic properties and an algorithm for identification in text. *Natural Language Engineering*, 1(1):9–27.

Mitsuhiro Kida, Masatsugu Tonoike, Takehito Utsuro, and Satoshi Sato. 2007. Domain classification of technical terms using the web. *Systems and Computers in Japan*, 38(14):11–19.

Adam Kilgariff. 2014. Finding terms in corpora for many languages with the Sketch Engine. *14th Conference of the European Chapter of the Association for Computational Linguistics*.

Su Nam Kim, Timothy Baldwin, and Min-Yen Kan. 2009. An unsupervised approach to domain-specific term extraction. In *Australasian Language Technology Association Workshop 2009*, page 94.

Christopher D Manning, Prabhakar Raghavan, and Hinrich Schütze. 2008. *Introduction to information retrieval*, volume 1. Cambridge university press Cambridge.

Małgorzata Marciniak and Agnieszka Mykowiecka. 2013. Terminology extraction from domain texts in polish. In *Intelligent Tools for Building a Scientific Information Platform*, pages 171–185. Springer.

Maria Teresa Pazienza, Marco Pennacchiotti, and Fabio Massimo Zanzotto. 2005. Terminology extraction: an analysis of linguistic and statistical approaches. In *Knowledge Mining*, pages 255–279. Springer.

Mārcis Pinnis, Nikola Ljubešić, Dan Ştefănescu, Inguna Skadiņa, Marko Tadić, and Tatiana Gornostay. 2012. Term extraction, tagging, and mapping tools for under-resourced languages. In *Proceedings of the 10th Conference on Terminology and Knowledge Engineering (TKE 2012), June*, pages 20–21.

Gerard Salton and Michael E Lesk. 1968. Computer evaluation of indexing and text processing. *Journal of the ACM (JACM)*, 15(1):8–36.

Inguna Skadiņa, Ahmet Aker, Nikos Mastropavlos, Fangzhong Su, Dan Tufis, Mateja Verlic, Andrejs Vasiļjevs, Bogdan Babych, Monica Paramita, Paul Clough, Robert Gaizauskas, and Nikos Glaros. 2012. Collecting and using comparable corpora for statistical machine translation. In *Proceedings of the 8th International Conference on Language Resources and Evaluation (LREC), Istanbul, Turkey*.

Fangzhong Su and Bogdan Babych. 2012. Measuring comparability of documents in non-parallel corpora for efficient extraction of (semi-) parallel translation equivalents. In *Proceedings of the Joint Workshop on Exploiting Synergies between Information Retrieval and Machine Translation (ESIRMT) and Hybrid Approaches to Machine Translation (HyTra)*, pages 10–19. Association for Computational Linguistics.

Takehito Utsuro, Mitsuhiro Kida, Masatsugu Tonoike, and Satoshi Sato. 2006. Collecting novel technical terms from the web by estimating domain specificity of a term. In *Computer Processing of Oriental Languages. Beyond the Orient: The Research Challenges Ahead*, pages 173–180. Springer.

Identification of Bilingual Terms from Monolingual Documents for Statistical Machine Translation

Mihael Arcan[1] **Claudio Giuliano**[2] **Marco Turchi**[2] **Paul Buitelaar**[1]

[1] Unit for Natural Language Processing, Insight @ NUI Galway, Ireland
{mihael.arcan , paul.buitelaar}@insight-centre.org
[2] FBK - Fondazione Bruno Kessler, Via Sommarive 18, 38123 Trento, Italy
{giuliano, turchi}@fbk.eu

Abstract

The automatic translation of domain-specific documents is often a hard task for generic Statistical Machine Translation (SMT) systems, which are not able to correctly translate the large number of terms encountered in the text. In this paper, we address the problems of automatic identification of bilingual terminology using Wikipedia as a lexical resource, and its integration into an SMT system. The correct translation equivalent of the disambiguated term identified in the monolingual text is obtained by taking advantage of the multilingual versions of Wikipedia. This approach is compared to the bilingual terminology provided by the Terminology as a Service (TaaS) platform. The small amount of high quality domain-specific terms is passed to the SMT system using the XML markup and the Fill-Up model methods, which produced a relative translation improvement up to 13% BLEU score points

1 Introduction

Translation tasks often need to deal with domain-specific terms in technical documents, which require specific lexical knowledge of the domain. Nowadays, SMT systems are suitable to translate very frequent expressions but fail in translating domain-specific terms. This mostly depends on a lack of domain-specific parallel data from which the SMT systems can learn. Translation tools such as Google Translate or open source phrase-based SMT systems, trained on generic data, are the most common solutions and they are often used to translate manuals or very specific texts, resulting in unsatisfactory translations.

This problem is particular relevant for professional translators that work with documents coming from different domains and are supported by generic SMT systems. A valuable solution to help them in handling domain-specific terms is represented by online terminology resources, e.g. IATE - Inter-Active Terminology for Europe,[1] which are continuously updated and can be easily queried. However, the manual use of these services can be very time demanding. For this reason, the identification and embedding of domain-specific terms in an SMT system is a crucial step towards increasing translator productivity and translation quality in highly specific domains.

In this paper, we propose an approach to automatically detect monolingual domain-specific terms from a source language document and identify their equivalents using Wikipedia cross-lingual links. For this purpose we extend The Wiki Machine API,[2] a tool for linking terms in text to Wikipedia pages, adding two more components able to first identify domain-specific terms, and to find their translations in a target language. The identified bilingual terms are then compared with those obtained by TaaS (Skadinš et al., 2013). The embedding of the domain-specific terms into an SMT system is performed by use of the XML markup approach, which uses the terms as preferred translation candidates at run time, and the Fill-Up model (Bisazza et al., 2011), which emphasizes phrase pairs extracted from the bilingual terms.

Our results show that the performance of our technique and TaaS are comparable in the identification of monolingual and bilingual domain-specific terms. From the machine translation point of view, our experiments highlight the benefit of integrating bilingual terms into the SMT system, and the relative improvement in BLEU score of the Fill-Up model over the baseline and the XML markup approach.

[1] http://iate.europa.eu/ [2] https://bitbucket.org/fbk/thewikimachine/

Proceedings of the 4th International Workshop on Computational Terminology, pages 22–31,
Dublin, Ireland, August 23 2014.

2 Methodology

Given a source document, it is processed by our pipeline that: (*i*) with the help of The Wiki Machine, it identifies, disambiguates and links all terms in the document to the Wikipedia pages; (*ii*) the terms and their links are used to identify the domain of the document and filter out the terms that are not domain-specific; (*iii*) the translation of such terms is obtained following the Wikipedia cross-lingual links; (*iv*) the bilingual domain-specific terms are embedded into the SMT system using different strategies. In the rest of this section, each step is described in detail.

2.1 Bilingual Term Identification

Term Detection and Linking The Wiki Machine is a tool for linking terms in text to Wikipedia pages and enriching them with information extracted from Wikipedia and Linked Open Data (LOD) resources such as DBPedia or Freebase. The Wiki Machine has been preferred among other approaches because it achieves the best performance in term disambiguation and linking (Mendes et al., 2011), and facilitates the extraction of structured information from Wikipedia.

The annotation process consists of a three-step pipeline based on statistical and machine learning methods that exclusively uses Wikipedia to train the models. No linguistic processing, such as stemming, morphology analysis, POS tagging, or parsing, is performed. This choice facilitates the portability of the system as the only requirement is the existence of a Wikipedia version with a sufficient coverage for the specific language and domain. The first step identifies and ranks the terms by relevance using a simple statistical approach based on *tf-idf* weighting, where all the n-grams, for n from 1 to 10, are generated and the *idf* is directly calculated on Wikipedia pages. The second step links the terms to Wikipedia pages. The linking problem is cast as a supervised word sense disambiguation problem, in which the terms must be disambiguated using Wikipedia to provide the sense inventory and the training data (for each sense, a list of phrases where the term appears) as first introduced in (Mihalcea, 2007). The application uses an ensemble of word-expert classifiers that are implemented using the kernel-based approach (Giuliano et al., 2009). Specifically, domain and syntagmatic aspects of sense distinction are modelled by means of a combination of the latent semantic and string kernels (Shawe-Taylor and Cristianini, 2004). The third step enriches the linked terms using information extracted from Wikipedia and LOD resources. The additional information relative to the pair term/Wikipedia page consists of alternative terms (i.e., orthographical and morphological variants, synonyms, and related terms), images, topic, type, cross language links, etc. For example, in the text "click right mouse key to pop up menu and Gnome panel", The Wiki Machine identifies the terms *mouse*, *key*, *pop up menu* and *Gnome panel*. For the ambiguous term *mouse*, the linking algorithm returns the Wikipedia page 'Mouse_(computing)', and the other terms used to link that page in Wikipedia with their frequency, i.e., *computer mouse*, *mice*, and *Mouse*.

In the context of the experiments reported here, we were specifically interested in the identification of domain-specific bilingual terminology to be embedded into the SMT system. For this reason, we extend The Wiki Machine adding the functionality of filtering out terms that do not belong to the document domain, and of automatically retrieving term translations.

Domain Detection To identify specific terms, we assign a domain to each linked term in a text, after that we obtain the most frequent domain and filter out the terms that are out of scope. In the example above, the term *mouse* is accepted because it belongs to the domain *computer_science*, as the majority of terms (*mouse*, *pop up menu* and *Gnome panel*), while the term *key* in the domain *music* is rejected.

The large number of languages and domains to cover prevents us from using standard text classification techniques to categorize the document. For this reason, we implemented an approach based on the mapping of the Wikipedia categories into the WordNet domains (Bentivogli et al., 2004). The Wikipedia categories are created and assigned by different human editors, and are therefore less rigorous, coherent and consistent than usual ontologies. In addition, the Wikipedia's category hierarchy forms a cyclic graph (Zesch and Gurevych, 2007) that limits its usability. Instead, the WordNet domains are organized in a hierarchy that contains only 164 items with a degree of granularity that makes them suitable for Natural Language Processing tasks. The approach we are proposing overcomes the Wikipedia category sparsity, allows us reducing the number of domains to few tens instead of some hundred thousands (800,000 categories in the English Wikipedia) and does not require any language-specific training data. Wikipedia categories that contain more pages (~1,000) have been manually mapped to WordNet domains. The domain for a term is obtained as follows. First, for each term, we extract its set of categories, C, from the Wikipedia page linked to it. Second, by means of a recursive procedure, all possible outgoing paths (usually in a large number) from each category in C are followed in the graph of Wikipedia categories. When one of the mapped categories to a WordNet domain is found, the approach stops and associates the relative WordNet domain to the term. In this way, more and more domains are assigned to a single term. Third, to isolate the most relevant one, these domains are ranked according the number of times they have been found following all the paths. The most frequent domain is assigned to the terms. Although this process needs the human intervention for the manual mapping, it is done once and it is less demanding than annotating large amounts of training documents for text classification, because it does not require the reading of the document for topic identification.

Bilingual Term Extraction The last phase consists in finding the translation of the domain terminology. We exploit the Wikipedia cross-language links, which, however, provide an alignment at page level not at term level. To deal with this issue we introduced the following procedure. If the term is equal to the source page title (ignoring case) we return the target page; otherwise, we return the most frequent alternative form of the term in the target language. From the previous example, the system is able to return the Italian page *Mouse* and all terms used in the Italian Wikipedia to express this concept of *Mouse* in *computer_science*. Using this information, the term *mouse* is paired with its translation into Italian.

2.2 Integration of Bilingual Terms into SMT

A straightforward approach for adding bilingual terms to the SMT system consists of concatenating the training data and the terms. Although it has been shown to perform better than more complex techniques (Bouamor et al., 2012), it is still affected by major disadvantages that limits its use in real applications. In particular, when small amounts of bilingual terms are concatenated with a large training dataset, terms with ambiguous translations are penalised, because the most frequent and general translations often receive the highest probability, which drives the SMT system to ignore specific translations.

In this paper, we focus on two techniques that give more priority to specific translations than generic ones: the Fill-Up model and the XML markup approach. The Fill-Up model has been developed to address a common scenario where a large generic background model exists, and only a small quantity of in-domain data can be used to build an in-domain model. Its goal is to leverage the large coverage of the background model, while preserving the domain-specific knowledge coming from the in-domain data. Given the generic and the in-domain phrase tables, they are merged. For those phrase pairs that appear in both tables, only one instance is reported in the Fill-Up model with the largest probabilities according to the tables. To keep track of a phrase pair's provenance, a binary feature that penalises if the phrase pair comes from the background table is added. The same strategy is used for reordering tables. In our experiments, we use the bilingual terms identified from the source data as in-domain data. Word alignments are computed on the concatenation of the data. Phrase extraction and scoring are carried out separately on each corpus. The XML markup approach makes it possible to directly pass external knowledge to the decoder, specifying translations for particular spans of the source sentence. In our scenario, the source term is used to identify a span in the source sentence, while the target term is directly passed to the decoder. With the setting *exclusive*, the decoder uses only the specified translations ignoring other possible translations in the translation model.

3 Experimental Setting

In our experiments, we used different English-Italian and Italian-English test sets from two domains: (*i*) a small subset of the GNOME project data[3] (4,3K tokens) and KDE4 Data[4] (9,5K) for the IT domain and (*ii*) a subset of the EMEA corpus (11K) for the medical domain.

In order to assess the quality of the monolingual and bilingual terms, we create a terminological gold standard. Two annotators with a linguistic background and English and Italian proficiency were asked

[3] `https://l10n.gnome.org/` [4] `http://i18n.kde.org/`

to mark all domain-specific terms in a set of 66 English and Italian documents of the GNOME corpus, and a set of 100 paragraphs (4,3K tokens) from the KDE4 corpus.[5] Domain-specificity was defined as all (multi-)words that are typically used in the IT domain and that may have different Italian translations in other domains. The average Cohen's Kappa of GNOME and KDE_anno computed at token level was 0.66 for English and 0.53 for Italian. Following Landis and Koch (1977), this corresponds to a substantial and moderate agreement between the annotators.

Finally the gold standard dataset was generated by the intersection of the annotations of the two annotators. In detail, for the GNOME dataset the annotators marked 93 single-word and 134 multi-word expressions (MWEs), resulting 227 terms in overall. For the KDE_anno dataset, 321 monolingual terms for the GNOME dataset were annotated, whereby 192 of them were multi-word expressions. This results in 190 unique bilingual terms for the GNOME corpus and 355 for the KDE_anno dataset.

We compare the monolingual and bilingual terms identified by our approach to the terms obtained by the online service TaaS,[6] which is a cloud-based platform for terminology services based on the state-of-the-art terminology extraction and bilingual terminology alignment methods. TaaS provides several options in term identification, of which we selected TWSC, Tilde wrapper system for CollTerm, (Pinnis et al., 2012). TWSC is based on linguistic analysis, i.e. part of speech tagging and morpho-syntactic patterns, enriched with statistical features. TaaS allows for lookup in several manually and automatically built monolingual and bilingual terminological resources and for our experiment we use EuroTermBank (ETB), Taus Data and Web Data. Accessing several resources, TaaS may provide several translations for a unique source term, but not an indicator of their translation quality. To avoid assigning the same probability to all the translations of the same source term, we prioritise a translation by the resource it was provided. In our case, we favour first the translation provided by ETB. If no translation is available, we use the translation provided by Taus Data or eventually from Web Data. Before starting the term extraction approach, TaaS requires manual specification of the source and target languages, the domain, and the source document. Since we focused on the IT and medical domains we set the options to 'Information and communication technology' and 'Medicine and pharmacy', respectively.

For each translation task, we use the statistical translation toolkit Moses (Koehn et al., 2007), where the word alignments were built with the GIZA++ toolkit (Och and Ney, 2003). The IRSTLM toolkit (Federico et al., 2008) was used to build the 5-gram language model. For a broader domain coverage, we merged parts of the following parallel resources: JRC-Acquis (Steinberger et al., 2006), Europarl (Koehn, 2005) and OpenSubtitles2013 (Tiedemann, 2012), this results in a generic training corpus of $\sim$37M tokens and a development set of $\sim$10K tokens.

In our experiments, an instance of Moses trained on the generic parallel dataset was used in three different scenarios: *(i)* as baseline SMT system without embedded terminology; *(ii)* in the XML markup approach for translating remaining parts that were not covered by the embedded terminology; *(iii)* in the Fill-Up method as background translation model.

4 Evaluation

In this Section, we report the performance of the different term identification tools and term embedding methods for the two domains: IT and the medical domain. For evaluating the extracted monolingual and bilingual terms, we calculate precision, recall and f-measure using the manually labelled KDE_anno and GNOME datasets. In addition, we perform a manual inspection of a subset of the bilingual identified terms. The BLEU metric (Papineni et al., 2002) was used to automatically evaluate the quality of the translations. The metric calculates the overlap of n-grams between the SMT system output and a reference translation, provided by a professional translator.

4.1 Monolingual Term Identification

In Table 1, the column 'Ident.' represents the number of identified terms for each tool, whereby we observed TaaS always extracts more terms than The Wiki Machine. While extracting Italian terms, TaaS extracts twice as more terms as The Wiki Machine, which can be explained by the overall lower

[5] In the rest of the paper, we refer to the annotated part of KDE4 as KDE_anno

[6] `https://demo.taas-project.eu/`

	English						Italian					
KDE_anno	Ident.	unigram	MWE	Precision	Recall	F1	Ident.	unigram	MWE	Precision	Recall	F1
TaaS	431	144	287	0.442	0.594	0.507	518	147	371	0.326	0.511	0.398
The Wiki Machine	327	247	80	0.400	0.406	0.403	207	184	23	0.429	0.268	0.330
GNOME	Ident.	unigram	MWE	Precision	Recall	F1	Ident.	unigram	MWE	Precision	Recall	F1
TaaS	311	119	192	0.260	0.355	0.301	359	110	249	0.272	0.415	0.329
The Wiki Machine	275	199	76	0.303	0.364	0.330	196	167	29	0.331	0.275	0.301

Table 1: Evaluation of monolingual term identification for the KDE_anno and GNOME dataset.

amount of Italian pages in Wikipedia compared to the English version. Focusing on the amount of identified single-word and multi-word expressions, it is interesting to notice that TaaS, independently of the language, extracts around twice as more MWEs than single words. Differently, The Wiki Machine identifies mostly single-word terms, whereby they represent around three-fourth of all identified terms for English and around 12% for Italian.

For the KDE_anno dataset, TaaS in most cases (except in precision for the Italian KDE_anno dataset) outperforms The Wiki Machine approach in all metrics. Especially we observed a higher recall produced by the TaaS approach, which can be deduced from the higher number of extracted MWEs compared to The Wiki Machine approach. On the English GNOME dataset, The Wiki Machine performs comparable results to TaaS, with a slightly higher recall and F1. On the Italian side, The Wiki Machine identifies less MWEs than TaaS, which results in a low recall and F1.

In summary, we observe that TaaS performs best on the KDE_anno dataset, whereas The Wiki Machine and TaaS perform comparable results on the GNOME dataset. Analysing the overall results, we notice that precision, recall and F1 are generally better in English than in Italian. This is due to the fact that Italian tends to use more words to express the same concept compared to English.

4.2 Bilingual Term Identification

Table 2 reports the performance of The Wiki Machine and TaaS in the identification of bilingual terms evaluated against the manually produced list of terms. In both language pairs and datasets, TaaS and The Wiki Machine mostly identify similar amounts of bilingual terms (column 'Ident.') and match with the gold standard (column 'Mat.'). Only for KDE_anno, It→En, TaaS identifies almost 50% more bilingual terms than The Wiki Machine.

It is worth noticing that, although TaaS is accessing high quality manually-produced termbases, e.g. ETB in our results, there is no evidence that it works significantly better than The Wiki Machine accessing Wikipedia. In fact, in terms of F1, The Wiki Machine performs best on the GNOME annotated test set, while it is outperformed by TaaS on KDE_anno. In both cases, differences in performance are minimal. According to the precision measure, The Wiki Machine seems to be able to produce more accurate bilingual terms.

The automatic evaluation shows difficulties (low F1 scores) for The Wiki Machine and TaaS in identifying bilingual terms that perfectly match the gold standard. To better understand the quality of term translations, we asked one of the annotators involved in the creation of the gold standard to perform a manual evaluation of a subset of fifty bilingual terms randomly selected from each list. We used the four error categories proposed in (Aker et al., 2013): 1) The terms are exact translations of each other in the domain; 2) Inclusion: Not an exact translation, but an exact translation of one term is entirely contained within the term in the other language; 3) Overlap: Not category 1 or 2, but the terms share at least one translated word; 4) Unrelated: No word in either term is a translation of a word in the other. The percentages of bilingual terms assigned to each class are shown in Table 3.

In terms of comparison between the two tools, the manual evaluation confirms that there is no evidence that a tool produces better term translations than the other in all the test sets. In fact, except for KDE_anno En→It where TaaS outperforms The Wiki Machine, the percentage of bilingual terms assigned to class 1 for both the tools is almost similar. In terms of absolute scores, the manual evaluation shows that the quality of the identified bilingual terms is relatively high (merging the terms assigned to classes 1

GNOME En→It	Ident.	Mat.	Precision	Recall	F1
TaaS	145	20	0.138	0.105	0.119
The Wiki Machine	156	25	0.160	0.130	0.144
GNOME It→En	**Ident.**	**Mat.**	**Precision**	**Recall**	**F1**
TaaS	139	21	0.151	0.110	0.127
The Wiki Machine	140	23	0.164	0.121	0.139
KDE_anno En→It	**Ident.**	**Mat.**	**Precision**	**Recall**	**F1**
TaaS	249	65	0.261	0.183	0.215
The Wiki Machine	229	49	0.202	0.138	0.164
KDE_anno It→En	**Ident.**	**Mat.**	**Precision**	**Recall**	**F1**
TaaS	228	58	0.254	0.163	0.199
The Wiki Machine	155	48	0.292	0.135	0.185

Table 2: Automatic evaluation of bilingual terms extracted from GNOME and KDE_anno.

GNOME En→It	1	2	3	4
TaaS	0.66	0.08	0.00	0.26
The Wiki Machine	0.70	0.08	0.06	0.16
GNOME It→En	**1**	**2**	**3**	**4**
TaaS	0.78	0.08	0.02	0.12
The Wiki Machine	0.68	0.12	0.04	0.16
KDE_anno En→It	**1**	**2**	**3**	**4**
TaaS	0.90	0.00	0.06	0.04
The Wiki Machine	0.70	0.10	0.06	0.14
KDE_anno It→En	**1**	**2**	**3**	**4**
TaaS	0.70	0.10	0.10	0.10
The Wiki Machine	0.64	0.22	0.08	0.06

Table 3: Manual evaluation of bilingual terms based on four error categories (1-4).

and 2, we reach a score, in most of the cases, larger than 80%). This is in contrast with the automatic evaluation, which reports limited performances (F1 $\sim$ 0.2) for both methods. The main reason is that the automatic evaluation requires a perfect match between the identified and the gold standard bilingual terms to measure an improvement in F1, while the manual evaluation can reward bilingual terms that do not perfectly match any gold standard terms but are correct translations of each other. An example is the multi-word bilingual term "settings of the network connection → impostazioni della connessione di rete" that is present in the gold standard as a single multi-word term, while it is identified by The Wiki Machine as two distinct bilingual terms, i.e. "network connection → connessione di rete" and "settings → impostazioni". From the translation point of view, both the distinct terms are correct and they are assigned to class 1 during the manual evaluation, but they are ignored by the automatic evaluation.

The analysis of terms assigned to error class four shows that both methods are affected by similar problems. The main source of error is the correct detection of the source term domain, which results in a translated term that does not belong to the correct domain. For instance, in the bilingual term "stringhe → shoe and boot laces", the term "stringhe" ("strings" in the IT domain) is translated into "laces". Similarly, the English term "launchers" ("lanciatori" in Italian in the IT domain) is translated into "lanciarazzi multiplo" ("multiple rocket launchers" in English), which is clearly not an IT term. Furthermore, The Wiki Machine seems to have more problems in identifying the right morphological variation, e.g. "indirizzi ip → ip address", where "indirizzi" is a plural noun and needs to be translated into "addresses". This is expected because page titles in Wikipedia are not always inflected. An interesting example highlighted by the annotator in the TaaS translations is: "percorso di ricerca" → "how do i access refresh grid texture?", where the Italian term ("search path" in English) is translated with a completely wrong translation. In the next Section we evaluate whether the automatic identified bilingual terms can improve the performance of an SMT system and if it is robust to the aforementioned errors.

4.3 Embedding Terminology into SMT

Our further experiments focused on the automatic evaluation of the translation quality of the EMEA, GNOME and KDE test sets (Table 4). The obtained bilingual terminology from TaaS and The Wiki Machine was embedded through the Fill-Up and XML markup approaches. The approximate randomization approach in MultEval (Clark et al., 2011) is used to test whether differences among system performances are statistically significant with a p-value < 0.05. The parameters of the baseline method and the Fill-Up models were optimized on the development set.

Injecting the obtained TaaS bilingual terms improves the BLEU score in several cases. XML markup outperforms the general baseline approach in three (out of eight) datasets, whereby three of them are statistically significant (GNOME En→It, KDE_anno En↔It). Embedding the same bilingual terminology into the Fill-Up model helped to outperform the baseline approach for all test sets, whereby only the result for EMEA En→It is not statistically significant.

	GNOME		KDE_anno		EMEA		KDE4	
	En→It	It→En	En→It	It→En	En→It	It→En	En→It	It→En
general baseline	15.39	21.62	15.58	22.64	25.88	25.75	19.22	23.54
XML Mark-up (TaaS)	15.87	22.45*	**17.62***	**23.88***	25.84	25.74	18.97	24.27*
Fill-Up Model (TaaS)	**16.22***	**22.73***	17.61*	23.45*	25.95	26.02*	**19.69***	**24.56***
XML Mark-up (The Wiki Machine)	15.49	20.57	17.19*	23.44*	25.59	24.97	17.74	22.16
Fill-Up Model (The Wiki Machine)	15.82	21.70	16.48*	23.28*	**26.35***	**26.44***	19.61*	24.14*

Table 4: Automatic BLEU Evaluation on GNOME, KDE and EMEA datasets with different term embedding strategies (bold results = best performance ; * statistically significant compared to baseline).

Finally, we investigate the impact of embedding the identified terms provided by The Wiki Machine. When we suggest translation candidates with the XML markup, it only slightly outperforms the baseline approach for GNOME En→It, but statistically significant improves the translations for the KDE_anno test set for both language directions. Similarly to previous observations, the Fill-Up model improves further the translations, i.e. the translations are statistically significant better than the baseline for both language pairs of both KDE test sets as well as for EMEA.

To better understand our translation results, we manually inspected the EMEA En→It sentences, which have the best translation performance. For each of the source sentence and the translation method, we analyse the translated sentences and the bilingual terms that match at least one word in the source sentence. Both translation strategies tried to encapsulate the bilingual terms, but there is clear evidence that the Fill-Up model better embeds the target terms in the context of the translation. For instance in the following example, the target sentence produced by the XML markup (XML trg) does not contain the article "la", uses a wrong conjunction ("di" instead of "per") and wrongly orders the adjective with the noun ("adulti pazienti" instead of "pazienti adulti"). All these issues are correctly addressed by the Fill-Up model (Fill-Up trg) which produces a smoother translation.

source sentence: adult patients receive therapy for tumours

reference sentence: pazienti adulti ricevono la terapia per i tumori

bilingual terms: therapy → terapia, patients → pazienti, adult → adulti

XML trg: adulti pazienti ricevono terapia di tumori

Fill-Up trg: pazienti adulti ricevono la terapia per i tumori

Analysing the number of suggested bilingual terms per sentence, we notice that The Wiki Machine tends to propose more terms than TaaS (on average, The Wiki Machine 3.1, TaaS 2.5 per sentence). Of these terms, TaaS provides on average more translations for each unique source term than The Wiki Machine (on average, TaaS 1.51, The Wiki Machine 1).

In addition to evaluating the performance of TaaS and The Wiki Machine separately, for the EMEA dataset we concatenate the terminological lists provided by the tools and supply it to the XML markup and the Fill-Up approach. Embedding the combined terminology with the XML markup produces a BLEU score of 25.59 for En→It and 24.92 for It→En. This performance is similar to the scores obtained using the terminology provided by The Wiki Machine, but worse compared to TaaS. Passing the whole terminology to the Fill-Up model, the BLEU score increases up to 26.57 for En→It and 27.02 for It→En, which are the best BLEU scores for the EMEA test set. This experiment shows the complementarity of the two term identification methods and suggests a novel research direction.

5 Related Work

The main focus of our research is on bilingual term identification and the embedding of this knowledge into an SMT system. Since previous research (Wu et al. (2008); Haddow and Koehn (2012)) showed that an SMT system built by using a large general resource cannot be used to translate domain-specific terms, we have to provide the system domain-specific lexical knowledge.

Wikipedia with its rich lexical and semantic knowledge was used as a resource for bilingual term identification in the context of SMT. Tyers and Pieanaar (2008) describe method for extracting bilingual dictionary entries from Wikipedia to support the machine translation system. Based on exact string matching they query Wikipedia with a list of around 10,000 noun lemmas to generate the bilingual dictionary. Besides the interwiki link system, Erdmann et al. (2009) enhances their bilingual dictionary by using redirection page titles and anchor text within Wikipedia. To filter out incorrect term translation pairs, the authors use the backward link information to prove if a redirect page title or an anchor text represents a synonymous expression. Niehues and Waibel (2011) analyse different methods to integrate the extracted Wikipedia titles into their system, whereby they explore methods to disambiguate between different translations by using the text in the articles. In addition, the authors use morphological forms of terms to enhance the extracted bilingual dictionary. The results show that the number of out-of-vocabulary words could be reduced by 50% on computer science lectures, which improved the translation quality by more than 1 BLEU point. Arcan et al. (2013) restrict term identification to the observed domain by using the frequency information of Wikipedia categories. Different from these approaches we focus on domain-specific dictionary generation, ignoring identified terms which do not belong to the domain to be observed. Furthermore, we take advantage of the Wikipedia category graph representation and its linking to WordNet domain, which allowed us to identify the domain we were interested in.

Furthermore, research has been done on the integration of domain-specific parallel data into SMT, either by retraining small domain-specific and large general resources as one concatenated parallel data (Koehn and Schroeder, 2007), adding new phrase pairs directly into the phrase table (Langlais, 2002; Ren et al., 2009; Haddow and Koehn, 2012) or assigning adequate weights to the in- and out-of-domain translation models (Foster and Kuhn (2007); Läubli et al. (2013)). Bouamor et al. (2012) address the problem of finding the best approach to integrate new obtained knowledge in an SMT system, and show that they should be used as additional parallel sentences to train the translation model. In our approach, we use the XML markup and the Fill-Up approach, which handles the in-domain parallel data equally to the out-domain data. Furthermore, Okita and Way (2010) investigate the effect of integrating bilingual terminology in the training step of an SMT system, and analyse in particular the performance and sensitivity of the word aligner. As opposed to their approach, we do not have prior knowledge about the bilingual terminology, since we extract it from the document to be translated.

6 Conclusion

In this paper we presented an approach to identify bilingual domain-specific terms starting from a monolingual text and to integrate these into an SMT system. With the help of terminological and lexical resources, we are able to discover a small amount ($\sim$200) of high-quality domain-specific terms and enhanced the performance of an SMT system trained on large amounts (1.8M) of parallel sentences. Monolingual and bilingual term evaluation showed no evidence that one of the tested tools (The Wiki Machine or TaaS) produces better terms than the other in all the test sets. Depending on the manual mapping between the Wikipedia categories and WordNet domains and the existence of a Wikipedia version, our approach is language and domain independent, does not need training data and is able to overcome the sparseness and coherence problems of the Wikipedia categories. Evaluation of the two systems on different language directions and domains shows significant improvements over the baseline in terms of two BLEU scores (up to 13%) and confirms the applicability of such techniques in a real scenario. It is interesting to notice that the Fill-Up technique regularly outperforms the XML markup approach, taking advantage of all terms and not only the overlapping terms in the text to be translated. Our contribution shows a different context of using Fill-Up and extends the usability of it in terms of embedding terminological knowledge into SMT. In future work, we plan to focus on exploiting morphological term variations taking advantage of the alternative terms (i.e., orthographical and morphological variants, synonyms, and related terms) provided by The Wiki Machine. This will make it possible to increase the coverage adding new terms and the accuracy of the proposed method for bilingual term identification.

Acknowledgments

This publication has emanated from research supported in part by a research grant from Science Foundation Ireland (SFI) under Grant Number SFI/12/RC/2289 and by the European Union supported projects EuroSentiment (Grant No. 296277), LIDER (Grant No. 610782) and MateCat (ICT-2011.4.2-287688).

References

Ahmet Aker, Monica Paramita, and Robert Gaizauskas. 2013. Extracting bilingual terminologies from comparable corpora. In *Proceedings of ACL*, Sofia, Bulgaria.

Mihael Arcan, Susan Marie Thomas, Derek De Brandt, and Paul Buitelaar. 2013. Translating the FINREP taxonomy using a domain-specific corpus. In *Machine Translation Summit XIV*, pages 199–206.

Luisa Bentivogli, Pamela Forner, Bernardo Magnini, and Emanuele Pianta. 2004. Revising the wordnet domains hierarchy: semantics, coverage and balancing. In *Proceedings of the Workshop on Multilingual Linguistic Ressources*, pages 101–108. Association for Computational Linguistics.

Arianna Bisazza, Nick Ruiz, and Marcello Federico. 2011. Fill-up versus Interpolation Methods for Phrase-based SMT Adaptation. In *Proceedings of IWSLT*.

Dhouha Bouamor, Nasredine Semmar, and Pierre Zweigenbaum. 2012. Identifying bilingual multi-word expressions for statistical machine translation. In *Proceedings of the Eight International Conference on Language Resources and Evaluation (LREC'12)*, Istanbul, Turkey, may. European Language Resources Association (ELRA).

Jonathan Clark, Chris Dyer, Alon Lavie, and Noah Smith. 2011. Better Hypothesis Testing for Statistical Machine Translation: Controlling for Optimizer Instability . In *Proceedings of the Association for Computational Lingustics*.

Maike Erdmann, Kotaro Nakayama, Takahiro Hara, and Shojiro Nishio. 2009. Improving the extraction of bilingual terminology from wikipedia. *ACM Trans. Multimedia Comput. Commun. Appl.*, 5(4):31:1–31:17, November.

Marcello Federico, Nicola Bertoldi, and Mauro Cettolo. 2008. Irstlm: an open source toolkit for handling large scale language models. In *INTERSPEECH*, pages 1618–1621. ISCA.

George Foster and Roland Kuhn. 2007. Mixture-model adaptation for smt. In *Proceedings of the Second Workshop on Statistical Machine Translation*, StatMT '07, pages 128–135, Stroudsburg, PA, USA. Association for Computational Linguistics.

Claudio Giuliano, Alfio Massimiliano Gliozzo, and Carlo Strapparava. 2009. Kernel methods for minimally supervised wsd. *Computational Linguistics*, 35(4):513–528.

Barry Haddow and Philipp Koehn. 2012. Analysing the Effect of Out-of-Domain Data on SMT Systems. In *Proceedings of the Seventh Workshop on Statistical Machine Translation*, Montréal, Canada. Association for Computational Linguistics.

Philipp Koehn and Josh Schroeder. 2007. Experiments in domain adaptation for statistical machine translation. In *Proceedings of the Second Workshop on Statistical Machine Translation*, StatMT '07, pages 224–227, Stroudsburg, PA, USA. Association for Computational Linguistics.

Philipp Koehn, Hieu Hoang, Alexandra Birch, Chris Callison-Burch, Marcello Federico, Nicola Bertoldi, Brooke Cowan, Wade Shen, Christine Moran, Richard Zens, Chris Dyer, Ondřej Bojar, Alexandra Constantin, and Evan Herbst. 2007. Moses: open source toolkit for statistical machine translation. In *Proceedings of the 45th Annual Meeting of the ACL on Interactive Poster and Demonstration Sessions*, ACL '07, pages 177–180, Stroudsburg, PA, USA. Association for Computational Linguistics.

Philipp Koehn. 2005. Europarl: A Parallel Corpus for Statistical Machine Translation. In *Conference Proceedings: the tenth Machine Translation Summit*, pages 79–86. AAMT.

J. Richard Landis and Gary G. Koch. 1977. Measurement of Observer Agreement for Categorical Data. In *Biometrics*, volume 33, pages 159–174.

Philippe Langlais. 2002. Improving a general-purpose statistical translation engine by terminological lexicons. In *Proceedings of the 2nd International Workshop on Computational Terminology (COMPUTERM) '2002, Taipei, Taiwan*, pages 1–7.

Samuel Läubli, Mark Fishel, Martin Volk, and Manuela Weibel. 2013. Combining statistical machine translation and translation memories with domain adaptation. In Stephan Oepen, Kristin Hagen, and Janne Bondi Johannesse, editors, *Proceedings of the 19th Nordic Conference of Computational Linguistics (NODALIDA 2013), May 22?24, 2013, Oslo University, Norway*, Linköping Electronic Conference Proceedings, pages 331–341, Oslo, May. Linköpings universitet Electronic Press.

Pablo N Mendes, Max Jakob, Andrés García-Silva, and Christian Bizer. 2011. Dbpedia spotlight: shedding light on the web of documents. In *Proceedings of the 7th International Conference on Semantic Systems*, pages 1–8. ACM.

Rada Mihalcea. 2007. Using Wikipedia for Automatic Word Sense Disambiguation. In *Proceedings of NAACL-HLT*, pages 196–203.

Jan Niehues and Alex Waibel. 2011. Using Wikipedia to Translate Domain-specific Terms in SMT. In *nternational Workshop on Spoken Language Translation*, San Francisco, CA, USA.

Franz Josef Och and Hermann Ney. 2003. A systematic comparison of various statistical alignment models. *Computational Linguistics*, 29.

Tsuyoshi Okita and Andy Way. 2010. Statistical Machine Translation with Terminology. In *Proceedings of the First Symposium on Patent Information Processing (SPIP)*, Tokyo, Japan.

Kishore Papineni, Salim Roukos, Todd Ward, and Wei-Jing Zhu. 2002. Bleu: a method for automatic evaluation of machine translation. In *Proceedings of the 40th Annual Meeting on Association for Computational Linguistics*, ACL '02, pages 311–318.

Mārcis Pinnis, Nikola Ljubešić, Dan Ştefănescu, Inguna Skadiņa, Marko Tadić, and Tatiana Gornostay. 2012. Term extraction, tagging, and mapping tools for under-resourced languages. In *Proceedings of the Terminology and Knowledge Engineering (TKE2012) Conference.*

Zhixiang Ren, Yajuan Lü, Jie Cao, Qun Liu, and Yun Huang. 2009. Improving statistical machine translation using domain bilingual multiword expressions. In *Proceedings of the Workshop on Multiword Expressions: Identification, Interpretation, Disambiguation and Applications*, MWE '09, pages 47–54, Stroudsburg, PA, USA. Association for Computational Linguistics.

John Shawe-Taylor and Nello Cristianini. 2004. *Kernel Methods for Pattern Analysis.* Cambridge University Press, New York, NY, USA.

Raivis Skadinš, Marcis Pinnis, Tatiana Gornostay, and Andrejs Vasiljevs. 2013. Application of online terminology services in statistical machine translation. In *Proceedings of the XIV Machine Translation Summit*, Nice, France.

Ralf Steinberger, Bruno Pouliquen, Anna Widiger, Camelia Ignat, Tomaz Erjavec, Dan Tufis, and Dániel Varga. 2006. The jrc-acquis: A multilingual aligned parallel corpus with 20+ languages. In *Proceedings of the 5th International Conference on Language Resources and Evaluation (LREC'2006).*

Jörg Tiedemann. 2012. Parallel data, tools and interfaces in opus. In Nicoletta Calzolari (Conference Chair), Khalid Choukri, Thierry Declerck, Mehmet Uğur Doğan, Bente Maegaard, Joseph Mariani, Jan Odijk, and Stelios Piperidis, editors, *Proceedings of the Eight International Conference on Language Resources and Evaluation (LREC'12)*, Istanbul, Turkey, may. European Language Resources Association (ELRA).

Francis M. Tyers and Jacques A. Pieanaar. 2008. Extracting bilingual word pairs from wikipedia. In *Collaboration: interoperability between people in the creation of language resources for less-resourced languages (A SALTMIL workshop).*

Hua Wu, Haifeng Wang, and Chengqing Zong. 2008. Domain adaptation for statistical machine translation with domain dictionary and monolingual corpora. In *Proceedings of the 22nd International Conference on Computational Linguistics - Volume 1*, COLING '08, pages 993–1000.

Torsten Zesch and Iryna Gurevych. 2007. Analysis of the wikipedia category graph for nlp applications. In *Proceedings of the TextGraphs-2 Workshop (NAACL-HLT)*, pages 1–8, Rochester, April. Association for Computational Linguistics.

Gap in pagination due to unavailable paper.

Pages 32

NPMI driven recognition of nested terms

Małgorzata Marciniak
Institute of Computer Science, PAS
Jana Kazimierza 5,
01-248 Warsaw, Poland
mm@ipipan.waw.pl

Agnieszka Mykowiecka
Institute of Computer Science, PAS
Jana Kazimierza 5,
01-248 Warsaw, Poland
agn@ipipan.waw.pl

Abstract

In the paper, we propose a new method of identifying terms nested within candidates for the terms extracted from domain texts. The list of all terms is then ranked by the process of automatic term recognition. Our method of identifying nested terms is based on two aspects: grammatical correctness and normalised pointwise mutual information (NPMI) counted for all bigrams on the basis of a corpus. NPMI is typically used for recognition of strong word connections but in our solution we use it to recognise the weakest points within phrases to suggest the best place for division of a phrase into two parts. By creating only two nested phrases in each step we introduce a binary hierarchical term structure. In the paper, we test the impact of the proposed nested terms recognition method applied together with the C-value ranking method to the automatic term recognition task.

1 Introduction

The Automatic Term Recognition (ATR) task consists in identifying linguistic expressions that refer to domain concepts. This is usually realised in two steps. In the first one, candidates for terms are identified in a corpus of domain texts. This step usually consists in identifying grammatically correct phrases by means of linguistically motivated grammars describing noun phrases in a given language. However, sometimes no linguistic knowledge is utilised and candidates for terms are just frequent n-grams as in (Wermter and Hahn, 2005). The second processing step consists in ranking the extracted candidates and selecting those which are most important for a considered domain. This task is usually based on statistics.

The ranking procedure can be based on different measures which are characterised as either "termhood-based" or "unithood-based". Kageura and Umino (1996) defined the termhood-based methods measure as "the degree that a linguistic unit is related to domain-specific concepts", i.e. the likelihood that a phrase is a valid domain term. The unithood-based methods measure the collocation strength of word sequences, usually with the help of log-likelihood, pointwise mutual information or T-score measures, described in (Manning and Schütze, 1999), while ATR applications based on them are described in e.g., (Pantel and Lin, 2001), (Sclano and Velardi, 2007). A comparison of these approaches is given in (Pazienza et al., 2005). Some hybrid solutions to the ATR problem have also been proposed (Vu et al., 2008) or (Ventura et al., 2014). In the paper (Korkontzelos et al., 2008), the comparison between these two groups of methods led the authors to the conclusion that the termhood-based methods outperform the unithood-based ones.

This paper is devoted to the problem of selecting candidates for terms from an annotated domain corpus. Our approach is based on the C-value method, (Frantzi et al., 2000). An important feature of this method that attracted our attention was the focus on nested terms. Frantzi *et al.* (2000) described nested terms as terms that appear within other longer terms, and may or may not appear by themselves in the corpus. They show that recognition of nested terms is very important in terms extraction, but they also give examples when a nested phrase constructed according to the grammar rules is not a term. One of

Proceedings of the 4th International Workshop on Computational Terminology, pages 33–41,
Dublin, Ireland, August 23 2014.

these examples is the phrase *real time clock* which has two nested phrases: *real time* and *time clock*, but the second one is not a good term. The authors define the C-value measure that is used to rank candidate terms extracted from a domain corpus, together with their nested terms. It is counted on the basis of the frequency of the term as a whole phrase in the corpus, its frequency as a nested phrase in other terms, the number of different phrases in which that nested phrase occurred, and its length. The authors expect that phrases that aren't considered as terms should be placed at the end of the list ordered according to this coefficient value.

We applied the C-value method to extract terminology from a corpus of hospital discharge documents in Polish. Experiments, where different methods of counting the C-value were tested, are described in (Marciniak and Mykowiecka, 2014). Unfortunately, a few grammatically correct but semantically odd phrases were always placed in the top part of the ranking list of terms. Examples of such phrases, placed among the 200 top positions, are: *USG jamy* 'USG of cavity' being a nested phrase of the very frequent phrase *USG jamy brzusznej* 'USG of abdominal cavity', *infekcja górnych dróg* 'infection of upper tract' or *powiększony węzeł* 'enlarged node'.

We propose a method that prevents the creation and promotion of such nested phrases to be considered as terms. The main idea is to use a unithood-based method e.g., Normalised Pointwise Mutual Information (NPMI) (Bouma, 2009) for driving recognition of nested phrases. Our solution is based on the division of each considered phrase into only two parts. The places where a phrase is divided must create nested phrases that are consistent with grammar rules. Usually, there are several possible places for division of a phrase. From all of them, we choose the weakest point according to NPMI counted for bigrams on the basis of the whole corpus. So, as a bigram constitutes a strong collocation, it prevents the phrase from being dividing in this place, and does not usually lead to the creation of semantically odd nested phrases, of which examples are given above.

The analysed corpus of Polish medical texts is described in Section 2. In the following two sections we present the method in detail. Then, in Section 5, we describe the comparison of the resulting lists of terms ranked according to the C-value measure, for two methods of recognition of nested phrases , i.e.: for all possible phrases fulfilling grammatical rules, and for the method proposed in the paper.

2 Corpus description

The domain corpus consists of 3116 hospital discharge documents gathered at a hospital in Poland. Texts came from six departments and were written by several physicians of different specialties. The collected texts were analysed using standard general purpose NLP tools. The morphological tagger Pantera (Acedański, 2010), cooperating with the Morfeusz analayser (Woliński, 2006), was used to divide the text into tokens and annotate them with morhosyntactic tags. They included a part of speech name (POS), a base form, as well as case, gender and number information, where they were appropriate. This information is used by shallow grammars recognising the boundaries of nominal phrases — term candidates and, also,sources for nested phrases. The corpus consists of about 2 million tokens in which a shallow grammar recognised more than 22 thousand noun phrases.

The corpus contains quite a lot of words unrecognised by Morfeusz as the vocabulary of the clinical documents significantly differs from general Polish texts. Additionally, the texts are not very well edited despite the spelling correction tools being usually turned on, so they contain quite a lot of misspelled words. This results in 22,000 unrecognised tokens (many of them are medications, acronyms and units) that are not taken into account when nominal phrases are recognised. Consequently, it lowers the number of phrases, and affects the quality of some of them. In (Marciniak and Mykowiecka, 2011), the problems of morphological annotation of hospital documents in Polish are presented and the reasons for the many unrecognised tokens are highlighted.

3 Nested phrases recognition

In this section, we describe the way to create a list of term candidates that takes into account nested phrases. This task is usually supported by linguistic knowledge that allows for identifying candidates for terms which are syntactically valid.

In the extraction step, we identified complex noun phrases consisting of nouns with adjectival and nominal modifiers obeying Polish grammar rules (in particular, case, gender and number agreement). The types of Noun Phrases under consideration can be schematically defined as below:

AdjPhrase Noun AdjPhrase
AdjPhrase Noun
Noun AdjPhrase
NounPhrase NounPhrase-in-genitive

Noun Phrases were extracted from the corpus using a cascade of shallow grammars. As Polish is a highly inflected language, we operate on simplified base forms of phrases in our computations, consisting of lemmas of subsequent words. This approach, proposed for ATR in Polish in (Marciniak and Mykowiecka, 2013), allows us to unify forms of phrases in different cases and numbers. For example: *przewlekłe zapalenie gardła, przewlekłe zapalenia gardła, przewlekłego zapalenia gardła, przewlekłych zapaleń gardła* are forms of 'chronic pharyngitis' in nominative singular and plural and genitive in both numbers.[1] The extracted phrases constitute a foundation for creating the list of term candidates. Then we add nested phrases, recognised within those phrases, to the list of term candidates. The rules for identifying nested terms are described in the rest of this section.

3.1 Motivations

The original C-value method (Frantzi et al., 2000) recommends that all grammatical phrases, created from the maximal phrases identified in a corpus, should be considered as term candidates. But using this method, we quite frequently obtain nested grammatical subphrases which are syntactically correct, but semantically odd. One such phrase is *infekcja górnych dróg* 'infection (of the) upper tract' that is created from *infekcja górnych dróg oddechowych* 'infection (of the) upper respiratory tract'.[2] The last phrase has many different longer phrases in which it is nested, eg: *(częsta, drobna, ostra, bakteryjna...) infekcja górnych dróg oddechowych* '(often, minor, acute, bacterial...) infection (of the) upper respiratory tract', but it always concerns *drogi oddechowe* 'respiratory tract'. We observe that the bigram *drogi oddechowe* 'respiratory tract' constitutes a strong collocation. So the original phrase shouldn't be divided in this place to create a phrase containing the word *drogi* 'tract' without adding its type, i.e., *oddechowe* 'respiratory' in this case. Nominal phrases are usually constructed from two parts (except for coordinated phrases and nouns with more complex subcategoriaztion frames, which usually do not fulfill agreement constraints in Polish). For nominal phrases from domain corpora, we suggest that the best place for the division is indicated by the weakest bigram.

After considering patterns of nominal phrases in Polish, we realised that the weakest connections are usually between two nominal phrases (the last pattern). So, an adjective more likely modifies the nearest noun and not the whole phrase, as in: $\textit{prawidłowa}_{adj}$ $\textit{mikroflora}_{noun}$ $\textit{górnych}_{adj}$ $\textit{dróg}_{noun}$ $\textit{oddechowych}_{adj}$ 'normal microflora (of the) upper respiratory tract'. In this phrase, all the outermost adjectives are important parts of nominal phrases constructed around their nearest nouns, and it should be divided into two nominal phrases: *prawidłowa mikroflora* 'normal microflora' and *górne drogi oddechowe* 'upper respiratory tract'. However, it is not the universal rule. Let us consider another example: *częste infekcje górnych dróg oddechowych* 'frequent infections (of the) upper respiratory tract', where *częste* 'frequent' modifies the whole phrase. To account for this observation, we may slightly prefer divisions into two nominal phrases instead of an adjective and a nominal phrase.

3.2 Algorithm

From several methods for counting the strength of bigrams we chose the normalised pointwise mutual information proposed by Bouma, (2009), as it is less sensitive to occurrence frequency. We were looking for a method for which the bigram, consisting of a rare and a frequent token, will be high if the rare token only appears in connection with the frequent token, as, for example, for *esowate skrzywienie* 'S-shaped curvature'. The definition of this measure for the 'x y' bigram, where x and y are lemmas of sequence

---

[1] Further in the paper we will use phrases in the nominal case and singular number forms. These forms may differ slightly from the same phrases being nested ones (in genitive).

[2] The word order of the translation is different.

tokens, is given in (1), where p(x,y) is a probability of the 'x y' bigram in the considered corpus, and p(x), p(y) are probabilities of 'x' and 'y' unigrams respectively.

$$NPMI(x,y) = \left(ln \ \frac{p(x,y)}{p(x)p(y)} \right) \Big/ - ln \ p(x,y) \qquad (1)$$

First, we extract all the grammatical phrases from the corpus, taking into account only the maximal one. Then, for each phrase we identify all places where it can be divided according to grammar rules. We count NPMI for those and indicate the weakest connection in the phrase. Then, we divide it into two parts in this position. There are two possible situations: the first, when the phrase is divided into two nominal phrases; the second, when one phrase is a nominal phrase while the second one is an adjective phrase. In the first case, we add both parts to the list of term candidates and process the obtained parts of the phrase in the same way. In the second case, only a nominal phrase is added to the list and only this phrase is further divided.

```
nested_phrases (phr)
  if length(phr) > 1
    find all i positions where phr can be divided according to the grammatic rules
    for all i positions
      count NPMI(i-th bigram of phr)
    sort NPMIs from the lowest to the highest value
    j := position with the lowest NPMI
    if the j-th position divides phr into two nominal phrases
      divide phr into phr1 and phr2 on j-th position
      add phr1 and phr2 to the list of nested terms
      nested_phrases(phr1)
      nested_phrases(phr2)
    else
      n := position with the lowest NPMI where phr is divided into two nominal phrases
      if (120% NPMI(j)) > NPMI (n)
        divide phr into phr1 and phr2 on n-th position
        add phr1 and phr2 to the list of nested terms
        nested_phrases(phr1)
        nested_phrases(phr2)
      else
        if phr is divided on j position into adjective phrase to the left of nominal phrase
          cut off the outermost left element from phr
        else
          cut off the outermost right element from phr
        add phr to the list of nested terms
        nested_phrases(phr)
```

Figure 1: Procedure of nested phrases recognition

To take into account the specificity of adjectives in Polish nominal phrases described in 3.1, we decided to introduce a slight modification to the basic algorithm. If the weakest connection prefers the cutting of an adjective part from a phrase, we find the nearest place where the phrase is divided into two nominal phrases. Then, we compare the NPMI value referring to this bigram with 120% (fixed experimentally) of the lowest NPMI value. If it is still lower, we cut off one outermost element (adjective or adverb) from this adjectival part of the phrase and add the slightly shorter phrase to the term list. In other case, we divide the original phrase in that second place into two nominal phrases. The algorithm is given in Figure 1.

The grammatically correct nested phrases				The nested phrases divided with help of NPMI			
'infection'	'upper'	'tract'	'respiratory'	'infection'	'upper'	'tract'	'respiratory'
infekcja	*górnych*	*dróg*	*oddechowych*	*infekcja*	*górnych*	*dróg*	*oddechowych*
infekcja	*górnych*	*dróg*		—			
infekcja				*infekcja*			
	górne	*drogi*	*oddechowe*		*górne*	*drogi*	*oddechowe*
	górne	*drogi*		—			
		drogi	*oddechowe*			*drogi*	*oddechowe*
		drogi				*drogi*	

Table 1: The nested phrases for two methods

bigram	translation	NPMI
infekcja górna	'infection upper'	0.65658
górna droga	'upper tract'	0.78773
droga oddechowy	'tract respiratory'	0.95089

Table 2: The NPMI value for the bigrams of the phrase: *infekcja górnych dróg oddechowych*

3.3 Examples

Let us consider examples illustrating the method. We compare nested phrases obtained from the phrase *infekcja górnych dróg oddechowych* 'infection (of the) upper respiratory tract' for the two following methods: creating all grammatically correct nested phrases, and the NPMI driven method. The considered phrase is constructed according to the following pattern: Noun_j Adj_i Noun_i Adj_i where indexes indicate agreement constraints, so a grammatically correct phrase may consist of: Noun_j Adj_i Noun_i, but can't be constructed as: Noun_j Adj_i. Thus, *infekcja górnych dróg* 'infection of the upper tract' is grammatically correct, while *infekcja górnych* 'infection of upper' is not. The phrase can be divided in one of two places indicated by the '|' character: *infekcja | górnych dróg | oddechowych*, 'infection | upper tract | respiratory'[3] and it is possible to create six grammatically correct phrases, see Table 1. Applying our method, we first count NPMI for the places of possible divisions. The NPMI value for two bigrams *infekcja górny* 'infection upper' and *droga oddechowy* 'tract respiratory' counted for the corpus described in Section 2 are given in Table 2. The lower value is for the first bigram so the phrase can be divided into: *infekcja* 'infection' and *górne drogi oddechowe* 'upper respiratory tract'. Both parts constitute nominal phrases so the phrase is divided in this place and both parts are added to the list of term candidates. In the next step only the second phrase can be recursively divided. The weaker connection is for: *górny droga* 'upper tract'. So the adjective *górna* 'upper' is cut off the phrase and only the nested phrase *drogi oddechowe* 'respiratory tract' is accepted as a term candidate. Table 1 contains all the nested phrases obtained by both methods for the considered phrase. It may be noted that our method, correctly, does not extract two semantically odd nested phrases from the six obtained by the first method.

Let us consider a phrase where the lowest NPMI indicates division into an adjective and a nominal phrase: *boczne*$_{adj}$ *skrzywienie*$_{noun}$ *kręgosłupa*$_{noun}$ 'lateral curvature (of the) spine'. The phrase can be divided in both places: *boczne | skrzywienie | kręgosłupa* 'lateral | curvature | spine'. The weakest connection is for the bigram: *boczny skrzywienie* 'lateral curvature', it indicates division into the nominal phrase *skrzywienie kręgosłupa* 'curvature (of the) spine', and the adjective *boczne* 'lateral'. The other place of division causes the phrase to be divided into two nominal phrases. So we compare the NPMI for *skrzywienie kręgosłup* 'curvature spine', with 120% NPMI *boczny skrzywienie* 'lateral curvature', see Table 3. As the first value is lower than the second one, the method prefers to divide the phrase into two nominal phrases *boczne skrzywienie* 'lateral curvature' and *kręgosłup* 'spine'. The basic algorithm, without multiplying NPMI values in some cases by 120%, creates a good term *skrzywienie kręgosłupa* 'curvature (of the) spine' instead of two nominal phrases: *boczne skrzywienie* 'lateral curvature' and

[3]The word for word translation.

bigram	translation	NPMI	120% NPMI
boczny skrzywienie	'lateral curvature'	0.67619	0.81143
skrzywienie kręgosłup	'curvature spine'	0.80151	

Table 3: The NPMI value for the bigrams of the phrase: *boczne skrzywienie kręgosłupa*

kręgosłup spine.

There are a few cases when the phrase division driven by the NPMI value prefers cutting off an adjective in the first step instead of dividing it into two nominal phrases, see: *okołoporodowe*$_{adj}$ *uszkodzenie*$_{noun}$ *splotu*$_{noun}$ *ramiennego*$_{adj}$ *prawego*$_{adj}$ 'perinatal damage (of) right brachial plexus'. Despite the fact that *okołoporodowe uszkodzenie splotu ramiennego* 'perinatal damage (of) brachial plexus' is a good term, we would prefer the division into two nominal phrases *okołoporodowe uszkodzenie* 'perinatal damage' and *splot ramienny prawy* 'right brachial plexus'. The last division reflects the internal construction of the phrase that might be important in an ontology construction task which is one of the intended uses of the method. In this case, we want to recognise nested phrases representing two concepts which are in a relationship. The method still (correctly) cuts off the adjective *częsty* 'frequent' from the phrase *częste infekcje górnych dróg oddechowych* 'frequent infections (of the) upper respiratory tract'.

4 Terms ordering

To test to what extent our approach to the phrase selection problem influences the ultimate results of the term selection algorithm, we used the C-value coefficient (Frantzi et al., 2000) to order extracted phrases. The standard equation for this coefficient is given in (2) where p is the phrase under consideration, freq(p) is a number of occurrences of this phrase both nested and in isolation, LP is a set of phrases containing p, r(LP) – the number of different phrases in LP, and l(p) = $log_2(length(p))$.

$$C\text{-}value(p) = \begin{cases} l(p) * (freq(p) - \frac{1}{r(LP)} \sum_{lp \in LP} freq(lp)), & if\ r(LP) > 0, \\ l(p) * freq(p), & if\ r(LP) = 0 \end{cases} \quad (2)$$

The C-value ranking method is focused on deciding which nested phrases should be considered as terms. It assigns higher values to phrases which, having the same frequency rate, occur more frequently in isolation or occur in a larger number of different longer phrases, i.e., have different lexical contexts within a set of initially extracted phrases. To account for the fact that long phrases tend to occur more rarely than shorter ones, the result is multiplied by the logarithm of the phrase length. If a phrase occurs only in isolation, its frequency rate defines the C-value. When a phrase occurs only in one context, its C-value gets the value 0 as it is properly assumed to be incomplete. If a nested phrase occurs in a lot of different contexts, its chances of constituting a domain term increase. A slight modification of the method also allows for processing phrases of length 1, which originally all got a 0 value. For this purpose, for one word phrases, the logarithm of the length (used in the original solution) is replaced with a non zero constant. In (Barrón-Cedeno et al., 2009), where this method was applied to Spanish texts, the authors set it to 1, arguing that if it is lower, one word terms are located too low on the ranking list (it cannot be greater than 1 for obvious reasons). Our experiments proved that in our data, such a change results in very many one word elements at the top of the list, we used a 0.1 value as the equivalent of logarithm of length for one word phrases.

The results obtained using the C-value method depend on the details concerning the way in which we distinguish different phrases, i.e., how we count r(LP). First, for inflectional languages like Polish, a method for recognising inflected forms of a multiword phrase has to be established. In our experiment, we used base form sequences for this purpose. Secondly, the way of counting contexts has to be elaborated. For example, it should be decided, whether *red blood cells* and *white blood cells* are two different contexts for *cell* or only one. For languages with more relaxed word order, like Polish, the same phrase can appear in different orders, e.g., *liczne krwinki białe* 'numerous white blood cells' or *krwinki białe liczne* 'white blood cells numerous'. As the C-value coefficient is drastically different for frequent phrases which occur in one and in two different contexts, we tried to limit the number of phrase types

length	all	=1	=2	3–5	>5
s-phrases	32809	4918	13442	13984	465
npmi-phrases	28328	4918	11693	11313	393
s&npmi-phrases	26671	4918	10420	10929	404

frequency	=1	2-10	11-50	51-100	101-1000	>1000
in isolation	13304	6776	1506	300	415	81
s-phrases	18572	10417	2461	523	704	132
s&npmi-phrases	15210	8296	2002	420	625	118

C-value	0	0<c<1	1≤c<5	5≤c<10	10 ≤c<100	>100
s-phrases	8946	2500	16891	1804	2312	357
s&npmi-phrases	3428	2508	16652	1672	2074	337

Table 4: The number of recognised phrases

	total	removed		lowered			
changes		all	correctly	all	incorrectly	correctly	questionable
nmpi/s-phrases	39	39	30	0	-	-	-
s&nmpi$_1$/s-phrases	137	28	26	109	19	73	17
s&nmpi/s-phrases	132	27	27	105	20	70	15

Table 5: The number of correct changes for the first 2000 positions

which differ only in order or are included one in another. We discussed different methods of counting contexts in (Marciniak and Mykowiecka, 2014) and concluded there that none of the tested ranking procedures were able to filter out all semantically odd noun phrases from the top of the list of terms. The best results we obtained taking only the nearest context of a phrase into account, i.e. the closest word to the left or to the right of a phrase. We used the greater number of these different left and right contexts. This solution can lower the actual number of contexts, but it prevents us from counting the same context words placed before and after the phrase twice.

5 Results and evaluation

We applied the C-value method to two sets of term candidates. The first set contains all possible phrases fulfilling the grammatical rules, while the second one is obtained by the method described in the previous sections. It is worth noting that we consider contexts of nested phrases only when they are recognised in phrases by the method. As both methods recognised different numbers of phrases,[4] Table 4 gives the comparison of their numbers. In this table, *s-phrases* refers to the baseline solution in which all grammatically correct nested phrases are taken into account, *npmi-phrases* refers to the solution obtained while recognising nested phrases using only NPMI value and *s&nmpi-pharses* is a name used for the final solution in which both grammar rules and NPMI values are utilised. Initially, 32809 phrases were extracted. The number of candidate phrases was significantly lower after applying NPMI selection (by 15%), but some of them were not grammatically correct. When applying both selection criteria we obtained about 80% of the phrases (only grammatically correct) from the *s-phrases* set. The reduction concerned phrases irrespective of their occurrences within texts. As to the distribution of the C-value, it may be seen that we finally obtained much fewer phrases with a 0 C-value.

In the paper (Marciniak and Mykowiecka, 2014), an evaluation of different aspects of the original C-value method applied to the same domain corpus is given. In this paper, we want to verify the tendencies

[4]The set of phrases recognised by the proposed method is included in that consisting of phrases recognised by the standard method based on all valid phrases.

of changes introduced by the proposed method. To focus on this task, we analysed all phrases that were included in the top 2000 positions ranked by the first method and whose position was moved below the 3000 in the final list, see Table 5. This comparison shows that our solution removed 6.6% (132) of phrases from the top of the list of terms, and 73.5% (97) among them were semantically odd phrases. We compared the baseline with the version in which, the minimum of NPMI value was always used to indicate phrase division ($s\&nmpi_1$) and with the final version, in which the division into two noun phrases was preferred (i.e. if the NPMI at the division position was not significantly higher than the minimum inside phrase). In the first case, we observed the elimination of only 39 phrases from the top 2000. From these sequences, 9 were incorrectly removed from the candidates list. Using both NPMI value and grammaticality test resulted in 137 changes inside the top 2000. This time, from 28 removed elements only 2 could be considered correct. In the final solution, all 27 phrases eliminated form the first 2000 were correctly eliminated, while from the remaining 105 phrases, whose positions were significantly lowered, 70 were not terms. For some phrases it is difficult to judge whether they are domain related phrases or are rather related to other topics. These cases were labelled as "questionable" in the table.

As the proposed method does not change the way of counting whole phrases recognised in the corpus, we cannot expect that every incorrect phrase will be eliminated. For example, the phrase *infekcja górnych dróg* 'infection (of the) upper tract' cannot disappear from our list of term candidates, as it occurred three times as a whole phrase due to a spelling error in the word *oddechowy* 'respiratory'. We only expect that its position is similar to the position of this phrase ranked according to the frequency of the whole phrase. We obtained this required effect. The semantically odd phrase, considered above, changed its position from 144 to 4374.

The presented results show that integrating NPMI with syntactic rules resulted both in better selection and ranking of candidates. The final decision to prefer division into two noun phrases had rather small but positive effects.

6 Conclusion

In the paper, we described a method for recognising nested phrases based on normalised pointwise mutual information. We proved that the method has a strong tendency not to recognise semantically odd phrases once they are nested, and allows for the elimination of incorrect unfinished phrases from the top part of the ranking list. The method can be applied to any language: it requires the existence of a POS tagger and several rules describing noun phrase structure. Taking into account information on the internal syntactic structure of terms improved the results.

There are several possible directions for further research. First, we plan to test the method on different datasets. Then, some extensions of the method are planned. The potentially easiest one concerns the problem of how to extend the method to take into account more complex phrases (i.e. prepositional phrases and coordinated phrases) and count NPMI effectively for them. The second problem refers to longer phrases that are strongly connected but only when all elements appear together. An example of such a phrase is *wykładnik stanu zapalnego* 'inflammation exponent' where *stan zapalny* 'inflammation' can appear in different contexts, but *wykładnik stanu* 'exponent (of the) state' implies the word *zapalny* 'inflammatory'. The third problem is to explore whether the proposed method provides a good starting point for recognising pieces of information that should be represented in a domain ontology.

References

Szymon Acedański. 2010. A morphosyntactic Brill tagger for inflectional languages. In Hrafn Loftsson, Eiríkur Rögnvaldsson, and Sigrún Helgadóttir, editors, *Advances in Natural Language Processing*, volume 6233 of *Lecture Notes in Computer Science*, pages 3–14. Springer.

Alberto Barrón-Cedeno, Gerardo Sierra, Patrick Drouin, and Sophia Ananiadou. 2009. An improved automatic term recognition method for Spanish. In *Computational Linguistics and Intelligent Text Processing, LNCS 5449*, pages 125–136. Springer.

Gerlof Bouma. 2009. Normalized (pointwise) mutual information in collocation extraction. In *From Form to*

Meaning: Processing Texts Automatically, Proceedings of the Biennial GSCL Conference 2009, volume Normalized, pages 31–40, Tübingen.

Katerina Frantzi, Sophia Ananiadou, and Hideki Mima. 2000. Automatic recognition of multi-word terms: the C-value/NC-value method. *Int. Journal on Digital Libraries*, 3:115–130.

Kyo Kageura and Bin Umino. 1996. Method for automatic term recognition. A review. *Terminology*, 3:2:259–289.

Ioannis Korkontzelos, Ioannis P. Klapaftis, and Suresh Manandhar. 2008. Reviewing and evaluating automatic term recognition techniques. In *Advances in Natural Language Processing, LNAI 5221*, volume 5221, pages 248–259. Springer.

Christopher D. Manning and Hinrich Schütze. 1999. *Foundations of Statistical Natural Language Processing*. MIT Press, Cambridge, MA, USA.

Małgorzata Marciniak and Agnieszka Mykowiecka. 2011. Towards Morphologically Annotated Corpus of Hospital Discharge Reports in Polish. In *Proceedings of BioNLP 2011*, pages 92–100.

Małgorzata Marciniak and Agnieszka Mykowiecka. 2013. Terminology extraction from domain texts in Polish. In R. Bembenik, L. Skonieczny, H. Rybinski, M. Kryszkiewicz, and M. Niezgodka, editors, *Intelligent Tools for Building a Scientific Information Platform. Advanced Architectures and Solutions*, volume 467 of *Studies in Computational Intelligence*, pages 171–185. Springer-Verlag.

Małgorzata Marciniak and Agnieszka Mykowiecka. 2014. Terminology extraction from medical texts in polish. *Journal of Biomedical Semantics*, 5:24.

Patrick Pantel and Dekang Lin. 2001. A statistical corpus-based term extractor. In *Proceedings of the 14th Biennial Conference of the Canadian Society on Computational Studies of Intelligence: Advances in Artificial Intelligence*, pages 36–46, London, UK, UK. Springer-Verlag.

Maria T. Pazienza, Marco Pennacchiotti, and Fabio M. Zanzotto. 2005. Terminology Extraction: An Analysis of Linguistic and Statistical Approaches. In S. Sirmakessis, editor, *Knowledge Mining Series: Studies in Fuzziness and Soft Computing*. Springer Verlag.

Francesco Sclano and Paola Velardi. 2007. Termextractor: a web application to learn the shared terminology of emergent web communities. In Ricardo Jardim-Gonçalves, Jörg P. Müller, Kai Mertins, and Martin Zelm, editors, *Enterprise Interoperability II*, pages 287–290. Springer.

Juan A. Lossio Ventura, Clement Jonquet, Mathieu Roche, and Maguelonne Teisseire. 2014. Towards a mixed approach to extract biomedical terms from documents. *International Journal of Knowledge Discovery in Bioinformatics*, 4(1).

Thuy Vu, Ai Ti Aw, and Min Zhang. 2008. Term extraction through unithood and termhood unification. In *Proceedings of International Joint Conference on Natural Language Processing*.

Joachim Wermter and Udo Hahn. 2005. Massive biomedical term discovery. In *Discovery Science, LNCS 3735*, pages 281–293. Springer Verlag.

Marcin Woliński. 2006. Morfeusz — a practical solution for the morphological analysis of Polish. In *Intelligent Information Processing and Web Mining. Proceedings of the International IIS:IIPWM'06 Conference held in Ustron, Poland*. Springer-Verlag.

Bilingual Termbank Creation via Log-Likelihood Comparison and Phrase-Based Statistical Machine Translation

Rejwanul Haque, Sergio Penkale, Andy Way[†]
Lingo24, Edinburgh, UK
{rejwanul.haque, sergio.penkale}@lingo24.com
[†]CNGL, Centre for Global Intelligent Content
School of Computing, Dublin City University
Dublin 9, Ireland
away@computing.dcu.ie

Abstract

Bilingual termbanks are important for many natural language processing (NLP) applications, especially in translation workflows in industrial settings. In this paper, we apply a log-likelihood comparison method to extract monolingual terminology from the source and target sides of a parallel corpus. Then, using a Phrase-Based Statistical Machine Translation model, we create a bilingual terminology with the extracted monolingual term lists. We manually evaluate our novel terminology extraction model on English-to-Spanish and English-to-Hindi data sets, and observe excellent performance for all domains. Furthermore, we report the performance of our monolingual terminology extraction model comparing with a number of the state-of-the-art terminology extraction models on the English-to-Hindi datasets.

1 Introduction

Terminology plays an important role in various NLP tasks including Machine Translation (MT) and Information Retrieval. It is also exploited in human translation workflows, where it plays a key role in ensuring translation consistency and reducing ambiguity across large translation projects involving multiple files and translators over a long period of time. The creation of monolingual and bilingual terminological resources using human experts are, however, expensive and time-consuming tasks. In contrast, automatic terminology extraction is much faster and less expensive, but cannot be guaranteed to be error-free. Accordingly, in real NLP applications, a manual inspection is required to amend or discard anomalous items from an automatically extracted terminology list.

The automatic terminology extraction task starts with selecting candidate terms from the input domain corpus, usually in two different ways: (i) linguistic processors are used to identify noun phrases that are regarded as candidate terms (Kupiec, 1993; Frantzi et al., 2000), and (ii) non-linguistic *n*-gram word sequences are regarded as candidate terms (Deane, 2005).

Various statistical measures have been used to rank candidate terms, such as C-Value (Ananiadou et al., 1994), NC-Value (Frantzi et al., 2000), log-likelihood comparison (Rayson and Garside, 2000), and TF-IDF (Basili et al., 2001). In this paper, we present our bilingual terminology extraction model, which is composed of two consecutive and independent processes:

1. A log-likelihood comparison method is employed to rank candidate terms (*n*-gram word sequences) independently from the source and target sides of a parallel corpus,

2. The extracted source terms are aligned to one or more extracted target terms using a Phrase-Based Statistical Machine Translation (PB-SMT) model (Koehn et al., 2003).

We then evaluate our novel bilingual terminology extraction model on various domain corpora considering English-to-Spanish and low-resourced and less-explored English-to-Hindi language-pairs and see excellent performance for all data sets.

Proceedings of the 4th International Workshop on Computational Terminology, pages 42–51,
Dublin, Ireland, August 23 2014.

The remainder of the paper is organized as follows. In Section 2, we discuss related work. In Section 3, we describe our two-stage terminology extraction model. Section 4 presents the results and analyses of our experiments, while Section 5 concludes, and provides avenues for further work.

2 Related Work

Several algorithms have been proposed to extract terminology from a domain-specific corpus, which can be divided into three broad categories: linguistic, statistical and hybrid. Statistical or hybrid approaches dominate this field, with some of the leading work including the use of frequency-based filtering (Daille et al., 1994), NC-Value (Frantzi et al., 2000), log-likelihood and mutual information (Rayson and Garside, 2000; Pantel and Lin, 2001), TF-IDF (Basili et al., 2001; Kim et al., 2009), weirdness algorithm (Ahmad et al., 1999), Glossex (Kozakov et al., 2004) and Termex (Sclano and Velardi, 2007).

In this work, we focus on extracting bilingual terminology from a parallel corpus. He et al. (2006) demonstrate that using log-likelihood for term discovery performs better than TF-IDF. Accordingly, similarly to Rayson and Garside (2000) and Gelbukh et al. (2010), we extract terms independently from both sides of a parallel corpus using log-likelihood comparisons with a generic reference corpus. Some of the most influential research on bilingual terminology extraction includes Kupiec (1993), Gaussier (1998), Ha et al. (2008) and Lefever et al. (2009). Lefever et al. (2009) proposed a sub-sentential alignment-based terminology extraction module that links linguistically motivated phrases in parallel texts. Unlike our approach, theirs relies on linguistic analysis tools such as PoS taggers or lemmatizers, which might be unavailable for under-resourced languages (e.g., Hindi). Gaussier (1998) and Ha et al. (2008) applied statistical approaches to acquire parallel term-pairs directly from a sentence-aligned corpus, with the latter focusing on improving monolingual term extraction, rather than on obtaining a bilingual term list. In contrast, we build a PB-SMT model (Koehn et al., 2003) from the input parallel corpus, which we use to align a source term to one or more target terms. While Rayson and Garside (2000) and Gelbukh et al. (2010) only allowed the extraction of single-word terms, we focus on extraction of up to 3-gram terms.

3 Methodology

In this section, we describe our two-stage bilingual terminology extraction model. In the first stage, we extract monolingual terms independently from either side of a sentence-aligned domain-specific parallel corpus. In the second stage, the extracted source terms are aligned to one or more extracted target terms using a PB-SMT model.

3.1 Monolingual Terminology Extraction

The monolingual term extraction task involves the identification of terms from a list of candidate terms formed from all n-gram word sequences from the monolingual domain corpus (i.e. in our case, each side of the domain parallel corpus, cf. Section 4.1). On both source and target sides, we used lists of language-specific stop-words and punctuation marks in order to filter out anomalous items from the candidate termlists. In order to rank the candidate terms in those lists, we used a log-likelihood comparison method that compares the frequencies of each candidate term in both the domain corpus and the large general corpus used as a reference.[1]

The log-likelihood (LL) value of a candidate term ($\mathrm{C_n}$) is calculated using equation (1) from Gelbukh et al. (2010).

$$\mathrm{LL} = 2 * ((\mathrm{F_d} * \log(\mathrm{F_d}/\mathrm{E_d})) + (\mathrm{F_g} * \log(\mathrm{F_g}/\mathrm{E_g}))) \tag{1}$$

where $\mathrm{F_d}$ and $\mathrm{F_g}$ are the frequencies of $\mathrm{C_n}$ in the domain corpus and the generic reference corpus, respectively. $\mathrm{E_d}$ and $\mathrm{E_g}$ are the expected frequencies of $\mathrm{C_n}$, which are calculated using (2) and (3).

$$\mathrm{E_d} = \mathrm{N_d^n} * (\mathrm{F_d} + \mathrm{F_g})/(\mathrm{N_d^n} + \mathrm{N_g^n}) \tag{2}$$

$$\mathrm{E_g} = \mathrm{N_g^n} * (\mathrm{F_d} + \mathrm{F_g})/(\mathrm{N_d^n} + \mathrm{N_g^n}) \tag{3}$$

[1]Before the term-extraction process begins, we apply a number of preprocessing methods including tokenisation to the input domain corpus and the generic reference corpus.

where $\mathrm{N}_\mathrm{d}^\mathrm{n}$ and $\mathrm{N}_\mathrm{g}^\mathrm{n}$ are the numbers of n-grams in the domain corpus and reference corpus, respectively. Thus, each candidate term is associated with a weight (LL value) which is used to sort the candidate terms: those candidates with the highest weights have the most significant differences in frequency in the two corpora. However, we are interested in those candidate terms that are likely to be terms in the domain corpus. Gelbukh et al. (2010) used the condition in (4) in order to filter out those candidate terms whose relative frequencies are bigger in the domain corpus than in the reference corpus, and we do likewise.

$$\mathrm{F_d}/\mathrm{N}_\mathrm{d}^\mathrm{n} > \mathrm{F_g}/\mathrm{N}_\mathrm{g}^\mathrm{n} \tag{4}$$

In contrast with Gelbukh et al. (2010), we extract multi-word terms up to 3-grams, whereas they focused solely on extracting single word terms.

3.2 Creating a Bilingual Termbank

We obtained source and target termlists from the bilingual domain corpus using the approach described in Section 3.1. We use a PB-SMT model (Koehn et al., 2003) to create a bilingual termbank from the extracted source and target termlists.

This section provides a mathematical derivation of the PB-SMT model to show how we scored candidate term-pairs using the PB-SMT model. We built a source-to-target PB-SMT model from the bilingual domain corpus using the Moses toolkit (Koehn et al., 2007). In PB-SMT, the posterior probability $\mathrm{P}(e_1^I|f_1^J)$ is directly modelled as a (log-linear) combination of features (Och and Ney, 2002), that usually comprise M translational features, and the language model, as in (5):

$$\log \mathrm{P}(e_1^I|f_1^J) = \sum_{m=1}^{M} \lambda_m h_m(f_1^J, e_1^I, s_1^K) + \lambda_{\mathrm{LM}} \log \mathrm{P}(e_1^I) \tag{5}$$

where $e_1^I = e_1, ..., e_I$ is the probable candidate translation for the given input sentence $f_1^J = f_1, ..., f_J$ and $s_1^K = s_1, ..., s_k$ denotes a segmentation of the source and target sentences respectively into the sequences of phrases $(\hat{f}_1, ..., \hat{f}_k)$ and $(\hat{e}_1, ..., \hat{e}_k)$ such that (we set $i_0 := 0$):

$$\begin{aligned} \forall k \in [1, K] \quad & s_k := (i_k; b_k, j_k), (b_k \text{ corresponds to starting index of } f_k) \\ & \hat{e}_k := \hat{e}_{i_{k-1}+1}, ..., \hat{e}_{i_k}, \\ & \hat{f}_k := \hat{f}_{b_k}, ..., \hat{f}_{j_k} \end{aligned}$$

Each feature h_m in (5) can be rewritten as in (6):

$$h_m(f_1^J, e_1^I, s_1^K) = \sum_{k=1}^{K} \hat{h}_m(\hat{f}_k, \hat{e}_k, s_k) \tag{6}$$

Therefore, the translational features in (5) can be rewritten as in (7):

$$\sum_{m=1}^{M} \lambda_m h_m(f_1^J, e_1^I, s_1^K) = \sum_{m=1}^{M} \lambda_m \sum_{k=1}^{K} \hat{h}_m(\hat{f}_k, \hat{e}_k, s_k) \tag{7}$$

In equation (7), $\hat{h}_m$ is a feature defined on phrase-pairs $(\hat{f}_k, \hat{e}_k)$, and λ_m is the feature weight of $\hat{h}_m$. These weights (λ_m) are optimized using minimum error-rate training (MERT) (Och, 2003) on a held-out 500 sentence-pair development set for each of the experiments.

We create a list of probable source–target term-pairs by taking each source and target term from the source and target termlists, respectively, provided that those source–target term-pairs are present in the PB-SMT phrase-table. We calculate a weight (w) for each source–target term-pair (essentially, a phrase-pair, i.e. $(\hat{e}_k, \hat{f}_k)$) using (8):[2]

$$w(\hat{e}_k, \hat{f}_k) = \sum_{m=1}^{M} \lambda_m \hat{h}_m(\hat{f}_k, \hat{e}_k) \tag{8}$$

[2] Equation (8) is derived from the right-hand side of equation (7) for a single source–target phrase-pair.

In order to calculate w, we used the four standard PB-SMT translational features ($\hat{h}_m$), namely forward phrase translation log-probability ($\log \mathrm{P}(\hat{e}_k|\hat{f}_k)$), its inverse ($\log \mathrm{P}(\hat{f}_k|\hat{e}_k)$), the lexical log-probability ($\log \mathrm{P}_{\mathrm{lex}}(\hat{e}_k|\hat{f}_k)$), and its inverse ($\log \mathrm{P}_{\mathrm{lex}}(\hat{f}_k|\hat{e}_k)$). We considered a higher threshold value for weights and considered those term-pairs whose weights exceeded this threshold. For each source term, we considered a maximum of the four highest-weighted target terms.

Domain Parallel Corpus		
Domain	Sentences	Words (English)
English-to-Spanish		
Banking, Finance and Economics	50,112	548,594
Engineering	91,896	1,165,384
IT	33,148	367,046
Tourism and Travel	50,042	723,088
Science	79,858	1,910,482
Arts and Culture	9,124	100,620
English-to-Hindi		
EILMT	7,096	173,770
EMILLE	9,907	159,024
Launchpad	67,663	380,546
KDE4	84,089	324,289
Reference Corpus		
Language	Sentences	Words
English	4,000,000	82,048,154
Spanish	4,132,386	128,005,190
Hindi	10,000,000	182,066,982

Table 1: Corpus Statistics.

4 Experiments and Discussion

4.1 Data Used

We conducted experiments on several data domains for two different language-pairs, English-to-Spanish and English-to-Hindi. For English-to-Spanish, we worked with client-provided data taken from six different domains in the form of translation memories. For English-to-Hindi, we used three parallel corpora from three different sources (EILMT, EMILLE and Launchpad) taken from HindEnCorp[3] (Bojar et al., 2014) released for the WMT14 shared translation task,[4] and a parallel corpus of KDE4 localization files[5] (Tiedemann, 2009). The EMILLE corpus contains leaflets from the UK Government and various local authorities. The domain of the EILMT[6] corpus is tourism.

We used data from a collection of translated documents from the United Nations (MultiUN)[7] (Tiedemann, 2009) and the European Parliament (Koehn et al., 2005) as the monolingual English and Spanish reference corpora. We used the HindEnCorp monolingual corpus (Bojar et al., 2014) as the monolingual Hindi reference corpus. The statistics of the data used in our experiments are shown in Table 1.

4.2 Runtime Performance

Our terminology extraction model is composed of two main processes: (i) Moses training and tuning (restricting the number of iterations of MERT to a maximum of 6), and (ii) terminology extraction. In Table 2, we report the actual runtimes of these two processes on the six domain corpora. As Table

[3]http://ufallab.ms.mff.cuni.cz/ bojar/hindencorp/
[4]http://www.statmt.org/wmt14/
[5]http://opus.lingfil.uu.se/KDE4.php
[6]English-to-Indian Language Machine Translation (EILMT) is a Ministry of IT, Govt. of India sponsored project.
[7]http://opus.lingfil.uu.se/MultiUN.php

2 demonstrates, both MT system-building (training *and* tuning combined) and terminology extraction processes are very short on each corpus. Given the crucial influence of bilingual terminology on quality in translation workflows, we believe that the creation of such assets from scratch in less than 30 minutes may prove to be a significant breakthrough for translators.

	MT System Building	Terminology Extraction
English-to-Spanish		
Banking, Finance and Economics	05:49	04:23
Engineering	06:47	04:33
IT	04:10	04:31
Tourism and Travel	05:34	04:24
Science	15:26	04:52
Arts and Culture	03:20	04:16
English-to-Hindi		
EILMT	12:41	15:47
EMILLE	05:41	17.18
Launchpad	04:37	24.11
KDE4	04:05	16:50

Table 2: Runtimes (minutes:seconds) for MT system-building and bilingual terminology extraction on the different domain data sets.

4.3 Human Evaluation

Of course, it is one thing to rapidly create translation assets such as bilingual termbanks, and another entirely to ensure the quality of such resources. Accordingly, we evaluated the performance of our bilingual terminology extraction model on each English-to-Spanish and English-to-Hindi domain corpus reported in Table 1, with the evaluation goals being twofold: (i) measuring the accuracy of the monolingual terminology extraction process, and (ii) measuring the accuracy of our novel bilingual terminology creation model.

As mentioned in Section 3.2, a source term may be aligned with up to four target terms. For evaluation purposes, we considered the top-100 source terms based on the LL values (cf. (1)) and their target counterparts (i.e. one to four target terms). The quality of the extracted terms was judged by native Spanish and Hindi speakers, both with excellent English skills, and the evaluation results are reported in Table 3. Note that we were not able to measure recall of the term extraction model on the domain corpora due to the unavailability of a reference terminology set. The evaluator counted the number of valid terms in the source term list for the domain in question, and the percentage of valid terms with respect to the total number of terms (i.e. 100) is reported in the second column in Table 3. We refer to this as VST (Valid Source Terms). For each valid source term there are one to four target terms that are ranked according to the weights in (8). In theory, therefore, the top-ranked target term is the most suitable target translation of the aligned source term. The evaluator counted the number of instances where the top-ranked target term was a suitable target translation of the source term; the percentage with respect to the number of valid source terms is shown in the third column in Table 3, and denoted as VTT (Valid Target Terms). The evaluator also reported the number of cases where any of the four target terms was a suitable translation of the source term; the percentage with respect to the number of valid source terms is given in the fourth column in Table 3. Furthermore, the evaluator counted the number of instances where any of the four target terms with minor editing can be regarded as suitable target translation; the percentage with respect to the number of valid source terms is reported in the last column of Table 3. In Table 4, we show three English–Spanish term-pairs extracted by our automatic term extractor where the target terms (Spanish) are slightly incorrect. In all these examples the edit distance between the correct term and the one proposed by our automatic extraction method is quite low, meaning that just a few keystrokes can transform the candidate term into the correct one. In these cases editing the candidate term is much cheaper (in terms of time) than creating the translations from scratch.

	VST (%)	VTT1 (%)	VTT4 (%)	VTTME4 (%)
English-to-Spanish				
Banking, Finance and Economics	76	92.1	93.4	94.7
Engineering	84	90.5	91.7	94.1
IT	89	90.0	97.8	97.8
Tourism and Travel	72	86.1	93.1	93.1
Science	94	93.6	93.6	93.6
Arts and Culture	89	91.9	96.5	96.5
English-to-Hindi				
EILMT	91	81.3	83.5	96.7
EMILLE	79	62.1	83.5	98.7
Launchpad	88	95.4	98.8	98.8
KDE4	79	88.6	89.8	94.9

Table 3: Manual evaluation results obtained on the top-100 term pairs. VST: Valid Source Terms, VTT1: Valid Target Terms (1-best), VTT4: Valid Target Terms (4-best), VTTME4: Valid Target Terms with Minor Editing (4-best).

Source Terms	Target Terms (using Bilingual Term Extractor)	Target Terms corrected with Minor Editing	Edit Distance
Shutter	Obturación	Obturador	5
comment: wrong choice of inflection is likely caused by the term being most frequently used as 'shutter speed'			
Lenses	Objetivos EF	Objetivos	3
comment: The qualifier 'EF' should not be present in the target, as it is not in the source			
Leave Cancel	Cancelación Vacaciones	Cancelación de Vacaciones	3
comment: The preposition 'de' is missing in the target term			

Table 4: Slightly wrong target terms corrected with minor editing.

In Table 3, we see that the accuracy of the monolingual term extraction model varies from 72% to 94% for both English-to-Spanish and English-to-Hindi. For English-to-Spanish, the accuracy of our bilingual terminology creation model ranges from 86.1% to 93.6%, 91.7% to 97.8% and 93.1% to 97.8% when the 1-best, 4-best and 4-best with slightly edited target terms are considered, respectively. For English-to-Hindi, the accuracy of our bilingual terminology creation model ranges from 62.1% to 95.4%, 83.5% to 98.8% and 94.9% to 98.8% when the 1-best, 4-best and 4-best with slightly edited target terms are considered, respectively.

We are greatly encouraged by these results, as they demonstrate that our novel bilingual termbank creation method is robust in the face of the somewhat noisy monolingual term-extraction results; as a consequence, if better methods for suggesting monolingual term candidates are proposed, we expect the performance of our bilingual term-creation model to improve accordingly.

We calculated the distributions of unigram, bigram and trigram in the valid source terms (cf. Table 3) and reported in Table 5. We also calculated the percentages of their distributions in the valid source terms averaged over all 10 data sets. As can be seen from Table 3, the percentage of the average distribution of the trigram terms is quite low (i.e. 2.5%). This result justifies our decision for extraction of up to 3-gram terms.

	Unigram	Bigram	Trigram
English-to-Spanish			
Banking, Finance and Economics	55	20	1
Engineering	64	18	2
IT	75	12	2
Tourism and Travel	49	18	5
Science	91	3	0
Arts and Culture	76	10	3
English-to-Hindi			
EILMT	73	17	1
EMILLE	35	37	7
Launchpad	85	3	0
KDE4	74	5	0
Average	80.4%	17.0 %	2.5%

Table 5: Distributions of unigram, bigram and trigram in the valid source term pairs (cf. second column in Table 3).

4.4 Comparison: Monolingual Terminology Extraction

In this section we report the performance of our monolingual terminology extraction model (cf. Section 3.1) comparing with the performance of several state-of-the-art terminology extraction algorithms capable of recognising multiword terms. In order to extract monolingual multiword terms we used the JATE toolkit[8] (Zhang et al., 2008). This toolkit first extracts candidate terms from a corpus using linguistic tools and then applies term extraction algorithms to recognise terms specific to the domain corpus. The JATE toolkit is currently available only for the English language. For evaluation purposes, we considered the source-side of the English-to-Hindi domain corpora.

Algorithm	Reference	EILMT	EMILLE	Launchpad	KDE4
LLC (Bilingual)	cf. VST in Table 3	91	79	88	79
LLC		77	53	80	71
STF		46	04	54	44
ACTF		42	15	62	48
TF-IDF		50	36	45	17
Glossex	Kozakov et al. (2004)	76	43	76	71
JK	Justeson & Katz (1995)	42	13	58	42
NC-Value	Frantzi et al. (2000)	46	34	52	25
RIDF	Church & Gale (1995)	27	16	23	21
TermEx	Sclano et al. (2007)	42	08	46	41
C-Value	Ananiadou (1994)	49	44	62	40
Weirdness	Ahmed et al. (1999)	77	57	82	63

Table 6: Monolingual evaluation results. LLC: Log-Likelihood Comparison, STF: Simple Term Frequency, ACTF: Average Corpus Term Frequency, JK: Justeson Katz

For comparison, we considered the top-100 source terms based on the log-likelihood values (cf. (1)). The automatic term extraction algorithms in JATE assign weights (domain representativeness) to the candidate terms giving an indication of the likelihood of being a good domain-specific term. The quality of the extracted terms (top-100 highest weighted) was judged by an evaluator with excellent English skills, and the evaluation results are reported in Table 6. The evaluator counted the number of valid terms

[8] https://code.google.com/p/jatetoolkit/

in the highest weighted 100 terms that were extracted using different state-of-the-art term extraction algorithms.

The third row of Table 6 represents the percentage of the valid source terms extracted by our log-likelihood comparison (LLC) based monolingual term extraction algorithm. The next three rows represent three basic monolingual term extraction algorithms (STF: simple term frequency, ACTF: average corpus term frequency and TF-IDF) available in the JATE toolkit. The last seven rows represent seven state-of-the-art terminology extraction algorithms. As can be seen from Table 6, LLC is the best-performing algorithm with the Weirdness (Ahmad et al., 1999) and the Glossex (Kozakov et al., 2004) algorithms on the EILMT and the KDE4 corpora, respectively. The LLC is also the second-best performing algorithm on the EMILLE and the Lauchpad corpora.

We see in Table 6 that the percentage of valid source terms is quite low on the EMILLE corpus. This might be caused by it containing information leaflets in a variety of domains (consumer, education, housing, health, legal, social), which might bring down the percentage of valid source terms on this corpus.

Note that the percentage of valid source terms (VST) reported in Table 3 is calculated taking the top-100 source terms from the bilingual term-pair list that were extracted using the method described in Section 3.2. For comparison purposes we again report this percentage (VST in Table 3) in the second row in Table 6. Our bilingual term extraction method discards any anomalous pairs from the initial candidate term-pair list (cf. Section 3.2). This essentially removes some of the source entries that are not pertinent to the domain. As a result, the percentage of the valid source terms extracted applying our bilingual terminology extraction method (Table 3) is higher than the percentage of the valid source terms extracted applying our monolingual terminology extraction algorithm (LLC) (Table 6). We clearly see from Tables 3 and 6 that this bilingual approach to term extraction not only achieves remarkable performance on the bilingual task, but that when used in a monolingual context it outperforms most state-of-the-art extraction algorithms, and is comparable with the best ones. We should also note that JATE's implementation of these algorithms (including Weirdness) uses language-dependent modules such as a lemmatizer, unlike our implementation of LLC which is language-independent.

5 Conclusions and Future Work

In this paper we presented a bilingual multi-word terminology extraction model based on two independent consecutive processes. Firstly, we employed a log-likelihood comparison method to extract source and target terms independently from both sides of a parallel domain corpus. Secondly, we used a PB-SMT model to align source terms to one or more target terms. The manual evaluation results on ten different domain corpora of two syntactically divergent language-pairs showed the accuracy of our bilingual terminology extraction model to be very high, especially in the light of the rather noisier monolingual candidate terms presented to it. Given the reported high levels of performance – minimum levels of 93.1% and 94.9% in the 4-best set-up across all six domains for English-to-Spanish and all four domains for English-to-Hindi, respectively – we are convinced that the extracted bilingual multiword termbanks are useful 'as is', and with a small amount of post-processing from domain experts would be completely error-free.

The proposed bilingual terminology extraction model has been tested on a highly investigated language-pair, English-to-Spanish, and a less-explored and low-resourced English-to-Indic language-pair, English-to-Hindi. Interestingly, the performance of the bilingual terminology extraction model is excellent for the both language-pairs. We also tested several state-of-the-art monolingual terminology extraction algorithms including our own (log-likelihood comparison) on the source-side of the four English-to-Hindi domain data sets. According to the manual evaluation results, our monolingual multi-word term extraction model proves to be the best-performing algorithm on two domain data sets and the second best-performing algorithm on the remaining two domain data sets. Our monolingual multiword terminology extraction method is clearly comparable to the state-of-the-art monolingual terminology extraction algorithms.

In this work, we considered all n-gram word sequences from the domain corpus as candidate terms.

In future work, we would like to incorporate the candidate phrasal term identification model of Deane (2005), which would omit irrelevant multiword units, and help us extend our evaluation beyond the top-100 terms. We also plan to demonstrate the impact of the created termbanks on translator productivity in a number of workflows – different language pairs, domains, and levels of post-editing – in an industrial setting.

Acknowledgements

This work was partially supported by the Science Foundation Ireland (Grant 07/CE/I1142) as part of CNGL at Dublin City University, and by Grant 610879 for the Falcon project funded by the European Commission.

References

S. Ananiadou. 1994. A methodology for automatic term recognition. In *COLING: 15th International Conference on Computational Linguistics*, pages 1034–1038.

K. Ahmad, L. Gillam and L. Tostevin. 1999. University of Surrey Participation in TREC8: Weirdness Indexing for Logical Document Extrapolation and Retrieval (WILDER). In *the Eighth Text REtrieval Conference (TREC-8)*. National Institute of Standards and Technology, Gaithersburg, MD., pp.717–724.

R. Basili, A. Moschitti, M. Pazienza and F. Zanzotto. 2001. A contrastive approach to term extraction. In *Proceedings of the 4th Conference on Terminology and Artificial Intelligence (TIA 2001)*. Nancy, France, 10pp.

K. Church and W. Gale. 1995. Inverse Document Frequency (IDF): A Measure of Deviation from Poisson. In *Proceedings of the 3rd Workshop on Very Large Corpora*, pages 121–130. Cambridge, MA.

B. Daille, E. Gaussier and J-M. Langé. 1994. Towards automatic extraction of monolingual and bilingual terminology. In *COLING 94, The 15th International Conference on Computational Linguistics, Proceedings*. Kyoto, Japan, pp.515–521.

P. Deane. 2007. A nonparametric method for extraction of candidate phrasal terms. In *ACL-05: 43rd Annual Meeting of the Association for Computational Linguistics*. Ann Arbor, Michigan, USA, pp.605–613.

K. Frantzi, S. Ananiadou and H. Mima. 2000. Automatic Recognition of Multi-word Terms: the C-value/NC-value Method. *International Journal of Digital Libraries*. **3**(2): 115–130.

E. Gaussier. 1998. Flow Network Models for Word Alignment and Terminology Extraction from Bilingual Corpora. In *COLING-ACL '98, 36th Annual Meeting of the Association for Computational Linguistics and 17th International Conference on Computational Linguistics, Proceedings of the Conference, Volume II*. Montreal, Quebec, Canada, pp.444–450.

A. Gelbukh, G. Sidorov, E. Lavin-Villa and L. Chanona-Hernandez. 2010. Automatic Term Extraction Using Log-Likelihood Based Comparison with General Reference Corpus. In *15th International Conference on Applications of Natural Language to Information Systems, NLDB 2010, Proceedings*. LNCS vol. 6177. Berlin: Springer. pp.248–255.

L. Ha, G. Fernandez, R. Mitkov and G. Corpas. 2008. Mutual bilingual terminology extraction. In *LREC 2008: 6th Language Resources and Evaluation Conference*. Marrakech, Morocco, pp.1818–1824.

T. He, T., X. Zhang and Y. Xinghuo. 2006. An Approach to Automatically Constructing Domain Ontology. In *Proceedings of the 20th Pacific Asia Conference on Language, Information and Computation, PACLIC 2006*. Wuhan, China, pp.150–157.

J. S. Justeson, and S. M. Katz. 1995. Technical terminology: some linguistic properties and an algorithm for identification in text. Natural language engineering, 1(1) 9–27.

S. Kim, T. Baldwin and M-Y. Kan. 2009. An Unsupervised Approach to Domain-Specific Term Extraction. In *Proceedings of the Australasian Language Technology Association Workshop 2009*. Sydney, Australia, pp.94–98.

P. Koehn. 2005. Europarl: a parallel corpus for statistical machine translation. In *MT Summit X: The Tenth Machine Translation Summit*. Phuket, Thailand, pp.79–86.

P. Koehn, H. Hoang, A. Birch, C. Callison-Burch, M. Federico, N. Bertoldi, B. Cowan, W. Shen, C. Moran, R. Zens, C. Dyer, O. Bojar, A. Constantin and E. Herbst. 2007. Moses: Open Source Toolkit for Statistical Machine Translation. In *ACL 2007, Proceedings of the Interactive Poster and Demonstration Sessions*. Prague, Czech Republic, pp.177–180.

P. Koehn, F. Och and H. Ney. 2003. Statistical Phrase-Based Translation. In *HLT-NAACL 2003: conference combining Human Language Technology conference series and the North American Chapter of the Association for Computational Linguistics conference series*. Edmonton, Canada, pp. 48–54.

L. Kozakov, Y. Park, T. H. Fin, Y. Drissi, Y. N. Doganata, and T. Cofino. 2004. Glossary extraction and knowledge in large organisations via semantic web technologies. In *Proceedings of the 6th International Semantic Web Conference and the 2nd Asian Semantic Web Conference*.

J. Kupiec. 1993. An algorithm for finding noun phrase correspondences in bilingual corpora. In *31st Annual Meeting of the Association for Computational Linguistics, Proceedings of the Conference*. Columbus, Ohio, USA, pp.17–22.

E. Lefever, L. Macken and V. Hoste. 2009. Language-Independent Bilingual Terminology Extraction from a Multilingual Parallel Corpus. In *EACL '09 Proceedings of the 12th Conference of the European Chapter of the Association for Computational Linguistics*. Athens, Greece, pp.496–504.

F. Och. 2003. Minimum Error Rate Training in Statistical Machine Translation. In *41st Annual Meeting of the Association for Computational Linguistics, Proceedings of the Conference*. Sapporo, Japan, pp.160–167.

F. Och and H. Ney. 2002. Discriminative Training and Maximum Entropy Models for Statistical Machine Translation. In *40th Annual Meeting of the Association for Computational Linguistics, Proceedings of the Conference*. Philadelphia, PA, USA, pp.295–302.

O. Bojar, V. Diatka, P. Rychlý, P. Straňák, A. Tamchyna, and D. Zeman. 2014. Hindi-English and Hindi-only Corpus for Machine Translation. In *Proceedings of the Ninth International Language Resources and Evaluation Conference (LREC'14)*. Reykjavik, Iceland.

P. Pantel and D. Lin. 2001. A Statistical Corpus-Based Term Extractor. In E. Stroulia and S. Matwin (eds.) *Advances in Artificial Intelligence, 14th Biennial Conference of the Canadian Society for Computational Studies of Intelligence, AI 2001, Ottawa, Canada, Proceedings*. LNCS vol. 2056. Berlin: Springer, pp.36–46.

P. Rayson and R. Garside. 2000. Comparing corpora using frequency profiling. In *Proceedings of the Workshop on Comparing Corpora, held in conjunction with the 38th Annual Meeting of the Association for Computational Linguistics (ACL 2000)*. Hong Kong, pp.1–6.

F. Sclano and P. Velardi. 2007. TermExtractor: a web application to learn the shared terminology of emergent web communities. In *Proceedings of the 3rd International Conference on Interoperability for Enterprise Software and Applications (I-ESA 2007)*. Funchal, Madeira Island, Portugal, pp.287–290.

J. Tiedemann. 2009. News from OPUS - A Collection of Multilingual Parallel Corpora with Tools and Interfaces. In N. Nicolov and K. Bontcheva and G. Angelova and R. Mitkov (eds.) Recent Advances in Natural Language Processing (vol V), pages 237–248, John Benjamins, Amsterdam/Philadelphia.

Z. Zhang, J. Iria, C. Brewster and F. Ciravegna. 2008. A Comparative Evaluation of Term Recognition Algorithms. In *Proceedings of The sixth international conference on Language Resources and Evaluation, (LREC 2008)*, pages 2108–2113, Marrakech, Morocco.

The ACL RD-TEC: A Dataset for Benchmarking Terminology Extraction and Classification in Computational Linguistics

Behrang Q. Zadeh* **and Siegfried Handschuh***†
*Insight Centre of Data Analytics
National University of Ireland, Galway
†Department of Computer Science and Mathematics
University of Passau, Germany
{behrang.qasemizadeh, siegfried.handschuh}@insight-centre.org

Abstract

This paper introduces ACL RD-TEC: a dataset for evaluating the extraction and classification of terms from literature in the domain of computational linguistics. The dataset is derived from the Association for Computational Linguistics anthology reference corpus (ACL ARC). In its first release, the ACL RD-TEC consists of automatically segmented, part-of-speech-tagged ACL ARC documents, three lists of candidate terms, and more than 82,000 manually annotated terms. The annotated terms are marked as either valid or invalid, and valid terms are further classified as *technology* and *non-technology* terms. Technology terms signify methods, algorithms, and solutions in computational linguistics. The paper describes the dataset and reports the relevant statistics. We hope the step described in this paper encourages a collaborative effort towards building a full-fledged annotated corpus from the computational linguistics literature.

1 Introduction

Computational terminology (CT) embraces a set of algorithms that extract terms from domain-specific corpora and arrange them in domain-specific knowledge structures such as a vocabulary, thesaurus or ontology. Modern methods in CT often take a corpus-based, distributional approach to fulfil their tasks. These methods exploit data-centric, data-sensitive techniques for mining and organizing terms. Evaluation of these methods—as described in Vivaldi and Rodrïguez (2007) and Nazarenko and Zargayouna (2009)—is inherently a difficult task. Regardless of the employed metric and method for the performance comparison of CT algorithms, however, choosing a shared dataset consisting of a fixed set of documents—which can be accessed freely and easily—is a major step towards alleviating a number of obstacles in the evaluation process. From a mathematical perspective, changes in the document set will alter the underlying distribution of words and terms in the benchmark dataset. Consequently, this can vary the performance of methods. From perspectives that involve meaning interpretation, as described in L'Homme (2014), terms are defined against a context. This context is the representative of a specialized subject field and reflects the requirements of the intended application for the extracted terms. In an evaluation dataset, the specialized subject field is largely defined by the set of documents in this dataset. Therefore, variation in the set of documents can result in variant set of terms.

Creating datasets for benchmarking CT techniques have been addressed in several research efforts. The GENIA corpus is a well-known example of such reference datasets in bio-text mining: a corpus of 2000 abstracts from scientific publications in biological literature that is accompanied by the annotations of 100,000 terms organized in a well-defined ontology (Kim et al., 2003). The Colorado Richly Annotated Full Text Corpus (CRAFT) is another example of a bio-text mining dataset, which consists of 97 articles from the PubMed Central Open Access subset annotated with biomedical concepts such as 'mouse genes' (Bada et al., 2012). In a more recent effort, Bernier-Colborne and Drouin (2014) report on creating a corpus for the evaluation of term extraction in the domain of automotive engineering.

Proceedings of the 4th International Workshop on Computational Terminology, pages 52–63,
Dublin, Ireland, August 23 2014.

The use of these datasets for CT research and terminology extraction has one obstacle: the minimal prerequisite knowledge that is required to understand these specialized discourse and literature. This understanding of text is, perhaps, essential to enable a CT researcher to first comprehend and then describe a linguistic phenomenon. Hence, conducting research in these specialized fields requires a training for terminologists. For example, research in bio-text mining is often conducted by a team that includes experts in biology, bioinformaticians and computational linguists who have specialized training in this field. Conducting CT research in these specialized domains, therefore, may not be the first choice for computational linguists who have a keen interest and specialized knowledge in the computational analysis of languages—or want to train themselves to gain this knowledge.[1]

In this paper, we introduce the ACL RD-TEC: a Reference Dataset for Terminology Extraction and Classification in the domain of computational linguistics. The ACL RD-TEC is drawn from the ACL ARC (Bird et al., 2008). The ACL ARC is a fixed set of scholarly publications in the domain of computational linguistics. It has been developed with an aim to provide a platform for benchmarking methods of scholarly document processing.[2] We report further processes and annotations that have been carried out on the ACL ARC in order to move a step closer to a reference dataset of familiar materials for the CT research community.

Before describing the dataset, Section 2 delineates the terms that are used in this paper and gives a brief summary of computational terminology. In Section 3, we explain the automatic and manual processes performed to create the ACL RD-TEC and summarize the statistics of the current release. Finally, we conclude and describe our goals for the immediate future in Section 4.

2 Computational Terminology

Computational terminology inherits its complexity from the difficulties in the interpretation of meaning in language. In terminology, these complications are often summarized by the question 'what counts as a *term*?' The Oxford Dictionary defines a term as

> 'a word or phrase used to describe a thing or to express a concept, specially in a particular kind of language or branch of study'.

According to the International Organization for Standardization (ISO), a term is

> 'a verbal designation of a general concept in a specific subject field (ISO 1087-1(2000))'.

As stated by Cabré (2010), linguistically, terms are *lexical units* and carry a special *meaning* in particular *contexts*. A lexical unit is often considered as a *lexical form*—a single token, part of a word, a word or a combination of these—that is paired with a single meaning and serves as the basic element of a language's vocabulary. As stated by L'Homme (2014), terms are the denomination of items of knowledge, i.e. concepts.

According to their lexical forms, terms are usually classified as *simple* or *complex*. Simple terms consist of one token; complex terms are composed of more than one token or word. For instance, 'lexicography' and 'multilingual terminology management' are, respectively, examples of a simple and a complex term in the domain of computational linguistics. The extracted lexical units constitute a *terminological resource*, also known as *terminology*: a specialized vocabulary of knowledge in a domain. Terms and their use are studied in a relatively young discipline, which is also called *terminology* (Cabré, 2003; Kageura, 1999):

> 'the field of activity concerned with the collection, description, processing and presentation of terms (Sager, 1990)'.

While terminology can be approached from several perspectives, e.g. as a branch of philosophy, sociology, or cognitive science, terminology is dominantly considered as a linguistic and cognitive activity.

[1] Considering that knowledge and vocabulary are highly correlated, and vocabulary can be gained by exposure to literature.

[2] With an intuition similar to "eating your own dog food", as proposed in Harrison (2006).

(a) General Theory of Terminology (b) Terms as Linguistic Units

Figure 1: Association of meaning in the GTT compared to recent theories of terminology: in the GTT, terms are linguistic labels and denote concepts that exist a priori. In recent theories of terminology, e.g. CTT, however, terms are treated like other linguistic units. They signify concepts in a communicative context. In the figures above, the dashed lines indicate the direction in which the meaning of a term is elaborated according to these theories. The indicated communicative context (the dotted triangle in Figure b) can be extended in a number of ways, e.g. by considering the application of terms.

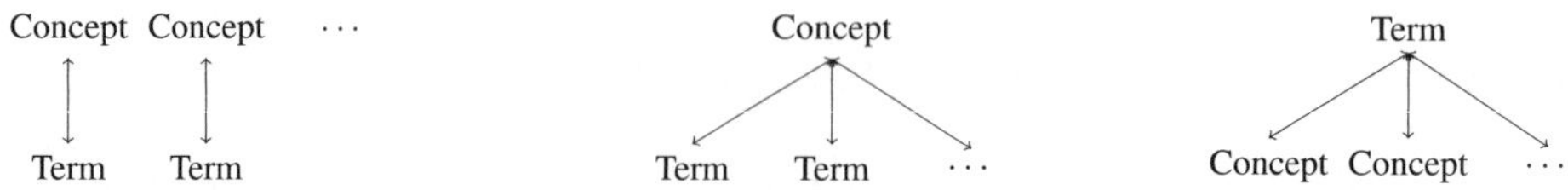

(a) One-to-One Relation (b) Synonymous Relation (c) Polysemous Relation

Figure 2: Relationships between terms and the concepts they signify: Figure 2a illustrates a mono-referential, unambiguous relationship between terms and concepts. Figure 2b shows an ambiguity that may arise when several terms denote the same concept in a synonymous relation. Figure 2c illustrates an ambiguous term-concept relation, a polysemous relationship where a term may denote several concepts.

Modern terminology is therefore pursued within a linguistic framework and as the study of specialized languages (Faber, 2012).

The meanings of terms and the process of concept denomination are studied within the framework of a 'theory of terminology'. As stated in Cabré (2003), a theory of terminology elaborates the fundamental problem of interpretation of meaning into a set of questions in which the definition of a terminological unit—and its characteristics—is the nucleus. The general theory of terminology (GTT) by Wüster (1974, as cited in Campo (2013, chap. 2)) is recognized as the first theory of terminology. The GTT, which is also known as traditional terminology, puts concepts first; terms are unambiguous linguistic labels that are defined independently of the context in which they are used (L'Homme, 2014) (Figure 1a). As implied by the given definition in ISO 1087-1(2000), the GTT is the most widely adopted theory amongst terminologists.[3] Consequently, the GTT regards terms and concepts as having mono-referential relationships (Figure 2a). The objective behind GTT, understandably, is to eliminate ambiguity in natural language to improve clarity in technical communication.

In an authoritative institutional organization that promotes or enforces standards, terms can be *made* and shared in a top-down manner; hence, the meaning of terms can be interpreted by the mechanism described in the GTT.[4] However, in practice and in many organizations, new terms are introduced in a bottom-up *synthesis* process. A lexical form (which may or may not be newly invented) in contexts that bear a concept (which may or may not be newly invented) is used frequently inasmuch as it becomes a term[5] in the organization. In practice, therefore, terms can be ambiguous: a term can refer to several concepts—similar to polysemy–homonymy in lexical semantics (Figure 2c); or, contrariwise, a particular concept can be denoted by several terms (Figure 2b). Heid and Gojun (2012) suggest that the rapid evolution of organizations as well as multi-players that are involved in an uncoordinated way, specifically in multidisciplinary domains, reinforces this situation and thus term ambiguity.

[3]Accordingly, Felber (1982) defines terminology as 'the combined action of groups of subject specialists (terminology commissions) of specialised organisations'.

[4]it is, perhaps, best demonstrated in the applications of controlled natural languages.

[5]That is, a norm.

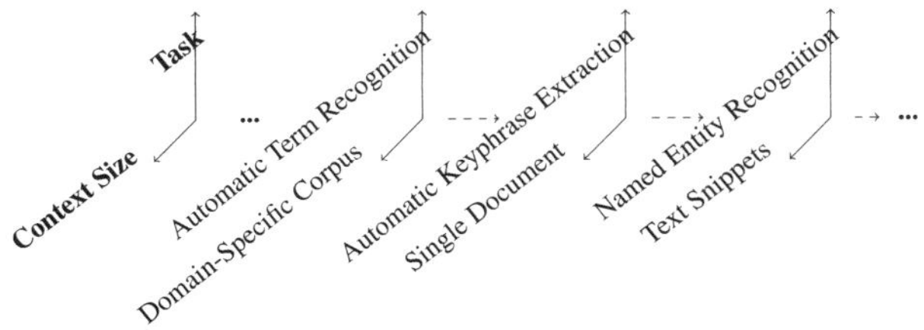

Figure 3: Lexical unit extraction tasks and the scope of the meaning: the diagram can be extended by adding new dimensions that take into the consideration characteristics of the communicative context other than the text size.

In contrast to the GTT, recent theories of terminology, e.g. the communicative theory of terminology (CTT) by Cabré (see 1999, chap. 3), acknowledges the situation stated above and takes a bottom-up distributional approach to terminology in the sense that the meanings of terms, thus the elements of domain knowledge, are not preconceived. Terms are linguistic units that are understood differently with regards to the communicative context, e.g. by the text surrounding them, the application they are used and so on. Terms signify concepts by syntagmatic and paradigmatic relations that they hold in a specialized communicative discourse (Figure 1b).[6] Methods that modern CT embraces, therefore, can be distinguished and classified by the communicative context in which they are employed.

In CT, the task of automatic term recognition (ATR) is at the centre of attention. The input of ATR is a large collection of documents, i.e. a domain-specific corpus, and the output is a terminological resource. In ATR, the meaning of the generated terms is interpreted in a wide spectrum of concepts in the domain that is being investigated and represented by the input corpus. ATR facilitates the automatic construction of terminological resources; hence, it is a significant processing resource in knowledge engineering tasks and applications such as information retrieval and machine translation.

As articulated by Kageura and Umino (1996), ATR deals with the computation of measures known as *unithood* and *termhood*. It is believed that the majority of terms in a domain are complex terms. Unithood indicates the degree to which a sequence of tokens can be combined to form a complex term. It is, thus, a measure of the *syntagmatic* relation between the constituents of complex terms: a lexical association measure to identify collocations. In the absence of explicit linguistic criteria for distinguishing complex terms from other natural language text phrases, a unithood measure construes the problem of complex term identification as the identification of *stable* lexical units (Sager, 1990).[7]

Termhood, on the other hand, 'is the degree to which a stable lexical unit is related to some domain-specific concepts' (Kageura and Umino, 1996). It characterizes a *paradigmatic* relation between lexical units—either simple or complex terms—and the communicative context that verbalizes domain-concepts. Termhood, thus, envisages the measurement of meaning. In the absence of a formal answer to the question 'what domain-specific concepts are?', devising a termhood measure for distinguishing terms and non-terms is a difficult and often conflictual task—hence, the evaluation of CT.

In ATR, the communicative context is a domain-specific corpus. ATR, therefore, should not be confused with other tasks in CT—such as keyword extraction, entity recognition, etc.—that bear a close resemblance to it. These tasks are similar to ATR in the sense that they extract stable lexical units from natural language text. However, they are different from ATR, because the meaning of the extracted lexical units, thus the termhood measure, is interpreted in a context other than a domain-specific corpus (Figure 3). For example, an automatic keyphrase extraction algorithm extracts lexical units from a single document that best describe the content of this document. Both unithood and termhood must be also measured in automatic keyphrase extraction. However, the criterion for their definition and the information available for their computation are different than ATR.

[6] As can be understood, the main difference between the GTT and the CTT is the interpretation of the process of pairing concepts and lexical forms that is mentioned in the definition of lexical units.

[7] See Evert (2004) on the application of lexical association measures for the identification of stable lexical units.

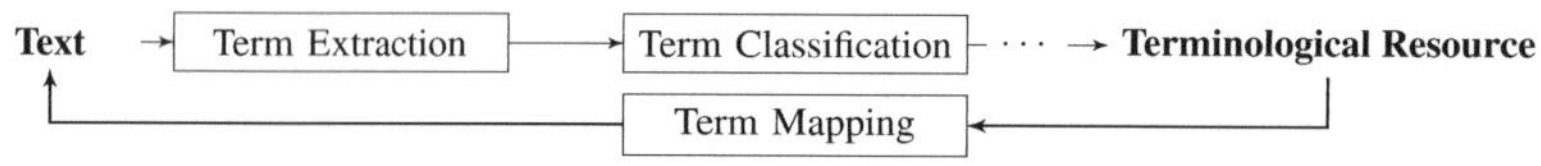

Figure 4: Significant processes in computational terminology and the direction in which they attach terms and natural language text.

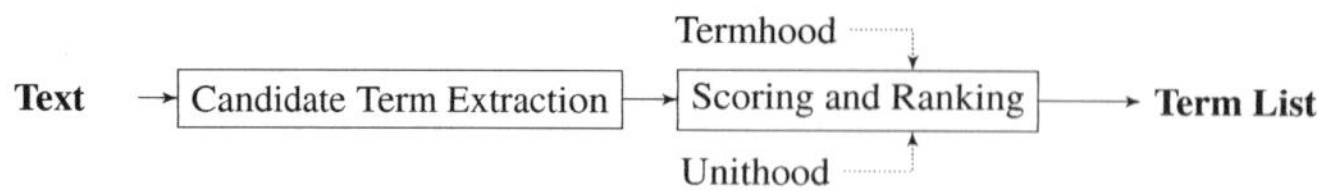

Figure 5: Prevalent architecture of the terminology extraction methods.

We can further distinguish CT methods based on the direction in which terms and text are related. Recent developments of ontological resources have stimulated a research strand that targets the reverse task of intermediary applications. The goal of these applications is to fill the gap between an available ontology, i.e. a knowledge base, and natural language text. In these tasks, given a particular concept in a knowledge base (e.g. a class and its instances in an ontology), a method—which we call *term mapping* following Krauthammer and Nenadic (2004)—decides if this concept or its instances has been mentioned in a given text snippet. Entity linking, which has been promoted through the series of Text Analysis Conferences,[8] is another term that characterizes these research efforts (see also Rao et al., 2013). The familiar task of named entity recognition (NER), as introduced at the Message Understanding Conference (Grishman and Sundheim, 1996), can also be placed in this category. In NER, the types of target terms are known prior to the extraction task, e.g. city, location and so on.

In contrast to term mapping techniques, there are methods that organize constituent terms of a terminological resource into a variety of classes. In these methods, the usage of terms in a given domain-specific corpus is assessed to decide about their membership in concept classes. If the classes are known prior to the assignment task, then the task is known as term classification; otherwise, if the classes are not known, the task is called term clustering. As suggested by Krauthammer and Nenadic (2004), these three tasks—i.e. term recognition, term classification and term mapping—are essential for automatic construction and maintenance of terminological resources and to form a closed loop between terminology and natural language text (Figure 4).

A more elaborate taxonomy of CT techniques can be obtained by distinguishing additional elements and characteristics of the communicative context, e.g. the way in which an end user benefits from the extracted terms, the role of background knowledge, linguistic characteristics of the extracted terms and so on. We leave this study for another occasion.

2.1 Prevalent Mechanism in Term Extraction Tasks

As suggested in Nakagawa (2001), the algorithms for term recognition are usually in the form of a two-step procedure: candidate term extraction followed by term scoring and ranking (Figure 5).

Candidate term extraction deals with the term formation and the extraction of candidate terms. In a few applications, candidate term extraction can assess the morphosyntactic structure of terms, e.g. as suggested in Ananiadou (1994) and Zweigenbaum and Grabar (1999), to identify candidate terms. In these methods, existing terminologies are often available before to the extraction task and employed to identify new candidate terms. Besides this, one can identify four major methods for the extraction of candidate terms: linguistic filtering based on part of speech (PoS) tag sequences, n-gram technique, linguistic filtering based on syntactic relations and techniques that rely on the presence of particular markers in text. Methods for the extraction of candidate terms are not limited to these categories. For instance, *contrastive approaches* exploit a reference corpus of general language to identify simple candidate terms (Drouin, 2004, 2003); for complex terms, the comparison between corpora is followed by one of the techniques listed above. A combination of these methods can also be employed to improve

[8] `http://www.nist.gov/tac/about/`

the results (e.g. see Aubin and Hamon, 2006).

Linguistic filters in the form of PoS tag sequence patterns are the most widely adopted technique for the extraction of candidate terms. In this method, any sequence of tokens with certain PoS tags are assumed as candidate terms (Justeson and Katz, 1995; Daille, 1995). Likewise, the knowledge about PoS patterns that *cannot* form candidate terms may be used to restrict the presence of token sequences in a list of candidate terms (Bourigault, 1992). In the n-gram technique, however, any sequences of tokens of length n, often $1 \leq n \leq 6$, that appear in the input text are considered as candidate terms. This method generates a large set of candidate terms. The number of candidate terms, therefore, is often reduced by filtering n-grams that contain tokens from a stop-word list. When linguistic processing tools are lacking, such as the case of under-resourced languages (see e.g. Pinnis et al., 2012), or the computational cost or accuracy hinders their usage, the n-gram technique is favourable.

Linguistic filters that employ syntactic relations have also been used for the extraction of candidate terms. The first sub-category of these methods use shallow parsing to identify noun phrases as candidate terms (Nakagawa, 2001). The second sub-category of these methods generate candidate terms from available terminological resources to identify term variations (Jacquemin and Tzoukermann, 1999). The third subcategory, which is often employed for multilingual term extraction, exploits the head-modifier principle to identify candidate terms (Hippisley et al., 2005). Finally, a category of candidate term extraction methods takes advantage of the presence of specific markers in input text that can be used to determine boundaries of terms, e.g. the presence of mark-up metadata in Hartmann et al. (2012).

Subsequent to candidate term extraction, a scoring procedure—which can be seen as a semantic weighting mechanism—is employed to indicate how likely it is that a candidate term is a term we would like to extract. As Figure 5 suggests, the scoring procedure usually combines termhood and unithood scores. Although several categorizations of the scoring and ranking methods can be given from a methodological point of view (e.g. statistics-based, machine learning-based, rule-based, etc.) or by the kind of information that is exploited for weighting (e.g. linguistic-based, statistical-based, hybrid) as stated earlier, all these techniques rely on the text and take a corpus-based distributional approach to score and rank terms. The usage of candidate terms in a communicative context (e.g. domain-corpus) is formulated in a machine-tractable format, e.g. in the form of a contingency table or a vector space model. It is then assessed using statistical measures, similarity metrics, language models or a set of rules, depending on the method employed and the objective of the task in hand, which defines the type of paradigmatic relation that the termhood measure characterizes.

The c-value algorithm, for instance, is an statistical method of assigning scores to candidate terms in an ATR task. It is used as a baseline in a number of ATR evaluation tasks. For each candidate term t, the c-value score of t is calculated using four criteria (Frantzi et al., 1998): the frequency of t in the corpus; the frequency of t when it appears nested in other terms longer than t; the number of those longer terms shown by T_t; and the number of the constituent words of t shown by $|t|$. The c-value score is given by

$$c\text{-}value(t) = \begin{cases} \log_2 |t| f(t) & \text{if } t \notin \text{nested} \\ \log_2 |t| \left(f(t) - \frac{1}{|T_t|} \sum_{b \in T_t} f(b)\right) & \text{otherwise} \end{cases}, \quad (1)$$

where T_t denotes the set of all the terms that contain t and are longer than t, and $f(s)$ denotes the frequency of an arbitary term s in the corpus. Other widely applied statistical measures for termhood assements in ATR include term frequency–inverse document frequency (tf-idf), term frequency (tf), and inverse document frequency (idf). We leave the study of scoring mechanisms for another occasion.

3 The ACL RD-TEC: Further Annotation Layers for ACL ARC

We introduce the ACL RD-TEC, a spin-off of the ACL ARC. In its first release, the ACL RD-TEC consists of manual annotations that can be used for the evaluation of ATR and term classification tasks that are explained in the previous section. The current release of the ACL ARC consists of 10,922 articles that were published between 1965 to 2006. The provided resources in the ACL ARC consist of three layers: (a) source publications in portable document format (PDF), (b) automatically extracted text from

Type	Token	Sentence	Paragraph	Section	Publication
704,085	36,729,513	1,564,430	510,366	92,935	10,922

Table 1: Summary statistics of the dataset derived from automatic processing of the ACL ARC.

PoS Tag	JJ	NN	NNP	VBG	FW	(Total)
Frequency	150	17,120	4,520	1255	2	(23,047)

Table 2: Summary statistics of the assigned PoS tags to the simple term 'parsing'. The PoS tags are from the *Penn Treebank PoS tagset.*

the articles and (c) bibliographic metadata and citation network. Each of the articles in the collection are assigned to a unique identifier that indicates the source (e.g. journal or conference) and the date (e.g. 1999, 2006, etc.) of publication.

In the preparation of ACL RD-TEC, we further employed the SectLabel module of Luong et al.'s (2010) ParsCit tool[9] for the automatic identification of logical text sections in ACL ARC's raw text files. Using a set of heuristics, sections such as 'bibliography' and 'acknowledgements' are removed from the corpus and are organized in separate files. In addition, text cleaning is performed, e.g. broken words and text segments are joined, footnotes and captions are removed and sections are organised into paragraphs. The sectioning process is followed by the text segmentation process using the OpenNLP sentence splitter[10] and the Stanford tokenizer. The text is then annotated by the Stanford PoS tagger.[11] The process is finalized by making an inverted index of the cleansed full-text documents and assigning unique identifiers to each one of the extracted linguistic units: types (i.e. PoS-tagged and lemmatized words), sentences, paragraphs and (sub)sections. All of these units are stored in separate flat tables, in which all units, except types, are presented as tuples, consisting of pairs of unique identifiers and their relative locations in the text units they constitute. Therefore, text units can be easily traced back to the publications that they appeared in. The statistics of the resulting data are given in Table 1.

Afterwards, candidate terms are extracted from the processed corpus using three methods: PoS-based filtering, n-gram-based technique and noun phrase (NP) chunking. In order to devise PoS sequence patterns and maximum length of candidate terms, we started with an observation of sample valid terms, their PoS sequences patterns and length in the corpus. We extracted 3301 sentences that contained the lemma 'technology'. We then identified 476 valid terms in these sentences, 65% of which had lengths of 2 and 3 tokens; only 5% were longer than 5 tokens.[12] Similar to the method proposed by Ittoo et al. (2010), to alleviate the problem of erroneous PoS tagging, we formulated the PoS patterns for candidate term extraction based on the actual output of the employed PoS tagger. All the occurrences of the identified terms were searched for in the corpus and all the PoS tag sequences assigned to them were extracted. Amongst the 100 extracted patterns, to keep a balance between correct and incorrect patterns resulted from erroneous PoS tagging, we chose 31 patterns P_l^i of maximum length 5 that satisfy the equation

$$\frac{f(P_l^i)}{\sum_{j:length(P^j)=l} f(P^j)} > \frac{1}{10^l}, \tag{2}$$

where f denotes the frequency of a PoS pattern and l is its length.

For example, the term 'parsing' is extracted as a valid term in this procedure. This simple term is encountered 23,047 times in the corpus. As shown in Table 2, the employed PoS tagger assigned several different PoS tags to this term. Assuming that these PoS tags are the only patterns of length 1, only *NN* and *NNP* satisfy the given formula in Equation 2 above and are added to the inventory of valid PoS patterns for terms of length $l = 1$. The rest of PoS patterns—*VBG*, *JJ* and *FW*—are discarded. As it can be understood from the right hand side of the equation, when the length of PoS patterns increases, the stated criteria for their selection process becomes easier (e.g. 0.01 for terms of length $l = 2$ instead of

[9]Release version 110505 (`http://aye.comp.nus.edu.sg/parsCit/`).

[10]Release version 1.5.2 (`http://opennlp.apache.org/`).

[11]Release date 9 July 2012; see Toutanova et al. (2003) for a description of the PoS tagger tagset.

[12]We eliminate definite and indefinite determiners from the terms.

Method	Total#	Length = 1	Length = 2	Length = 3	Length = 4	Length = 5
PoS-based	$1,322,445$	$271,064$	$741,448$	$284,725$	$23,384$	$1,824$
n-gram	$9,339,303$	$236,053$	$1,054,792$	$2,187,041$	$2,880,665$	$2,980,752$
NP Chunk	$1,813,222$	$142,636$	$706,051$	$623,633$	$248,505$	$92,397$

Table 3: Summary statistics of the extracted candidate terms.

0.1 for terms of length $l = 1$). The list of devised PoS patterns is included in the distributed package.

We repeated the procedure described above by extracting sentences that contain lemmas other than 'technology', e.g. 'algorithm', 'method', 'framework'and 'theory'. There is no evidence to support that the extracted patterns are specific to a category of terms (e.g. technology terms). These patterns seem to be generic enough to extract terms of any category. We support this claim based on the conducted manual verification of the extracted candidate terms. In these extracted sentences, the only terms that are longer than 5 tokens are various transliteration of the term 'very-large-vocabulary speaker-independent continuous speech recognition'. Based on these observations and the previous studies reported on the length of terms (e.g. see Maynard, 2000; Bonin et al., 2010), we believe the maximum length of 5 tokens is a fair trade-off between accuracy and recall in the process of candidate term extraction.

The sentences in the corpus are scanned for occurrences of the devised PoS patterns. Any sequences of tokens that conform to any of these patterns is considered as a candidate term. The extracted token sequences construct the list of PoS-based candidate terms. Based on the above observation, in the n-gram-based extraction of candidate terms, n is set to $1 \leq n \leq 5$ tokens. In addition, n-grams that begin with a token from a stop-word list[13] are discarded. The remaining n-grams form the second list of candidate terms. The extracted sentences from the corpus are also chunked by the OpenNLP chunker. NP chunks that are not longer than 5 tokens constitute the third list of candidate terms. As other lists of candidate terms, determiners are removed from the NP chunks. From all the above lists, we eliminate candidates that are shorter than 3 characters. Candidate terms are further augmented by their frequency in the corpus, distinct documents, sections, and paragraphs and stored separately. Table 3 shows a summary statistics of the extracted candidate terms.

In an ideal scenario, each occurrence of a candidate term in each sentence could have been annotated to identify the particular concept–class that the term signals in that context. Such annotations could have been used in all the tasks described in the previous section. In the absence of an agreed taxonomy of concepts and classes for computational linguistics and—more importantly—the required resources to carry out this complex manual annotation task, achieving the ideal goal at once and in a single step seems infeasible. In order to keep it manageable, we begin the manual annotation task by the verification of the candidate terms in vocabulary lists as is suggested in the previous evaluations of ATR algorithms.

To proceed with the annotation task, the extracted candidate terms are sorted using scores that are obtained from several ATR algorithms, e.g. the c-value score (Equation 1). The annotators are provided with an annotation guideline, consisting of basic definitions (such as the given description in the earlier sections), rules (e.g. how to deal with term variation, misspelled terms and so on) and examples.[14] During this process, the annotators are provided with a tool to access concordance view of candidate terms in the ACL ARC corpus.[15] The annotators are asked to envisage a mind map of computational linguistics topics and perceive the candidate terms in this map. For a given lexical form t in the list of candidate terms, if t refers to a significant concept in the computational linguistics domain,[16] the annotators are ask to mark t as valid. However, this does not guarantee that all the occurrences of t in the corpus are valid terms. For instance, 'natural language' is a lexical form that appears in the corpus as a term on several occasions, e.g. in

'$\cdots$ a *natural language* is a scheme of communication$\cdots$'.

[13]The SMART stop-word list built by Chris Buckley and Gerard Salton, which can be obtained from `goo.gl/rBQNbO`.

[14]The annotator guideline can be accessed in the distributed package.

[15]We used the preloaded version of the ACL ARC in the Sketch Engine Corpus Query System available at `https://the.sketchengine.co.uk/bonito/run.cgi/first_form?corpname=preloaded/aclarc_1`

[16]That is, if they can situate the term in their envisaged mind map.

	Total#	Length = 1	Length = 2	Length = 3	Length = 4	Length = 5
Technology Terms	13,832	757	8,674	3,822	538	41
Invalid Terms	61,818	15,908	33,502	11,027	1,211	170
Valid Terms	22,027	1,495	14,146	5,677	657	52
Total Annotated	83,845	17,403	47,648	16,704	1,868	222

Table 4: Summary statistics of the annotated candidate terms.

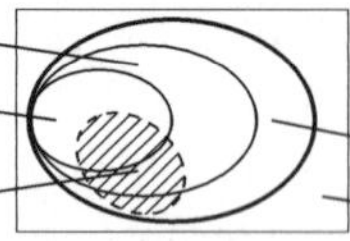

Figure 6: Relationships between candidate terms, valid terms, technology terms and annotated terms. Candidate term extraction extracts a subset of all possible terms. ATR targets the identification of valid terms amongst candidate terms. Technology terms are a subset of valid terms. The dashed area shows the set of annotated terms.

However, there are a number of occurrences of 'natural language' that cannot be considered as term, e.g.

'··· the speech and *natural language* groups at SRI reported results ···'.

On the other hand, if t is annotated as invalid, then there must be no occurrence of t in the corpus that can be counted as a term. In the current version, 83,845 terms are annotated as either valid or invalid.

Furthermore, valid terms in the annotated list of terms are classified as those that can signal a technology concept. If 'genes' are an essential category of concepts in an ontology that characterizes biological discipline, we speculate that the presence of technology as a category of concepts is essential in any ontology or terminological resource that describes an applied discipline like computational linguistics. As to our definition, technology terms indicate concepts such as methods, algorithms and processes that are designed, developed and employed to accomplish a certain task in order to fulfil a practical purpose, i.e. to address a research problem (see also the task in Kovaevi et al., 2012). In computational linguistics, examples of these terms are 'parsing', 'information retrieval', and more delicate terms such as 'linear interpolation'.

In order to distinguish technology terms amongst other categories of terms, annotators are provided with several definitions of technology and its known examples in computational linguistics.[17] In addition, the annotators are exposed to materials on philosophy of technology, e.g. Franssen et al. (2013), and introduced to the task of 'tech mining' in Porter and Cunningham (2005). Despite all these efforts, because establishing a precise definition of technology is infeasible, classification of valid terms to technology and non-technology terms, to a great extent, relies on the intuition of experts who participated in the annotation task. The annotators are allowed to use other sources of information than the ACL ARC, e.g. web search, in order to decide about the technology class membership of valid terms. The process of annotating technology terms in the lists of extracted candidate terms is facilitated by supervised machine learning-based methods of term weighting, e.g. as reported in Zadeh and Handschuh (2014a,b). Table 4 shows the current statistics of the annotated terms. Figure 6 illustrates relationships between candidate terms, valid terms and technology terms.

Similar to the valid terms, terms that are annotated as technology terms do not exclusively belong to this class. For example, 'computational linguistics' is a lexical form that can be classified as a technology term, e.g., in

'···promising area of application of *computational linguistics* techniques···'.

However, it can also signal other concepts such as a scientific discipline, e.g. in

'···theoretical work in *computational linguistics*···'

[17]Those terms that are explicitly named as technology in literature are taken as the examples of technology terms. To make a list of examples, we identified these terms using simple patterns such as '··· X is a technology···'.

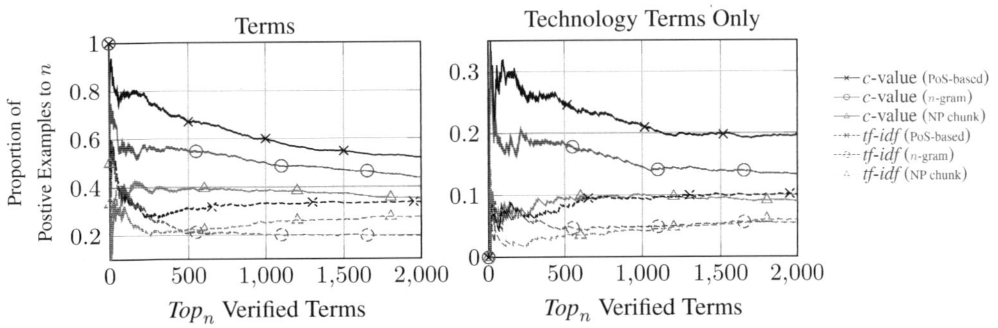

Figure 7: Comparison between c-value and $tf\text{-}idf$.

, as well as a community, e.g. in

'... pursued by the *computational linguistics* community ···'.

The data, perhaps, speaks better for itself. Thus, we invite the interested reader to explore the annotated set of terms in order to gain more insight into the performed annotation task. The dataset can be obtained freely from the European Language Resources Association, catalogue reference ELRA-T0375.[18]

While we hope more researchers become involved in the annotation task, in the current release, all the annotations are made by one person. In order to assess the quality and reliability of the annotations, we carried out two preliminary experiments. In the first experiment, a list of terms consisting of 250 terms that have been particularly difficult to annotate are annotated by a researcher who is familiar with terminology. For example, we particularly found it hard and conflicting to annotate terms that start with words such as 'automatic, automated, stat-of-the-art, scalable, rapid, full, fast' and so on, e.g. in terms such as 'fast clustering, 'fast classification, and 'fast prototyping. In addition, deciding on the inclusion of certain categories of terms is difficult. For example, one may consider 'people' and 'organizations' as valid domain terms, while another person—with her own specific interest and expertise—may consider these as invalid terms. This problem is more subtle about categories such as 'languages' and 'linguistic units'. For instance, one may consider 'English' and 'French' as well as 'clitic' and 'suffix' as terms; however, another person may not consider them as valid terms in the domain of computational linguistics (e.g. one may found them too generic to be considered as valid terms). As to our experience, the more specific we are about the concept categories, the easier it is to annotate the terms. We made sure sample of these terms are included in the assessment of the annotations. We report an observed agreement A_o of 0.758 and Cohen'kappa coefficient κ of 0.517 for this set of terms (see Artstein and Poesio, 2008, for definition of A_o and κ).

In the second experiment, two postgrad students in the area of natural language processing were given a list of 389 terms and asked to identify technology terms. The list of annotated terms were then compared with the annotations in the dataset. The results are $A_o = 0.840$ and $\kappa = 0.655$ for the first comparison and $A_o = 0.775$ and $\kappa = 0.533$ for the second comparison. These measures over the annotations generated by the participants in the evaluation task are $A_o = 0.828$ and $\kappa = 0.627$.

As a usage example of the constructed dataset, we use the annotations for the comparison of the top n terms in the list of candidate terms that are weighted and sorted using Frantzi et al.'s (1998) c-value and term frequency–inverse document frequency ($tf\text{-}idf$). We hope other researchers in the domain are intrigued by the numbers reported in Figure 7 and report the performance of other algorithms.

4 Conclusion and Future Work

The saying 'the shoemaker's son goes barefoot' is perhaps true when it comes to the state of terminological resources that characterize computational linguistics domain. We report a small action towards

[18] http://catalog.elra.info/index.php; the annotated terms are also available from https://github.com/languagerecipes/the-acl-rd-tec.

building a terminological resource from the ACL ARC, which can be used for the evaluation of computational terminology methods. There are currently three sets of candidate terms, which are augmented by their frequency in various logical text segments in the corpus and are presented in tabulated inverse index files. More than 82,000 of these terms are annotated manually as valid and invalid, in which valid terms are further classified as technology and non-technology terms. The built resource can facilitate the evaluation of a number of methods in computational terminology. We invite other researchers to embellish the dataset by adding their own lists of candidate terms and manual annotations.

During the annotation process we have identified several frequent concepts other than technology and methods in the computational linguistics domain, e.g. grammar formalism, theories, measures, language resources, tasks and applications. We hope to continue our effort by adding annotations for at least one of these concepts. Adding a new concept class will allow us to evaluate term disambiguation methods. The application of clustering techniques for identification of term variations amongst the annotated terms and their manual annotation is another goal that can be achieved in the near future. These small steps, collectively, can provide the shoemaker's son with a fine pair of leather boots.

Acknowledgements

We thank the anonymous reviewers for their constructive comments, which helped us to improve the paper. In addition, we thank Professor Marie-Claude L'Homme for her helpful advice. We also thank Kartik Asooja, Georgeta Bordea, Sapna Negi and Bianca Pereira who participated in the inter-annotator agreement experiment. This publication has emanated from research supported in part by a research grant from Science Foundation Ireland (SFI) under Grant Number SFI/12/RC/2289.

References

2000. ISO 1087-1:2000 terminology — vocabulary — part 1: Theory and application.

Sophia Ananiadou. 1994. A methodology for automatic term recognition. In *Proceedings of the 15th conference on Computational linguistics - Volume 2*, COLING '94, pages 1034–1038.

Ron Artstein and Massimo Poesio. 2008. Inter-coder agreement for computational linguistics. *Comput. Linguist.*, 34(4).

Sophie Aubin and Thierry Hamon. 2006. Improving term extraction with terminological resources. In *Advances in Natural Language Processing*, LNCS 4139, pages 380–387.

Michael Bada, Miriam Eckert, Donald Evans, Kristin Garcia, Krista Shipley, Dmitry Sitnikov, William Baumgartner, K Cohen, Karin Verspoor, Judith Blake, and Lawrence Hunter. 2012. Concept annotation in the craft corpus. *BMC Bioinformatics*, 13(1):161.

Gabriel Bernier-Colborne and Patrick Drouin. 2014. Creating a test corpus for term extractors through term annotation. *Terminology*, 20:1:5073.

Steven Bird, Robert Dale, Bonnie Dorr, Bryan Gibson, Mark Joseph, Min-Yen Kan, Dongwon Lee, Brett Powley, Dragomir Radev, and Yee Fan Tan. 2008. The ACL anthology reference corpus: A reference dataset for bibliographic research in computational linguistics. In *LREC'08*. Marrakech, Morocco.

Francesca Bonin, Felice Dell'Orletta, Simonetta Montemagni, and Giulia Venturi. 2010. A contrastive approach to multi-word extraction from domain-specific corpora. In *LREC'10*. ELRA, Valletta, Malta.

Didier Bourigault. 1992. LEXTER: a natural language tool for terminology extraction. In *COLING '92*. pages 977–981.

M. Teresa Cabré. 1999. *TERMINOLOGY: THEORY, METHODS AND APPLICATIONS*. John Benjamins.

M. Teresa Cabré. 2003. Theories of terminology their description, prescription and explanation. *Terminology*, 9:2:163–199.

M. Teresa Cabré. 2010. *Handbook of translation studies*, volume 1, chapter Terminology and translation, pages 356–365.

M. Teresa Cabré, Anne Condamines, and Fidelia Ibekwe-SanJuan. 2005. Introduction: Application-driven terminology engineering. *Terminology*, 11:1–19(18).

Ángela Campo. 2013. *The reception of Eugen Wsters work and the development of terminology*. Ph.D. thesis, Université de Montréal.

Beatrice Daille. 1995. Combined approach for terminology extraction: lexical statistics and linguistic filtering. Technical report, UCREL, Lancaster University.

Patrick Drouin. 2003. Term extraction using non-technical corpora as a point of leverage. *Terminology*, 9(1):99–115.

Patrick Drouin. 2004. Detection of domain specific terminology using corpora comparison. In *LREC'04*.

Stefan Evert. 2004. *The Statistics of Word Cooccurrences Word Pairs and Collocations*. Ph.D. thesis, Institut für maschinelle Sprachverarbeitung, Universität Stuttgart.

Pamela Faber. 2012. *A cognitive linguistics view of terminology and specialized language*, volume 20, chapter Terminology and Specialized Language, pages 13–33. Walter de Gruyter.

Helmut Felber. 1982. Computerized terminology in termnet: The role of terminological data banks. *Term banks for tomorrows world: Translating and the Computer*, 4:8–20.

Maarten Franssen, Gert-Jan Lokhorst, and Ibo van de Poel. 2013. Philosophy of technology. In *The Stanford Encyclopedia of Philosophy*. Winter 2013 edition.

KaterinaT. Frantzi, Sophia Ananiadou, and Junichi Tsujii. 1998. The c-value/nc-value method of automatic recognition for multi-word terms. In *Research and Advanced Technology for Digital Libraries*, LNCS 1513, pages 585–604.

Ralph Grishman and Beth Sundheim. 1996. Message understanding conference-6: A brief history. In *Proceedings of COLING (Vol. 96).*, pages 466–471.

Warren Harrison. 2006. Eating your own dog food. *IEEE Software*, 23(3):5–7.

Silvana Hartmann, György Szarvas, and Iryna Gurevych. 2012. Mining multiword terms from wikipedia. In *Semi-Automatic Ontology Development: Processes and Resources*, pages 226–258. IGI Global, Hershey, PA, USA.

Ulrich Heid and Anita Gojun. 2012. Term candidate extraction for terminography and cat: and overview of ttc. In *Proceedings of the 15th Euralex International Congress*. Oslo, Norway.

Andrew Hippisley, David Cheng, and Khurshid Ahmad. 2005. The head-modifier principle and multilingual term extraction. *Nat. Lang. Eng.*, 11(2):129–157.

Ashwin Ittoo, Laura Maruster, Hans Wortmann, and Gosse Bouma. 2010. Textractor: A framework for extracting relevant domain concepts from irregular corporate textual datasets. In *BIS*, LNBIP 47, pages 71–82. Springer.

Christian Jacquemin and Evelyne Tzoukermann. 1999. NLP for term variant extraction: synergy between morphology, lexicon and syntax. *Natural language information retrieval*, 7:25–74.

John S. Justeson and Slava M. Katz. 1995. Technical terminology: some linguistic properties and an algorithm for identification in text. *Nat. Lang. Eng.*, 1.1:9–27.

Kyo Kageura. 1999. On the study of dynamics of terminology: A proposal of a theoretical framework. *Research Bulletin of the NACSIS*, 11:1–10.

Kyo Kageura and Bin Umino. 1996. Methods of automatic term recognition: A review. *Terminology*, 3.2 (1996):259–289.

J. . D. Kim, T. Ohta, Y. Tateisi, and J. Tsujii. 2003. Genia corpus—a semantically annotated corpus for bio-textmining. *Bioinformatics*, 19(suppl 1):i180–i182.

Aleksandar Kovaevi, Zora Konjovi, Branko Milosavljevi, and Goran Nenadic. 2012. Mining methodologies from nlp publications: A case study in automatic terminology recognition. *Computer Speech & Language*, 26(2):105 – 126.

Michael Krauthammer and Goran Nenadic. 2004. Term identification in the biomedical literature. *J. of Biomedical Informatics*, 37(6):512–526.

Marie-Claude L'Homme. 2014. Terminologies and taxonomies. *Oxford Handbooks Online*.

Minh-Thang Luong, Thuy Dung Nguyen, and Min-Yen Kan. 2010. Logical structure recovery in scholarly articles with rich document features. *IJDLS*, 1(4):1–23.

Diana Maynard. 2000. *Term recognition using combined knowledge sources*. Ph.D. thesis, Manchester Metropolitan University.

Hiroshi Nakagawa. 2001. Automatic term recognition based on statistics of compound nouns. *Terminology*, 6.2:195–210.

Adeline Nazarenko and Haïfa Zargayouna. 2009. Evaluating term extraction. In *Proceedings of the International Conference RANLP-2009*, pages 299–304. Association for Computational Linguistics, Borovets, Bulgaria.

Mārcis Pinnis, Nikola Ljubešić, Dan Ştefănescu, Inguna Skadiņa, Marko Tadić, and Tatiana Gornostay. 2012. Term extraction, tagging, and mapping tools for under-resourced languages. In *TKE 2012*.

Alan L Porter and Scott W Cunningham. 2005. Tech mining. *Competitive Intelligence Magazine*, 8(1):30–36.

Delip Rao, Paul McNamee, and Mark Dredze. 2013. Entity linking: Finding extracted entities in a knowledge base. In *Multi-source, Multilingual Information Extraction and Summarization*, Theory and Applications of Natural Language Processing.

Juan C. Sager. 1990. *Practical Course in Terminology Processing*, chapter Term Formation: theory and practice, pages 61–87. John Benjamins Publishing Company.

Kristina Toutanova, Dan Klein, Christopher D. Manning, and Yoram Singer. 2003. Feature-rich part-of-speech tagging with a cyclic dependency network. In *NAACL '03*. pages 173–180.

Jorge Vivaldi and Horacio Rodrĭguez. 2007. Evaluation of terms and term extraction systems: A practical approach. *Terminology*. 13:225–248.

Eugen Wüster. 1974. Die allgemeine terminologielehre–ein grenzgebiet zwischen sprachwissenschaft, logik, ontologie, informatik und den sachwissenschaften. *Linguistics*, 12(119):61–106.

Behrang Q. Zadeh and Siegfried Handschuh. 2014a. Evaluation of technology term recognition with random indexing. *LREC'14*. ELRA, Reykjavik, Iceland.

Behrang Q. Zadeh and Siegfried Handschuh. 2014b. Investigating context parameters in technology term recognition. *COLING Workshop on Synchronic and Diachronic Approaches to Analyzing Technical Language (SADAATL)*.

Pierre Zweigenbaum and Natalia Grabar. 1999. Automatic acquisition of morphological knowledge for medical language processing. In *Artificial Intelligence in Medicine*, LNCS 1620, pages 416–420.

Building the interface between experts and linguists in the detection and characterisation of neology in the field of the neurosciences

Jesús Torres-del-Rey
Facultad de Traducción y Documentación
Universidad de Salamanca
C/ Francisco de Vitoria 6-16
37008 Salamanca (Spain)
jtorres@usal.es

Nava Maroto
CES Felipe II
Universidad Complutense de Madrid
C/ Capitán, s/n
28300 Aranjuez (Spain)
mmaro01@ucm.es

1 Introduction

The NeuroNEO Project (García Palacios et al, 2014) aims to collect and suggest new lexical units in close collaboration with specialists in the field and with specialised translators as necessary collaborators and decisive agents in the dissemination of neologisms. Neologisms are a powerful spearhead for science and, needless to say, for the language(s) of science.

Field specialists come in touch with new term creations and concepts both in the process of knowledge reception and knowledge production. In both cases, Spanish specialists' need to conceptualise, verbalise and stabilise the new concepts is often mediated by English as a scientific lingua franca. This results in a diminished capability of non-English speakers to both apprehend and exploit the potential of the new conceptual and linguistic coinages and to cast their own ideas and scientific constructions onto functionally adequate linguistic moulds. We acknowledge that science, at least for the foreseeable future, will be "created" mostly in English, but contend that it can be enriched and expanded by helping it "speak" other languages through translation from and into English.

In the first phase of our project we are concentrating on the knowledge-reception process alone. Our team of Spanish-speaking language, terminology and translation experts and researchers will be monitoring the way neuroscientists cognitively and linguistically cope and deal with conceptual and terminological neologisms when reading recent English articles. To gather this knowledge, we are experimenting with the design of a collaborative tool to collect relevant information of the specialists' encounter with neological occurrences.

2 Defining and detecting neologisms

Neologisms appear in order to fulfil denominative needs. They challenge a language code, pushing it to its limits, but, at the same time, provide the basis for its survival and development (Sánchez Ibáñez, 2013: 58-65). Linguistic classification of neologisms (e.g. morphosyntactic, semantic, loans, calques) would not be beneficial for neuroscientists while processing the scientific information they read, as this would detract from their concentration on the subject matter and "contaminate" the ecology of the activity, by letting an alien expert domain intrude into their habitual knowledge-reception task. We need to provide neuroscientists "ontologically clean" (Winograd and Flores, 1986: 165) linguistic means to help them identify and communicate their neological experiences.

A cognitive-ontological model that has successfully focused on "units of understanding" (rather than static, universal terms or concepts), historical determinations, diachronic evolution and domain expert participation, is Temmerman's sociocognitive approach to terminology (2000), which later led to "termontography" (see, for instance Temmerman and Kerremans, 2003; Kerremans, 2004). Their

Proceedings of the 4th International Workshop on Computational Terminology, pages 64–67,
Dublin, Ireland, August 23 2014.

main aim is to bring together the activities of terminography and ontology engineering from a socio-cognitive perspective, and to provide a conceptual and methodological basis for the development of applications for different human and semi-automatic terminology-related endeavours.

A "termontology" which defines and describes units of understanding in terms of categories (also specified as human language phrases), intracategorial aspects and intercategorial relationships in a categorisation framework (Kerremans, 2004) seems like an excellent idea if we want to empower domain experts with a familiar map of knowledge which they can contribute to and which can help us to identify systemic/viewpoint change leading to nascent neologisms.

3 Building the interface between field specialists and language experts

The design of the tool must start with the analysis of the activity where it is to be integrated, the concerns and the commitments of the users/actors, and their conceptual model (Liddle, 1996). It is crucial to get as much "practical understanding" (Ehn, 1992: 122-123) of the task that the users will undertake and of potential breakdown; to stimulate the task by not interfering too much in it, unencumbered but enhanced by the interactive and linguistic scaffolding of our tool.

The necessary (hopefully minimal but productive) interference with neuroscientists' cognitive process must be compensated for by satisfying other needs they may (consciously or unconsciously) have or providing them with a rewarding experience (Hassenzahl, 2010). They must be aware that their participation will help science (not only Spanish science) and Spanish as a language of science; at the same time, even those who have no linguistic inclinations must find that, by focusing on the way language represents and creates reality, the tool can help reinforce, deepen and enhance the understanding of the concepts they read and of their potential implications. Ideally, our tool should also become a friendly platform for neuroscientists to read and annotate all their articles.

In order to test what interface, actions, language and workflows could accomplish all this, we will turn to prototyping as a fundamental method in Human-Computer Interaction. "The ability to shape and reshape software requires a capacity for rapid prototyping – for turning an unarticulated idea into a working prototype quickly enough to be able to change it, to listen to it, even to throw it out and to go on to another" (Winograd, 1996: 206).

4 Prototype experiment for expert neologism detection and characterization

The outline of the experiment is as follows: first, our neuroscientist expert subjects will be assigned a recent journal article about some new development in the field in English. The approximate length of each unit of cognitive-textual processing should be one page (a section or a number of sections totalling that length or thereabouts).

As they read, subjects are encouraged to highlight what they consider to be key elements of the text (mono- or plurilexical terms). Afterwards, they will be required to mark concepts or terms that can be considered as new. These new concepts may be expressed through mono- or plurilexical terms, but they can also appear in the form of denominative periphrasis or other kinds of non-lexicalised expressions (García Palacios, 2009: 19; Sánchez Ibáñez, 2013: 295-308). A term or expression will be considered as a neologism if the expert has only been aware of its existence in recent years.

Once the candidate neologisms are identified, experts will have to decide to what broad category of the field of neuroscience the expression identified as new pertains. Then, they will be requested to explain in Spanish and in their own words the novel aspects discovered in the text. The subjects are expected to emphasise in what respect (activities, situations, cases...) new aspects could be relevant.

Finally, experts will have to suggest other terms or categories (both in English and in Spanish) related to the concept they are describing. This last task is meant to detect categories, conceptual frames to which the identified candidate neologism may belong or prototypical characteristics of the concept.

This first pilot experiment should measure the adequacy of the proposal, and in particular:

- The most adequate unit of cognitive processing (section, page, paragraph, time).
- The degree of distortion the experiment imposes on the process of reading, and whether the task implies a cognitive overload.
- To what extent experts are willing to engage in the experiment, whether they find it motivating.

- From a qualitative perspective, which elements experts identify as novel and which not, allowing us to get a feeling of the clues for the identification of new concepts.

5 Tools for the development of the prototype experiment

For the practical development of our prototype experiments we are considering to use the upper categories of the NIFSTD ontology and wikis as a collaborative tool. The availability and suitability for our research of the former has been considered in Maroto (2013).

NIFSTD (NIF Standard) ontology stands out as the most comprehensive ontology of the neurosciences available on the web. Its wide coverage and its degree of normalisation and reusability make this ontology particularly suitable for our research purposes. It is composed of several modules, each one covering a distinct domain of neuroscience (Bug et al, 2008) and reflecting the semantic domains covered by NIFSTD: organism taxonomy, molecules, macroscopic anatomy, sub-cellular anatomy, cell, nervous system function, nervous system dysfunction, phenotypic qualities and investigation.

The upper classes of the ontology will be used in our research as "tags" so that experts can categorise neologisms identified during the reception of specialised articles. Therefore, these upper classes will shape the initial framework of categories from which our top-down strategy starts, which in turn-will later be refined thanks to experts' contributions.

At this stage, we need to test to what extent the conceptual classes proposed by existing ontologies can be used as a valuable tool to help experts categorise new terms and concepts. As our research develops, we might want to integrate our findings within an ontology structure (either NIF's or our own).

We also need a collaborative tool for collecting and linking expert knowledge during the experiments. A wiki can be defined as collaborative software that allows different users to develop web sites in a simple way using a simplified mark-up language, based on linking interrelated concepts and tracking changes. A "wiki is a written-down memory with a lot more space than the built-in one, and it's a collective memory, too" (Stafford and Webb 2006). In a wiki "What You Think Is What You Get".

The main reasons that justify the use of wikis in our experiments are that most scientists are already familiar with this kind of software and the fact that wikis are accessible anytime from anywhere with a web connection. Besides, every detail about the editing is stored in the wiki, that is, we can later analyse how much time our experts spent editing, whether they made many or few changes, etc.

Finally, wikis offer the possibility to "tag" pages and to link concepts. Our experts will be required to categorise new terms and/or concepts, that is, to assign one or more cognitive "tags" to the newly discovered concept. Neuroscientists will be given a set of proposed tags from the upper level of NIFSTD ontology to label their responses to our experiments. In this way the suitability of upper-level ontological classes could be tested and, if necessary, the categories could be revised and/or refined.

This contribution presents the theoretical and methodological framework that is the basis of our research. However, a lot of work still lays ahead in order to check the validity of our proposal.

Acknowledgments

This work is supported by the Spanish Ministry of Economy and Competitiveness within the national project NeuroNEO "Regulación de los procesos neológicos y los neologismos en las áreas de neurociencias" (code FFI2012-34596).

Reference

William J. Bug, Giorgio A. Ascoli, Geffrey S. Grethe et al. 2008. The NIFSTD and BIRNLex Vocabularies: Building Comprehensive Ontologies for Neuroscience. *Neuroinformatics*. 6(3), 175-194. Available at: http://www.ncbi.nlm.nih.gov/pmc/articles/PMC2743139/. [Last access: April 2014].

Pelle Ehn. 1992. Scandinavian Design: On Participation and Skill. In: Paul S. Adler and Terry Winograd. (eds) *Usability: Turning Technologies into Tools*. Oxford University Press, New York, 96-132.

Joaquín García Palacios. 2009. La competencia neológica especializada en el estudio y la actuación sobre la neología terminológica. *Revue Française de Linguistique Appliquée XIV* (2), 17-30.

Joaquín García Palacios, Jesús Torres del Rey, Nava Maroto, Daniel Linder, Goedele De Sterck, and Miguel Sánchez-Ibáñez. 2014. NeuroNEO, una investigación multidisciplinar sobre la neología terminológica. In: Belén Santanta López and Críspulo Travieso Rodríguez (eds). *Puntos de encuentro: los primeros 20 años de la Facultad de Traducción y Documentación de la Universidad de Salamanca.* Ediciones Universidad de Salamanca, Salamanca, 241-260.

Marc Hassenzahl. 2010. *Experience Design: Technology for All the Right Reasons*. Morgan & Claypool. (Kindle Edition).

Koen Kerremans. 2004. Categorisation Frameworks in Termontography. *Linguistica Antverpiensia New Series* 3, 263–277.

David Liddle (An interview with). 1996. Design of the Conceptual Model. Reflective Conversation with Materials. In: Terry Winograd (ed). *Bringing Design to Software*. Addison-Wesley, Reading, MA, 17-131.

Nava Maroto. 2013. Reusing existing conceptual structures and lexica for neology characterization in the field of Neurosciences: the NeuroNEO project. *Proceedings 10th International Conference on Terminology and Artificial Intelligence TIA 2013*: 87-90. Available at: https://lipn.univ-paris13.fr/tia2013/Conference_Proceedings.html. [Last access: April 2014].

Miguel Sánchez Ibáñez. 2013. *Neología y traducción especializada: claves para calibrar la dependencia terminológica español-inglés en el ámbito de la Enfermedad de Alzheimer* (Doctoral thesis). Salamanca: University of Salamanca.

Rita Temmerman. 2000. *Towards New Ways of Terminology Description: The Sociocognitive-Approach*. John Benjamins, Amsterdam/Philadelphia.

Rita Temmerman and Koen Kerremans. 2003. Termontography: Ontology Building and the Sociocognitive Approach to Terminology Description. *Proceedings of CIL17*, Matfyzpress, Prague. Available at: http://taalkunde.ehb.be/sites/www2.ehb.be/files/u96/temmerman_art_prague03.pdf. [Last access: April 2014].

Tom Stafford and Matt Webb. 2006. What is a wiki (and how to use one for your projects). Available at: http://www.oreillynet.com/pub/a/network/2006/07/07/what-is-a-wiki.html?page=1. [Last access: April 2014].

Terry Winograd. 1996. Profile: Hypercard, Director and Visual Basic. In: Terry Winograd (ed). *Bringing Design to Software*. Addison-Wesley, Reading, MA, 206-213.

Terry Winograd and Fernando Flores. 1986. *Understanding Computers and Cognition. A New Foundation for Design*. Ablex, Norwood, New Jersey.

A comparative User Evaluation of Terminology Management Tools for Interpreters

Hernani Costa* **Gloria Corpas Pastor** **Isabel Durán Muñoz**
LEXYTRAD, University of Malaga, Spain
{hercos,gcorpas,iduran}@uma.es

Abstract

When facing new fields, interpreters need to perform extensive searches for specialised knowledge and terminology. They require this information prior to an interpretation and have it accessible during the interpreting service. Fortunately, there are currently several terminology management tools capable of assisting interpreters before and during an interpretation service. Although these tools appear to be quite similar, they provide different kind of features and as a result they exhibit different degrees of usefulness. This paper aims at describing current terminology management tools with a view to establishing a set of features to assess the extent to which terminology tools meet the specific needs of the interpreters. Subsequently, a comparative analysis is performed to evaluate these tools based on the list of features previously identified.

1 Introduction

Professional interpreters frequently face different settings and specialised fields in their interpretation services and yet they always need to provide excellent results. They might be called to work for specialists that share a background knowledge that is totally or partially unknown to laypersons and/or outsiders (Will, 2007). When interpreters lack the necessary background knowledge or experience, they usually need to perform extensive searches for specialised knowledge and terminology in a very efficient way in order to supply this deficit and acquire the required information.

Even though there are several modes of interpretation, depending mainly on the timing/delay of the interpretation, the direction and the setting (cf. Pöchhacker, 2007), it is not possible for interpreters to collect the relevant specialised information during the interpretation service itself. Interpreters are required to find the necessary information prior to interpretation and have it accessible during the service, even though they sometimes are able to carry out searches during the service.

According to Rodríguez and Schnell (2009), terminology work is present in the whole process of preparation prior to an interpretation service. For example, interpreters become familiar with the subject field by searching for specialised documents, by extracting terms and looking for synonyms and hyperonyms, by finding and developing acronyms and abbreviations and by compiling a glossary. According to these authors, interpreters tend to compile in-house glossaries tailor to their individual needs as the main way to prepare the terminology of a given interpretation.

2 Interpreters' Needs

The potentialities of computers for improving interpreters' working conditions was realised a long time ago by Gile (1987). However, very little progress has been made so far. Costa, Corpas Pastor and Durán-Muñoz (2014) offer a tentative catalogue of current language technologies for interpreters, divided into terminology tools for interpreters, note-taking applications for consecutive interpreting, applications for voice recording and training tools. This paper focus exclusively on terminology tools for interpreters with a view to performing a user evaluation.

As a rule, most interpreters seem to be unaware of the opportunities offered by language technologies. As far as terminology is concerned, interpreters continue to store information and terminology on scraps

*Hernani Costa is supported by the People Programme (Marie Curie Actions) of the European Union's Framework Programme (FP7/2007-2013) under REA grant agreement N° 317471.

Proceedings of the 4th International Workshop on Computational Terminology, pages 68–76,
Dublin, Ireland, August 23 2014.

of paper or excel spreadsheets, while the use of technologies and terminology management tools is still very low. A study conducted by Moser-Mercer (1992:507, quoted in Bilgen, 2009) rejected the assumption that "interpreters' needs are identical to those of translators and terminologists" and intended to "survey how conference interpreters handle terminology documentation and document control and to offer some guidelines as to the interpretation-specific software tools for terminology and documentation management". The results of this study includes some key findings, such as the conclusion that most of the respondents were interested in exchanging terminological information and that they were open to using computers in their profession. According to these findings, Moser-Mercer (1992) highlighted that "software developers targeting the conference interpreting market must provide a tool that meets the specific needs of the interpreters and not just market translation tools" (ibid:511). More recent studies have also studied interpreters' current needs and practices regarding terminology management (Rodríguez and Schnell, 2009; Bilgen, 2009), and they also share the same findings: interpreters require specific tools to meet their needs, which are different from translators and terminologists. According to a survey conducted by Bilgen (2009), 85% of respondents are open to using computers, yet conventional methods still prevail over the use of computerised methods of terminology management. The author observed that respondents had no or little experience with terminology management software, and those with some experience were most dissatisfied with the money and time they had to invest in them, and their overall experience was mediocre (ibid:66). Respondents indicated that their priorities were different from those identified in terminology literature in terms of terminological information stored, and the way in which term records are structured. This is an important aspect that differentiates the needs of interpreters and translators as regards definitions and contexts (Bilgen, 2009). Due to their working conditions, translators usually prefer to consult multiple definitions and contexts to find the best solution for the translation problem. On the contrary, interpreters will rarely have the time to go over multiple definitions, contexts, etc. to find the right one, and thus, they will need to store the most concise information to be able to consult it in the quickest and easiest way. Their responses in this survey also showed that the way they retrieve terminological information was context-specific, and that there was also a significant variation among individual interpreters. Flexibility is, therefore, of great importance to interpreters due to the variation of their context-specific terminology management practices, and on their individual preferences regarding the storage, organisation and retrieval of terminological information (ibid:92). Rodríguez and Schnell (2009), after a thorough analysis of interpreters' needs and in order to meet their requirements as regards terminology management tools, propose the possibility of developing small databases that vary according to the area of speciality or according to the conference and client. These mini-databases would be multilingual and include an option allowing the interpreter to switch the source and target languages. This assumption is in line with the Function Theory (Bergenholtz and Tarp, 2003; Tarp, 2008) and electronic multifunctional dictionaries (Spohr, 2009), which both defend the need to elaborate terminological entries according to the potential users. Rodríguez and Schnell (2009) recognise five features that would distinguish the interpreters' mini-databases from the terminology databases intended for translators: speed of consultation; intuitive navigation; possibility of updating the terminology record in the interpretation booth; considerable freedom to define the basic structure; and multiple ways of filtering data.

Accordingly, they also suggest the abandonment of the usual terminology methodology if the intention is to provide interpreters with specific glossaries tailored to their needs. The authors advance the use of a semasiological and associative methodology instead of the onomasiological approach, as "it does not adapt well to interpretation because the cognitive effort required by the onomasiological structures slows down the interpretation process" (ibid).

3 Terminology Management Tools for Interpreters

There are some specialised computer and mobile software that can be used to quickly compile, store, manage and search within glossaries. The most outstanding applications developed by/for interpreters are described in detail below. They can be typically used to prepare an interpretation, in consecutive interpreting or in a booth. These applications are quite similar to the look-up terminology tools currently used by translators (Durán Muñoz, 2012). In fact, some of them have been developed to cater for the needs of both translators and interpreters. Due to the lack of space, this article is focused on standalone applications, but other types of applications like Web-based (e.g. Interpreters' Help[1]) can also be used for the same purposes (Ruetten, 2014).

Intragloss[2] is a commercial Mac OS X software created specifically to help interpreters when preparing for an event by allowing them to manage glossaries. This application can be simply defined as a glossary and document management tool created to help the interpreter prepare, use and merge different glossaries with preparation documents, in more than 180 different languages. It allows to import and export glossaries from and to plain text, Microsoft Word and Excel formats. Every glossary imported to, or created in, is assigned to a domain glossary (considered the highest level of knowledge), which contains all the glossaries from the sub-areas of knowledge, named 'assignments'. The creation of an assignment glossary can be done in two different ways: either by extracting automatically all the terms from the domain glossary that appear in the imported documents, or by highlighting a term in the document, search for it on search sites (such as online glossaries, terminology databases, dictionaries and general Web pages) and manually add the new translated term to the assignment glossary. It is important to mention that the online search can be made within Intragloss. Another interesting feature is that Intraglosss permits to copy assignment glossaries and assignment entries from one assignment to another. The domain glossary may be multilingual as it can include several bilingual assignment glossaries. By a way of example, if we have two assignment glossaries English/French and Dutch/English, in the same domain, the domain glossary will be French/English/Dutch, i.e. multilingual. Finally, Intragloss also allows to manually add meta-information to each glossary entry (see Fig. 1a).

In short, Intragloss is an intuitive and easy-to-use tool that facilitates the interpreters' terminology management process by producing glossaries (imported or created ad hoc), by searching on several websites simultaneously and by highlighting all the terms in the documents that appear in the domain glossary. However, it is currently platform dependent and only works on Mac OS X platforms.

InterpretBank[3] is a simple terminology and knowledge management software tool designed both for interpreters and translators using Windows and Android. It helps to manage, learn and look up glossaries and term-related information. Due to its modular architecture (see Fig. 1b), it can be used to guide the interpreter during the entire workflow process, starting from the creation and management of multilingual glossaries (TermMode), passing through the study of these glossaries (MemoryMode), and finally allowing the interpreter to look up terms while in a booth (ConferenceMode). InterpretBank also has an Android version called InterpretBank Lite. This application is specifically designed to access bi- or trilingual glossaries previously created with the desktop version. It is useful when working as a consecutive, community or liaison interpreter, when a quick look up at the terminology list is necessary.

InterpretBank has a user-friendly, intuitive and easy-to-use interface. It allows us to import and export glossaries in different formats (Microsoft Word, Microsoft Excel, simple text files, Android and TMEX) and suggests translation candidates by taking advantage of online translation portal services, such as Wikipedia, MyMemory and Bing. However, it is platform-dependent (it only works on Windows and Android), does not handle documents, only glossaries and requires a commercial license.

Interplex UE[4] is a user-friendly multilingual glossary management programme that can be used easily and quickly in a booth while the interpreter is working. Instead of keeping isolated word lists, it allows to group all terms relating to a particular subject or field into multilingual glossaries that can be searched in an instant. As we can see in Fig. 1c, this programme permits to have several glossaries open at the same time, which is a very useful feature if the working domain is covered by more than one glossary. Similar to the previous analysed programmes, Interplex UE also allows to import and export glossaries from and to Microsoft Word, Excel, and simple text files. Interplex UE runs on Windows; nevertheless, it has a simpler version for iOS devices, one named Interplex Lite, for iPhone and iPod Touch, and another named Interplex HD, for iPad. Both glossaries and multi-glossary searchers offer the functionality of

[1] `www.interpretershelp.com`
[2] `intragloss.com`
[3] `www.interpretbank.de`
[4] `www.fourwillows.com`

viewing expressions in each of the defined languages.

In general, Interplex UE has a user-friendly interface and it is regularly updated. It allows to import and export glossaries from and to Microsoft Word and Excel formats. However, it, too, is platform dependent (only works on Windows and iOS), does not handle documents, only glossaries, and requires a commercial license.

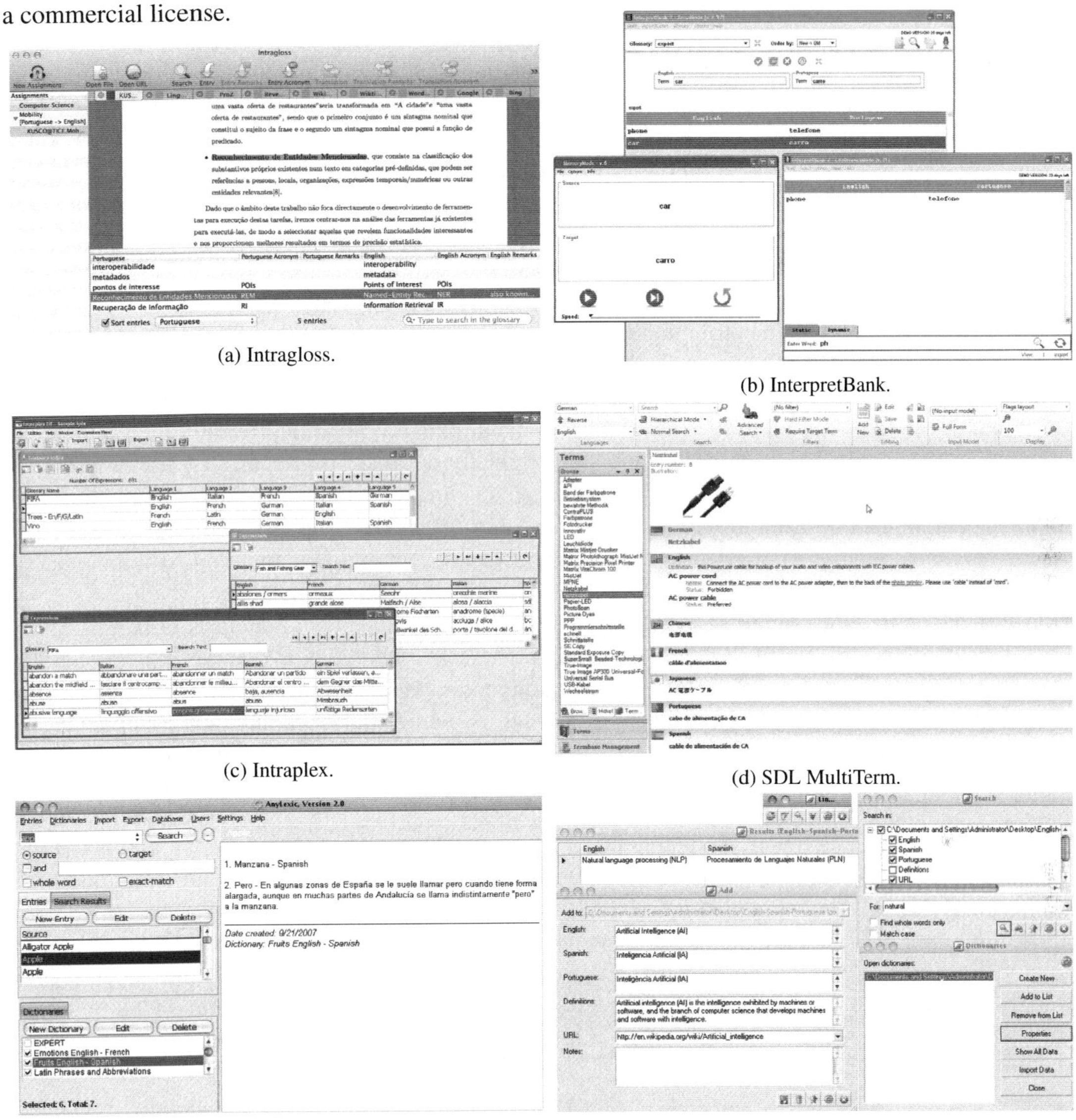

(a) Intragloss. (b) InterpretBank.

(c) Intraplex. (d) SDL MultiTerm.

(e) AnyLexic. (f) Lingo.

Figure 1: Screenshots of various terminology managment tools.

SDL MultiTerm Desktop[5] is a commercial terminology management tool developed for Windows that provides one solution to store and manage multilingual terminology. MultiTerm was first launched in 1990 by Tradós GmbH but in 2005 the company was acquired by SDL[6], which renamed MultiTerm to SDL MultiTerm. Today, SDL MultiTerm is a terminology management tool commercialised by SDL as a standalone application, which has been improved according to the translators' needs. Alternatively, MultiTerm can be used within the SDL Trados Studio[7] as an integrated tool. As translators can

[5] www.sdl.com/products/sdl-multiterm/desktop.html

[6] www.sdl.com

[7] www.sdl.com/products/sdl-trados-studio

easily edit and add terminology within SDL Trados Studio, MultiTerm helps to improve the efficiency of the translation process and promotes high-quality translated content with real-time verification of multilingual terminology. This application is very complete because it allows to store an unlimited number of terms in a vast number of languages; imports and exports glossaries from and to different technology environments, such as Microsoft Excel, XML, TBX and several other proprietary formats; permits to manually add a variety of meta-data information, such as synonyms, context, definitions, associated project, part-of-speech tags, URLs, etc. Apart from the previous mentioned descriptive fields, MultiTerm also allows the user to insert illustrations to the terms in the terminology database (which can be stored either locally or, for collaborative purposes, in a remote server). It is important to mention that this visual reference feature is very useful specially to interpreters and translators dealing with unfamiliar terms. Moreover, MultiTerm has an advanced search feature that permits to search not only the indexed terms but also in their descriptive fields, or create filters to make custom searches within specific fields, like language, definition, part-of-speech, etc. Nevertheless, the most interesting feature about MultiTerm is its concept-oriented feature, i.e. each entry in MultiTerm corresponds to a single concept, which can be described by different terms in both source and target language. This detail is very important because it allows the user to centralise and customise the terms with more information, such as different possible translations and their corresponding contexts (see Fig. 1d).

In general, MultiTerm can be seen as an advanced multilingual terminology tool with an intuitive and easy-to-use interface. Although MultiTerm was originally designed for translators, it can also be used by interpreters. Its main advantage to interpreters, when compared with other terminology tools, is twofold: it allows to add several translation terms in one entry and permits to customise a wide variety of descriptive fields, such as illustrations, associated projects, definitions, etc. However, it can only be used on Windows, does not handle documents and there is no demo version available.

AnyLexic[8] is an easy-to-use terminology management tool developed for Windows with a simple and intuitive interface. It was not designed to tie any particular terminological requirement, instead it aims to help the interpreter prepare, use and manage different glossaries or dictionaries. AnyLexic can be described as a robust terminology management tool, as it enables users to easily create and manage multiple mono-, bi- or multilingual glossaries in any language and to import and export glossaries from and to Microsoft Excel, plain text and AnyLexic Exchange Format (AEF). In addition, each entry in the glossary can have multiple translation equivalents in the target language along with notes. The search for records in the database allow users to combine different options, such as search for all source terms or translation candidates and associated notes. In addition, the search can be performed within one or multiple glossaries (see Fig. 1e). Another interesting feature in AnyLexic is the way that records can be displayed using different templates with configurable text colour, background colour, font size and text format. Besides, it is possible to create our own template for displaying the records. With the purpose of simplifying the teamwork process, this tool has an additional option to exchange any glossary with other AnyLexic users by either using the AEF proprietary format or by accessing a remote glossary, a very useful feature when co-operating with other interpreters or translators on a project.

In general, AnyLexic is an easy and convenient terminology database managing software for working with terminology, creating, editing and exchanging glossaries when working under one project both alone or with other working partners. However, it only works on Windows platforms and even though an evaluation version is available for 30 days, it requires a commercial license.

Lingo[9] is a commercial Windows terminology management tool designed to create and manage terminology databases, whether mono- or multilingual. It can import from and export to TMX and plain text. Its main features are: creation and management of any number of specialised glossaries/dictionaries in any language; can handle large files (i.e. over 50K entries); it allows users to have several glossaries open at the same time; and it has a rapid and easily configurable search functionality that can be customised to search for all terms, translation candidates and associated descriptive fields, either in all glossaries or in a specific one. Another interesting feature is the drag and drop functionality, which

[8] www.anylexic.com

[9] www.lexicool.com/soft_lingo2.asp

allows to easily insert words into Microsoft documents, for instance.

As we can see in Fig. 1f, Lingo is a simple and user-friendly software that offers an effective way to create and manage multilingual glossaries in any language. Additionally, it permits to manually add an infinite number of customised fields into each entry, such as definitions, URLs, synonyms, antonyms, contextual information, notes or any other desirable field. However, it is platform dependent and does not import from or export to common formats like Microsoft Word or Excel.

UniLex[10] is a free terminology management tool created by Acolada GmbH for Windows. It aims to help interpreters and translators prepare, use and manage bilingual glossaries or dictionaries in approximately 30 different languages. UniLex offers a variety of search functions and the possibility to combine user glossaries or dictionaries with a full range of dictionaries available in the UniLex series (e.g. Blaha: Pocket Dictionary of Automobile Technology German/English), which can be acquired as single user versions or as network versions for collaborative purposes. UniLex can also be used in a network environment, which allows users to exchange glossaries or dictionaries. Nevertheless, this additional feature requires a commercial license.

In general, UniLex is not only capable of managing user bilingual glossaries or dictionaries, but also dictionary titles from renowned publishers, which are sold by the company to be consulted within UniLex. However, it only works on Windows and does not handle multilingual glossaries.

The Interpreter's Wizard[11] is a free iPad application capable of managing bilingual glossaries in a booth. It is a simple, fast and easy-to-use application that helps the interpreter to search and visualise terminology in seconds. The system includes rapid and easily configurable search functionality that can be customised to search for all terms, translation candidates either in all glossaries or in a specific one. Nevertheless, all the imported glossaries need to be previously created and converted online to the proprietary format, and it does not allow users to export glossaries.

3.1 Comparative Analysis

Despite the aforementioned terminology tools can be used to prepare a given interpretation according to the interpreters' requirements identified in section 2, these systems differ from one another in their functionalities, practical issues and degrees of user-friendliness. Therefore, it is necessary to establish a set of specific and measurable features that permit us to assess and distinguish the different tools concerning users' needs in such a way that the results would be useful for both potential users as well as to the designers of such systems. Departing from the conclusions drawn from the literature review (see section 2) and the description of the terminology tools analysed in section 3, we provide in this section an analysis of these tools based on our own practical set of measurable features. For instance, the "freedom to define the basic structure" identified by Rodríguez and Schnell (2009) was reformulated into several practical measurable features, such as "N° of descriptive fields", "N° of working languages" and "N° of languages per glossary". Moreover, the possibility of "developing multilingual mini-databases", also identified in their study, was reconsidered as measurable features by means of the following criteria: "Manages multiple glossaries" and "N° of languages per glossary". Another example is the "Remote Glossary Exchange" measurable feature, which was inferred from the study conducted by Bilgen (2009), who identified the need to exchange terminological information.

After a careful analysis of the priorities for the design and features to be included in a terminology management tool for interpreters, 15 features were identified, 5 of which were classified as fundamental to a terminology tool (10 points) and 10 as secondary (5 points). Then, these features were used to evaluate the eight tools presented in section 3 and to investigate which one is the most complete. The first considered feature clarifies if the tools were designed to handle multiple glossaries in their interfaces at same time (**Manages multiple glossaries**). The next two features are somehow related. The **N° of possible working languages** describes how many different working languages are permitted by the application. Then, considering these working languages, how many of them can be used at the same time per glossary (**N° of languages per glossary allowed**). The next feature is related with

[10] www.acolada.de/unilex.htm
[11] the-interpreters-wizard.topapp.net

Feature/ Evaluation Criteria	**Intragloss** Pre-1.0 (2014)	**InterpretBank** 3.102 (2014)	**Intraplex** 2.1.1.47 (2012)	**SDL MultiTerm** 2014 (2013)	**AnyLexic** 2.0.0.2110 (2009)	**Lingo** 4 (2011)	**UniLex** 0.9 (2007)	**The Interpreter's Wizard** 2.0 (2011)
Manages multiple glossaries ⟨no=0; yes=10⟩	yes ⟨10⟩	yes ⟨10⟩	yes ⟨10⟩	yes ⟨10⟩	yes ⟨10⟩	yes ⟨10⟩	no ⟨0⟩	yes ⟨10⟩
N° of possible working languages ⟨≤100=4; >100=7; unlimited=10⟩	≈180 ⟨7⟩	≈35 ⟨4⟩	unlimited ⟨10⟩	unlimited ⟨10⟩	unlimited ⟨10⟩	unlimited ⟨10⟩	≈30 ⟨4⟩	unlimited ⟨10⟩
N° of languages per glossary allowed ⟨≤3=5; unlimited=10⟩	2 ⟨5⟩	2 ⟨5⟩	unlimited ⟨10⟩	unlimited ⟨10⟩	unlimited ⟨10⟩	unlimited ⟨10⟩	2 ⟨5⟩	2 ⟨5⟩
N° of descriptive fields ⟨non=0; 1=3; [2-5]=7; >5=10⟩	4 ⟨7⟩	4 ⟨7⟩	non ⟨0⟩	>5 ⟨10⟩	1 ⟨3⟩	>5 ⟨10⟩	2 ⟨7⟩	non ⟨0⟩
Handles documents ⟨no=0; yes=10⟩	yes (PDF, MS Word, Pages and Keynote files) ⟨10⟩	no ⟨0⟩	no ⟨0⟩	no ⟨0⟩	no ⟨0⟩	no ⟨0⟩	no ⟨0⟩	no ⟨0⟩
Unicode compatibility ⟨no=0; yes=5⟩	yes ⟨5⟩	yes ⟨5⟩	yes ⟨5⟩	yes ⟨5⟩	yes ⟨5⟩	yes ⟨5⟩	no ⟨0⟩	yes ⟨5⟩
Imports from ⟨1=1; 2=2; 3=3; [4-5]=4; >5=5⟩	MS Word, Excel and Plain Text ⟨3⟩	MS Word, Excel, TMEX and Plain Text ⟨4⟩	MS Word, Excel and Plain Text ⟨3⟩	MS Word, Excel and other CAT formats ⟨5⟩	MS Excel, Plain Text and AEF ⟨3⟩	TMX and Pain Text ⟨2⟩	Plain Text ⟨1⟩	Proprietary format ⟨1⟩
Exports to ⟨non=0; 1=1; 2=2; 3=3; [4-5]=4; >5=5⟩	MS Word and Excel ⟨2⟩	MS Word, Excel, TMEX, Android and Plain Text ⟨4⟩	MS Word, Excel and Plain Text ⟨3⟩	MS Word, Excel and other CAT formats ⟨5⟩	MS Excel, Plain Text and AEF ⟨3⟩	TMX and Plain Text ⟨2⟩	Plain Text ⟨1⟩	non ⟨0⟩
Embedded online search for translation candidates ⟨>no=0; yes=5⟩	yes ⟨5⟩	yes ⟨5⟩	no ⟨0⟩	no ⟨0⟩	no ⟨0⟩	no ⟨0⟩	no ⟨0⟩	no ⟨0⟩
Interface's supported languages ⟨1=1; [2-5]=3; >5=5⟩	English ⟨1⟩	English ⟨1⟩	English ⟨1⟩	English, German, French, Spanish, Japanese and Simplified Chinese ⟨5⟩	English, Simplified Chinese, German, Spanish, French, Italian, Dutch, Polish, Portuguese, Russian and Ukrainian ⟨5⟩	English ⟨1⟩	English, German, French and Spanish ⟨3⟩	English ⟨1⟩
Remote Glossary Exchange ⟨no=0; yes=5⟩	no ⟨0⟩	no ⟨0⟩	no ⟨0⟩	yes ⟨5⟩	yes ⟨5⟩	no ⟨0⟩	no ⟨0⟩	no ⟨0⟩
Well-documented ⟨no=0; yes=5⟩	yes ⟨5⟩	yes ⟨5⟩	yes ⟨5⟩	yes ⟨5⟩	yes ⟨5⟩	yes ⟨5⟩	no ⟨0⟩	no ⟨0⟩
Availability ⟨proprietary without demo=1; proprietary with demo=3; free=5⟩	proprietary with demo ⟨3⟩	proprietary with demo ⟨3⟩	proprietary with demo ⟨3⟩	proprietary without demo⟨1⟩	proprietary with demo ⟨3⟩	proprietary with demo ⟨3⟩	free ⟨5⟩	free ⟨5⟩
Operating System(s) ⟨1=1; 2=3; ≥3=5⟩	Mac OS X ⟨1⟩	Windows and Android ⟨3⟩	Windowns and iOS ⟨3⟩	Windows ⟨1⟩	Windows ⟨1⟩	Windows ⟨1⟩	Windows ⟨1⟩	iOS (only iPad) ⟨1⟩
Other relevant features ⟨subjective analysis=max. 5⟩	allows to highlight terms in the documents and merge a glossary with a document making it annotated to be printed ⟨5⟩	the MemoryMode helps to memorise bilingual glossaries ⟨4⟩	permits to have several glossaries open at the same time ⟨2⟩	it is a concept oriented-tool and permits to add illustrations into each entry ⟨5⟩	allows to share glossaries within a group of AnyLexic users ⟨1⟩	permits to add an unlimited number of descriptive fields ⟨2⟩	–	quick performance ⟨1⟩
Final Mark	69	60	55	77	64	61	27	39

Table 1: Comparative view and classification of several terminology management tools.

all types of descriptive fields that these tools allow to add to each glossary entry (**N° of descriptive fields**). The possibility of managing terminology with preparation documents (**Handles documents**) is another relevant feature for interpreters seeking for tools capable of highlighting terms in documents, for example. Equally import is the Unicode support (**Unicode compatibility**) as it provides a unique number for every character, no matter what the platform, the program, or the language is. In other words, an application that supports full Unicode means that it has support for any ASCII or non-ASCII language, such as Hebrew or Russian, two non-ASCII languages. **Imports from** and **Exports to**, as its name suggests, represents the supported input and output formats. The **Embedded online search for translation candidates** is a relevant add-in for terminology tools, as it permits to focus the search for terminological candidates within the tool. Despite the fact that all the tools have English as a default language, the support of multiple languages (**Interface's supported languages**) is another important feature as it allows to increase the number of potential users that a terminology tool can reach. The **Remote glossary exchange** feature is important when co-operating with other working partners remotely is required. The next three features are related with the available documentation, their availability and platform dependency (**Well-documented**, **Availability** and **Operating System(s)**, respectively). Finally, the last row presents some unique characteristics along with some relevant comments (**Other relevant features**).

Based on this comparative analysis, none of the investigated terminology tools exhibit all the proposed features. Nevertheless, SDL MultiTerm and Intragloss are the best classified with 77 and 69 points out of 100, respectively. This is not surprising because SDL MultiTerm is the most expensive tool nowadays available on the market and, apart from that, it has been developed for more than 20 years. Its flexibility to easily store, manage and search for multilingual terminology and definitions is just an example of the features that meet the specific needs of an interpreter. The score of Intragloss, released last year as a beta version, is neither surprising due to its novelty and design purposes, i.e. it was developed by interpreters for interpreters and thus corresponds better to their needs. On the other hand, UniLex and The Interpreter's Wizard tools got the worst scores due to the lack of features offered. About the remaining tools (AnyLexic, Lingo, InterpretBank and Intraplex) we can say that they have similar features, which resulted in similar scores (64, 61, 60 and 55, respectively).

4 Conclusion

This paper presents an overview of the most relevant features that terminology management tools should have in order to help interpreters before and during the interpretation process. Eight terminology tools are discussed and a comparative analysis is performed to evaluate them on the bases of the set of features previously identified. This comparative analysis not only aims at highlighting some of the features that interpreters can expect from the currently available terminology management tools on the market, but also intended to help them choose a specific tool for a given interpretation project. Table 1 provides interpreters with a comprehensive and up-to-date review of the currently available terminology tools on the market. It is envisaged to serve as a concise guide to help interpreters choose the terminology management tool that best caters for their specific needs, in order to help them work more efficiently, store and share terminology more easily, as well as save time when a looking for a specific feature most suited to a specific interpreting service.

Although most of the analysed tools could be considered to be very flexible when searching for terminology within glossaries, it appears that none of them fulfil all needs of interpreters. It is worth mentioning that some tools require a steep learning curve while others imply a significant financial investment (e.g. Lingo and SDL MultiTerm, respectively). Moreover, some tools are fairly basic and more orientated towards creating and managing bilingual or multilingual glossaries rather than more comprehensive terminology records with supporting information (e.g. UniLex and The Interpreter's Wizard).

Given that quality terminology management ranks high in their priorities, it would seem that there is a pressing need to design terminology management tools tailored to assist interpreters in the preparation stage, before their interpreting service or during it. In this respect, it would be necessary to identify the exact needs of interpreters (which are likely to be different from translators).

Acknowledgements

The research reported in this article has been partially carried out in the framework of the Educational Innovation Project TRADICOR (PIE 13-054, 2014-2015); the R&D project INTELITERM (nº FFI2012-38881, 2012-2015), and the R&D Project for Excelence TERMITUR (ref. nº HUM2754, 2014-2017).

References

Henning Bergenholtz and Sven Tarp. 2003. Two opposing theories: On H.E. Wiegand's recent discovery of lexicographic functions. *Hermes, Journal of Linguistics*, 31:171–196.

Baris Bilgen. 2009. *Investigating Terminology Management for Conference Interpreters*. MA dissertation, University of Otawa, Otawa, Canada.

Hernani Costa, Gloria Corpas Pastor, and Isabel Durán Muñoz. 2014. Technology-assisted Interpreting. *MultiLingual 143*, 25(3):27–32, April/May.

Isabel Durán Muñoz. 2012. Meeting Translators' Needs: Translation-oriented Terminological Management and Applications. *The Journal of Specialised Translation*, 18:77–92. Available at: `http://www.jostrans.org/issue18/art_duran.pdf` (Accessed 30 June 2014).

Daniel Gile. 1987. La terminotique en interprétation de conférence: un potentiel à exploiter. *Meta: Translators' Journal*, 32(2):164–169, June.

Barbara Moser-Mercer. 1992. Banking on Terminology: Conference Interpreters in the Electronic Age. *Meta: Translators' Journal*, 37(3):507–522, September.

Franz Pöchhacker. 2007. *Introducing Interpreting Studies*. London and New York: Routledge, 2nd edition.

Nadia Rodríguez and Bettina Schnell. 2009. A Look at Terminology Adapted to the Requirements of Interpretation. *Language Update*, 6(1):21–27. Available at: `http://www.btb.termiumplus.gc.ca/tpv2guides/guides/favart/index-eng.html?lang=eng&lettr=indx_autr8gijKBACeGnI&page=9oHAHvmFzkgE.html` (Accessed 30 June 2014).

Anja Ruetten. 2014, June 30. Booth-friendly terminology management revisited - 2 newcomers. Retrieved from: `http://blog.sprachmanagement.net/?p=305` (Accessed 30 June 2014).

Dennis Spohr. 2009. Towards a Multifunctional Electronic Dictionary Using a Metamodel of User Needs. In *eLexicography in the 21st century: New challenges, new applications*, Louvain-La-Neuve, Belgium. Presses Universitaires de Louvain.

Sven Tarp. 2008. *Lexicography in the Borderland Between Knowledge and Non-knowledge: General Lexicographical Theory with Particular Focus on Learner's Lexicography*. Lexicographica: Series maior. Walter de Gruyter, 1st edition.

Martin Will. 2007. Terminology Work for Simultaneous Interpreters in LSP Conferences: Model and Method. In Heidrun Gerzymisch-Arbogast and Gerhard Budin, editors, *Proc. of the Marie Curie Euroconferences MuTra: LSP Translation Scenario*, EU-High-Level Scientific Conference Series, Vienna, Austria.

Automatic Annotation of Parameters from Nanodevice Development Research Papers

Thaer M. Dieb
Graduate school of IST, Hokkaido University, Sapporo, Japan
diebt@kb.ist.hokudai.ac.jp

Masaharu Yoshioka
Graduate school of IST, Hokkaido University, Sapporo, Japan
yoshioka@ist.hokudai.ac.jp

Shinjiro Hara
RCIQE, Hokkaido University, Sapporo, Japan
hara@rciqe.hokudai.ac.jp

Marcus C. Newton
Physics & Astronomy, University of Southampton, Southampton, UK
M.C.Newton@soton.ac.uk

Abstract

In utilizing nanodevice development research papers to assist in experimental planning and design, it is useful to identify and annotate characteristic categories of information contained in those papers such as source material, evaluation parameter, etc. In order to support this annotation process, we have been working to construct a nanodevice development corpus and a complementary automatic annotation scheme. Due to the variations of terms, however, recall of the automatic annotation in some information categories was not adequate.
In this paper, we propose to use a basic physical quantities list to extract parameter information. We confirmed the efficiency of this method to improve the annotation of parameters. Recall for parameters increases between 4% and 7% depending on the type of parameter and analysis metric.

1 Introduction

"Nanoinformatics" is an emerging interdisciplinary research field in developing a computational framework to support nanoscale research (Karl et al. 2004). Nanoinformatics is the science and practice of determining which information is relevant to the nanoscale science and engineering community, and then developing and implementing effective mechanisms for collecting, validating, storing, sharing, analyzing, modeling, and applying this information (De la Iglesia et al. 2011). In order to support nanodevice development process, we have been working on a project that aims at analyzing the experiment results related to nanodevice development to provide insights for nanodevice novice researchers to help them planning their experiments more effectively (Yoshioka et al. 2010). In this project, we have proposed a framework to annotate useful information from research papers related to nanodevice development (e.g., source material, evaluation parameter, and so on), and use them for analyzing experiment results (Dieb et al. 2011). In order to speed up the annotation process, we have built an automatic annotation framework using machine-learning techniques to annotate research papers (Dieb et al. 2012).

However, due to the variations of terms, this framework may miss to annotate terms that are not in the training data set. Therefore, we have used chemical named entity recognition system to add generalized feature to extract "source material" terms. This generalized information is useful to extract "source material" terms and recall of this category increased. However, there are several other categories whose recall is inadequate.

Proceedings of the 4th International Workshop on Computational Terminology, pages 77–85,
Dublin, Ireland, August 23 2014.

In this paper, we propose to use a physical quantities list for adding generalized feature for extracting parameter terms in two categories ("evaluation parameter" and "experiment parameter"). In those two categories, since "experiment parameter" represents a control parameter for the experimental equipment and "evaluation parameter" represents ones measured by measuring devices, most of the terms are associated with physical quantities and they contains (a) term(s) that represent(s) its characteristics. We use 2 methods for the identification: first one we try to identify parameters (experiment and evaluation) using the new automatic annotated framework. The other one, we identify the parameters (in general) using the automatic annotation framework, and then classify the parameters into experiment and evaluation using SVM (Support Vector Machine) (Li 2005).

Several attempts have been made to use dictionary to enhance machine-learning performance. For example, Usié et al. (2013) is using a dictionary to assist in identifying certain categories of chemical entities in biomedical text. Our method is using the physical quantities list to enhance the identification of parameter information.

This paper has five sections. The first one is introduction. Second one introduces the nanodevice development papers corpus we have developed (Dieb et al, 2011) and the automatic annotation framework we have built (Dieb et al., 2012) in brief. Section 3 discusses parameter identification methods. In section 4, we demonstrate the experiment and discuss the results, and section 5 is a conclusion.

2 Automatic Annotation Framework for Nanodevice Development Papers

2.1 Nanodevice Development Papers Corpus

In order to analyze experiment results related to nanodevice development, we constructed nanodevice development papers corpus that annotates characteristic information from research papers Dieb et al. (2011). It was very critical to decide on what categories of information are necessary and adequate for the analysis of experiment results. Based on discussion with nanodevice development researchers, we were able to build an abstract for a development experiment in order to define the necessary terms for the analysis. We have defined eight categories of information for annotation as below:

- Source Material (SMaterial) e.g., As, InGaAs
- Source Material Characteristic (SMChar) e.g.,(111)B
- Experiment Parameter (ExP) e.g., total pressure
- Value of the Experiment parameter (ExPVal) e.g., 50 nm
- Evaluation Parameter (EvP) e.g., peak energy, FWHMs
- Value of the Evaluation Parameter (EvPVal) e.g., 1.22eV
- Manufacturing Method (MMethod) e.g., SA-MOVPE
- Final Product (TArtifact) e.g., semiconductor

The information in the papers is annotated using XML format. Figure 1 shows an example of an annotated paper.

We demonstrate the successful formation of <TArtifact> <SMChar>ferromagnetic</SMChar> <SMaterial>MnAs</SMaterial> nanoclusters </TArtifact> self-assembled on <SMaterial> GaInAs</SMaterial><SMChar> (1 1 1) B </SMChar> surfaces by <MMethod>metalorganic vapor phase epitaxy </MMethod><MMethod>MOVPE</MMethod>).
The <TArtifact><SMChar>hexagonal</SMChar> <SMaterial>MnAs</SMaterial>nanoclusters</TArtifact> show <EvPVal>strong</EvPVal> <EvP>ferromagnetic coupling</EvP><ExPVal>at room temperature </ExPVal> when the <ExP>external magnetic fields </ExP> are applied <ExPVal>in a direction parallel to the <SMaterial>InP</SMaterial><SMChar>(1 1 1) B</SMChar> wafer planes</ExPVal>.

Fig. 1: Example of annotated paper

Manual annotation of research papers is a time consuming process. Papers were first annotated by graduate students in nanodevice development domain. Several experiments and discussions have been held to improve the reliability of the corpus by resolving mismatches between different annotators. Papers then were corrected manually based on discussion with annotators. So far, we were able to complete five fully annotated papers, which can allow us to start our preliminary experiments concerning extracting and utilizing characteristic information in supporting nanodevice development. These papers are currently from the same research group (e.g., (Hara et al. 2006)). We also started to collaborate with other research groups to enlarge and include different research topics related to nanodevice development. Other information categories can be added to our model as needed along the way of the corpus development. Currently this corpus is still under construction, and not yet available.

2.2 Automatic Annotation Framework

In order to speed up the annotation process that also require domain expert, we have built an automatic annotation framework using the machine learning techniques to annotate the desired categories of information Dieb et al. (2012).

There are two main issues to be discussed in this automatic annotation framework:

(1) Chemical entity recognition:

In literature related to nanodevice development, most of the source material items are chemical compounds. If large training data set is available, the machine might be able to identify source material based on the training data only with no need to additional clue. However, since training data size is still very small, more clues are needed to identify Source Material. Identifying chemical entities can add more clues and will help the machine to recognize Source Material terms.

A new chemical entity recognizer called SERB-CNER (Syntactically Enhanced Rule-Based CNER) is used to enhance the identification of Source Material terms. SERB-CNER is a rule-based chemical entity recognizer that uses regular expressions to identify chemical compounds. In addition to that, SERB-CNER uses syntactic rules to eliminate some mismatches that might occur between chemical entities and general text.

(2) Overlapped term structure:

In nanodevice development domain, terms sometimes can overlap within each other, and not always simple. This might be a common issue in several other domains. Figure 2 shows an example of term overlapping.

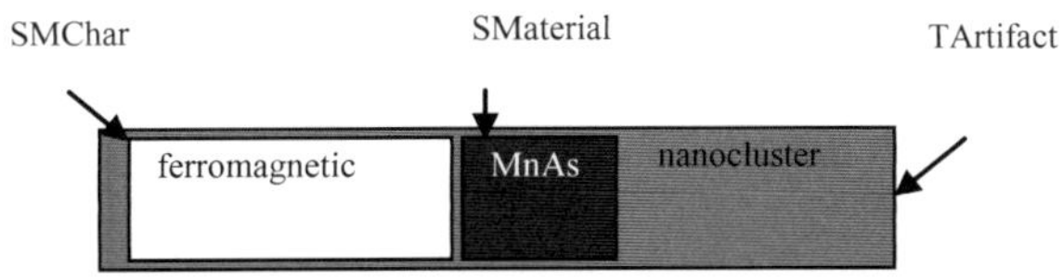

Fig. 2 Example of overlapped term structure

Because of this overlapping between different terms, same chunk of text might have information related to more than one term at the same time. That makes it difficult for the machine to learn to set the correct term information all at once. To tackle this issue, we have separated overlapped term categories into four groups where terms do not overlap within other terms from the same group. Based on these 4 groups, the machine learning process also divided into 4 cascading levels i.e. cascading named entity recognition (Kano et al. 2011).

For the automatic annotation framework, YamCha 0.33 (YamCha) was used, as a machine learning based sequence labelling tools. For the features, we use linguistic features like POS tag and orthogonal feature. POS tag was generated using rb tagger (rb tagger), which is A Simple Ruby Rule-Based Part of Speech Tagger based on the work of Eric Brill. Orthogonal feature was calculated using regular expressions. Chemical entity feature (CM) was calculated using SERB-CNER that identifies chemical entities as we discussed before. Term group's features were estimated in cascading style. In each level of this cascading style, we apply machine-learning technique to estimate the target feature for this level using information estimated from previous levels. For example, in cascading level 1, the machine will try to estimate term group 1 (TG1) using information of {Word, POS, Orth, CM}. In cascading level two, the machine will try to estimate term group 2 (TG2) using information of {Word, POS,

Orth, CM}, and TG1 that the machine estimated in cascading level 1. Figure 3 illustrates the cascading style annotation on an example of input data in IOB format.

Word	POS	Orth	CM	TG1	TG2	TG3	TG4
hexagonal	JJ	Lowercase	O	B-SMChar	B-TArtifact	O	O
MnAs	NNP	TwoCaps	B-CM	B-SMaterial	I-TArtifact	O	O
nanoclusters	NNS	Lowercase	O	O	I-TArtifact	O	O
show	VBP	Lowercase	O	O	O	O	O
strong	JJ	Lowercase	O	O	O	O	B-EvPVal
ferromagnetic	JJ	Lowercase	O	O	O	B-EvP	O

Note: POS=POS tag, Orth=orthogonal feature, CM=chemical compound, TG1, … TG4=term group.

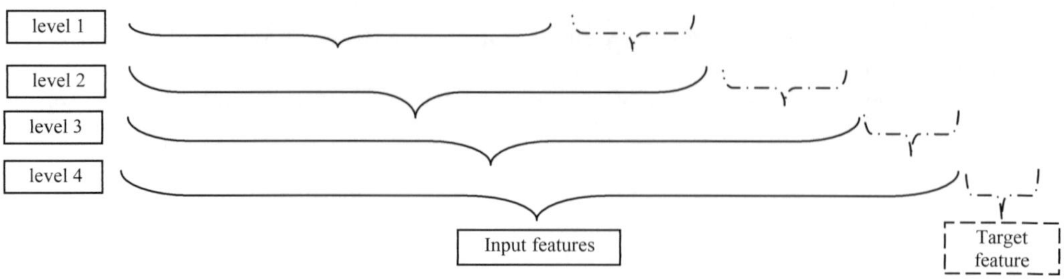

Fig. 3 Cascading style annotation on input data for the automatic annotation framework

We have tested this system using only two fully annotated papers with 10 fold cross validation. We use two metrics for analysis. One is tight agreement, which takes term category and term boundary into consideration and the other one is loose agreement, which checks term categories only. Table 1 shows the result of the automatic annotation framework. As we can see from the table, some categories have low recall, for example, EvP and EvPVal that depends on EvP for assessment.

Table 1: Automatic annotation framework performance

	Tight /precision	Tight /recall	Loose /precision	Loose /recall
SMaterial	0.99	0.96	0.99	0.96
SMChar	0.89	0.69	0.89	0.69
MMethod	0.93	0.86	0.95	0.88
TArtifact	0.86	0.73	0.93	0.79
ExP	0.91	0.81	0.97	0.86
EvP	0.76	0.60	0.87	0.69
ExPVal	0.72	0.57	0.85	0.67
EvPVal	0.86	0.60	0.97	0.67
Overall	0.89	0.76	0.94	0.80

3 Usage of Physical Quantities for Parameter Identification

3.1 Basic Idea

In the framework we proposed (Dieb et. al, 2012), recall and precision of each categories are evaluated, and recall and precision of "evaluation parameter" (EvP) is lower than average. One of the reasons about this problem is a variety of parameter terms used in the paper. Machine learning based sequence labelling tools is good at extracting terms that are also exists in the training data set, but it is necessary to extract more generalized clue to identify terms that do not appear in the training data set.

Identification of chemical named entity is helpful to extract such clue from the corpus, but it is not sufficient.

As Nakagawa and Mori (2003) discussed, most of the compound nouns are constructed from basic noun and identification of terms that contribute to make up compound noun is useful to extract terms.

Since "experiment parameter" (ExP) represents a control parameter for the experimental equipment and "evaluation parameter" (EvP) represents ones measured by measuring devices, most of the terms are associated with physical quantities and they contains (a) term(s) that represent(s) its characteristics. For example, "density of the nanoclusters" and "height of the nanoclusters" contains physical quantity term "density" and "height" respectively. Identification of physical quantities of test data may support to extract new terms. For example, identification of "size" as a physical quantity might support identification of "size of nanoclusters" as a parameter.

There are two types of parameters exist in this nanodevice development papers corpus; Experiment parameter that is used to control the conditions of the experiment like temperature, pressure, gas flow rate, and so on; The other type is evaluation parameter that is used to evaluate the quality of the experiment output like smoothness of the surface, conductivity, and so on. In this paper, a list of physical quantities is used to support extracting terms of those two types of parameters.

3.2 Physical Quantities List

In order to construct a list of physical quantities, we started with a basic list of physical properties of matter, collected by Dr. Anne Marie Helmenstine, Ph.D. in biomedical science. [1] This list includes but not limited to the physical properties of an object. For example, concentration, density, and so on. In addition to this list, we have added several other common parameters that commonly found in nanodevice development research papers. For example, height, conductivity, and so on. Additionally, we have added several keywords that usually in close relation with parameters like ratio, rate, percentage, and so on. We collected these keywords from research papers related to nanodevice development. The compiled list then checked by nanodevice researchers as a basic list for physical quantities.

3.3 Parameter Classification

In the automatic annotation framework, we proposed (Dieb et al, 2012), experiment and evaluation parameters (ExP and EvP) are exclusive categories and identified at the same time. However, in this approach, recall and word boundary identification rate of terms is lower than SMaterial and MMethod. In order to identify good term boundaries to identify parameter terms, it is better to have large variation of compound terms for representing parameter. However, since our corpus size is limited, it is better to merge two parameter categories into one "Parameter" category to enlarge training example for making compound parameter terms. After extracting parameter terms, another machine learning classifier is used for categorize each extracted parameter.

Since two parameter categories (ExP and EvP) represent role of parameter in the paper, it is better to include results of dependency analysis and verbs related to the terms. Therefore, in this paper, we use SVM with following features to identify its category.

1. Information about term
   A) Surface description of the term
   B) lemmatized element(s) of the term
   C) (a) term(s) that is (are) identified as physical quantity by a physical quantities list
2. Dependency structure results
   A) First verb that given parameter terms directly depends
   B) First preposition that given parameter terms directly depends
   C) Lemmas that parameter terms depends.

Following is example of extracted features for a sentence that contains parameter term "temperature"

Figure 4 represents an example of feature extraction. Stanford Core NLP tools are used for generating dependency analysis results. Features that start with "1stVB++", "1stIN++", "plemma++", and "PAR++" represents 2-A,B,C and 1-C respectively. Other elements correspond to 1-A and 1-B.

[1] This list of physical properties of matter is available online at: http://chemistry.about.com/od/matter/a/Physical-Properties-List.htm

Input: The size of the MnAs nanoclusters are controllable by optimizing MOVPE growth conditions.
Experiment parameter (ExP): MOVPE growth conditions

↓

MOVPE__growth__conditions MOVPE growth condition plemma++condition plemma++optimize 1stVB++optimize plemma++by 1stIN++by plemma++controllable PAR++size
Evaluation parameter (EvP): size of the MnAs nanoclusters

↓

The__size__of__the__MnAs the size of the mna plemma++size plemma++controllable

```
-> controllable-JJ (root)
 -> size-NN (nsubj)
  -> The-DT (det)
  -> of-IN (prep)
   -> nanoclusters-NNS (pobj)
    -> the-DT (det)
    -> MnAs-NNS (nn)
 -> are-VBP (cop)
 -> by-IN (prep)
  -> optimizing-VBG (pcomp)
   -> conditions-NNS (dobj)
    -> MOVPE-NNP (nn)
    -> growth-NN (nn)
```

Dependency analysis results

Fig. 4 Example of feature extraction for two parameters from a text

4 Experiments

4.1 Setup

In order to confirm the effectiveness of our proposed framework, we conduct automatic annotation experiments by using nanodevice development papers corpus with following three systems.

- Base line system: we use the automatic annotation framework we previously proposed (Dieb et al. 2012) without physical quantities list for parameter identification.
- Suggested system without parameter classification: we integrated the physical quantities list for parameter identification component in the automatic annotation framework. This component cannot separate experiment (ExP) from evaluation parameter (EvP) because that depends on the context, so the CRF will handle this separation based on training data.
- Suggested system with parameter classification using SVM: after annotating parameters using automatic annotation framework with physical quantities for parameter identification component integrated, SVM will handle the classification of parameters using statistical data into experiment (ExP) and evaluation parameter (EvP).

All systems use CRF++ (CRFpp) implementation of Conditional Random field (CRF) (John et al. 2001) as the machine learning system. Additionally, we have added one more level for the cascading for the SMChar term category, since we found some cases that caused overlap between SMChar and SMaterial that used to be in the same term group. Figure 5 shows an example of the input data in IOB format. Since chemical compound and parameters do not overlap between each other, we use the same feature column for both (CM is chemical entity feature, and PAR is parameter feature based on the physical quantity list).

For experiment 1: the feature CM/PAR has only CM type of values.

For experiment 3: the feature TG4 has Param type of values (general parameter replaces ExP, and EvP without separation. Classification is done independently with SVM)

4.2 Results and Discussion

We have five fully annotated papers. In order to check the performance of these three systems, we use five cross fold validation (training on four papers, and testing on the 5th) for each system. We use tight and loose agreement metrics for analysis (same as explained in section 2.2). Table 2 shows comparative average results for the three experiments. In this experiment, since it is necessary to identify new terms that are only exists in one paper; recall of baseline system is lower than the value in Table 1. Statistical significance test is conducted for the difference between value of baseline system and value of proposed system. "*" represents difference is statistically significant ($P<0.05$) in both side test.

Word	POS	Orth	CM/PAR	TG1	TG2	TG3	TG4	TG5
V/	NP	Other	O	O	O	O	B-ExP	O
Mn	NP	InitCap	B-CM	B-SMaterial	O	O	I-ExP	O
ratio	NN	Lowercase	B-PAR	O	O	O	I-ExP	O
were	VBD	Lowercase	O	O	O	O	O	O
850	CD	DigitNumber	O	O	O	O	O	B-ExPVal
°C	NN	Other	O	O	O	O	O	I-ExPVal

Note: POS=POS tag, Orth=orthogonal feature, CM/PAR=chemical compound/parameter list, TG1, ... TG5=term group.

Fig. 5 Example of input data for our suggested system

Table 2: Performance comparison between base line system and suggested one

	Base line system				**Our system without parameter classification**				**Our system with parameter classification using SVM**			
	T_pre	**T_rec**	**L_pre**	**L_rec**	**T_pre**	**T_rec**	**L_pre**	**L_rec**	**T_pre**	**T_rec**	**L_pre**	**L_rec**
SMaterial	0.94	0.92	0.97	0.95	0.94	0.92	0.97	0.95	0.94	0.92	0.97	0.95
MMethod	0.97	0.70	0.98	0.70	0.98	0.72	0.98	0.72	0.98	0.72	0.98	0.72
SMChar	0.87	0.68	0.90	0.70	0.87	0.69	0.90	0.71	0.87	0.69	0.90	0.71
TArtifact	0.88	0.72	0.93	0.76	0.89	0.72	0.93	0.75	0.89	0.72	0.93	0.75
Param	**0.67**	**0.45**	**0.86**	**0.58**	**0.67**	**0.49**	**0.87**	**0.64**	**0.66**	**0.52**	**0.85**	**0.67**
ExP	**0.85**	**0.59**	**0.91**	**0.63**	**0.84**	**0.62**	**0.91**	**0.67**	**0.80**	**0.63**	**0.88**	**0.70**
EvP	**0.50**	**0.32**	**0.78**	**0.51**	**0.50**	**0.35**	**0.78**	**0.55***	**0.50**	**0.38***	**0.76**	**0.57***
ExPVal	0.67	0.42	0.81	0.53	0.67	0.42	0.80	0.52	0.70	0.43	0.82	0.52
EvPVal	0.62	0.34	0.79	0.43	0.63	0.37	0.78	0.46	0.62	0.37	0.78	0.46
overall	0.82	0.63	0.90	0.69	0.82	0.64	0.90	0.71	0.81	0.64	0.89	0.71

Note: T_pre=Tight precision T_rec=Tight recall, L_pre=Loose, L_rec= Loose recall, param= general parameter resulted from merging ExP and EvP

From this result, identification of physical quantities may not affect earlier stage of cascading term extraction (SMaterial, MMethod, SMChar, and TArtifact). For both ExP and EvP, recall is increased when we use physical quantities list, and increase even more when we use SVM classification. Especially for EvP, improvement of recall for loose agreement of both suggested systems are statistically significant at the 5% level. In addition, improvement of recall for tight agreement of using SVM for parameter classification is also statistically significant. These improvements justify usage of physical quantities list is good for improving recall of ExP and EvP. In addition, using both examples of ExP and EvP for identification of compound word boundary is also helpful. Even though precision of ExP and EvP are decreased from baseline system, precision of parameter term (terms that belongs to ExP or EvP) identification is almost same as baseline system.

In order to evaluate detailed behaviour of our proposed system, we check the data whose annotation results are different from baseline system and proposed system. We confirm there are some cases in which new parameters terms that did not exist in training data are extracted. For example, "temperature of (MeCp)2Mn" did not exist at all in the training data, and was not able to be annotated by CRF in test data before adding physical quantities list. After marking "temperature" as parameter, CRF was able to find "temperature of (MeCp)2Mn" by learning compound term construction rule (i.e., PAR of CM may be a parameter term). On the other hand, merging parameters into one category then classifying them seems to be effective, because we can get use of a larger training data. For example, "partial pressure" (where "pressure" is in the physical quantities list) did not exist in the training data. It was not recognized neither by the baseline system nor by the suggested system without parameter classification; However, when we merge the parameters into one category (allowing for larger training data for the identification of parameter), the suggested system with parameter classification was able to identify such entity. Another example, "period of the mask openings" where "period" is in the physical quantities list. In this example also, only the suggested system with parameter classification were able to identify such entity using physical quantities list.

Regarding the precision, there are several cases whose parameter types are difficult to identify by using sentence information only. For example, "diameter" can be some cases as experiment parameter, and can be evaluation parameter in other cases depending on the context. In "the typical diameter of the initial circular opening" it is ExP, however, in “diameter of the NCs", it is EvP. Even though both texts have similar style, "diameter" can be of different types. In order to improve the quality of parameter type classification, it is better to use other information that cannot be extracted from one sentence (e.g., description of same parameter in other sentences of the same paper, position of first parameter term appearance).

5 Conclusion and Future Development

In this paper, we proposed to use a basic physical quantities list in combination with machine learning technique to improve the extraction of parameter information from research papers related to nanodevice development. We confirmed our proposed system improve recall of parameters between 4% and 7% depending on the type of parameter and analysis metric, and using both example of Experiment parameter and Evaluation parameter for term boundary identification is helpful.

In future studies, and as further manuscripts are annotated, we plan to make use of a larger corpus thus allowing us to evaluate our system on a larger text collection. Additionally, we are planning to develop a new POS tagger for the nanodevice development domain. Brill tagger is developed for general language POS tagging purposes, and changing it with specialized POS tagger might improve the results. It is beneficial to study the impact of each component of the system (POS tagger, the chemical named entity recognizer, or the machine learning system) on the overall performance (Kolluru et al, 2011)

Acknowledgements

This work was partially supported by MEXT/JSPS KAKENHI Grant Number 24240021 and 26540165.

Reference

CRFpp: available online at http://crfpp.googlecode.com/svn/trunk/doc/index.html

GPoSTTL: available online at http://gposttl.sourceforge.net.

Thaer M. Dieb, Masaharu Yoshioka, and Shinjiroh Hara. Automatic Information Extraction of Experiments from Nanodevices Development Papers, IIAIAAI 2012 Proceedings of 2012 IIAI International Conference on Advanced Applied Informatics,pp.42-47,2012

Thaer M. Dieb, Masaharu Yoshioka, and Shinjiroh Hara. Construction of Tagged Corpus for Nanodevices Development Papers, GrC, 2011 Proceedings of the 2011 IEEE International Conference on Granular Computing, pp. 167–170, 2011.

Shinjiroh Hara, and Takahashi Fukui. Hexagonal ferromagnetic MnAs nanocluster formation on GaInAs/InP (111) B layers by metal–organic vapor phase epitaxy. Applied Physics Letters, Vol. 89, 113111, 2006.

Diana de la Iglesia, Stacey Harper, Mark D. Hoover, Fred Klaessig, Phil Lippel, Bettye Maddux, Jeff Morse, André Nel, Krishna Rajan, Rebecca Reznik-Zellen, and Mark Tuominen, (2011, Apr.). Nanoinformatics 2020 Roadmap, National Nanomanufacturing Network. Amherst, MA 01003. [Online]. Available: http://eprints.internano.org/607/1/Roadmap_FINAL041311.pdf, 2011.

Yoshinobu Kano, Makoto Miwa, K Bretonnel Cohen, Lawrence E Hunter, Sophia Ananiadou, and Jun'ichi Tsujii. U-Compare: a modular NLP workflow construction and evaluation system. In IBM Journal of Research and Development, vol. 55, no. 3, pp. 11:1-11:10, 2011.

BalaKrishna Kolluru, Lezan Hawizy, Peter Murray-Rust, Junichi Tsujii, Sophia Ananiadou. Using Workflows to Explore and Optimise Named Entity Recognition for Chemistry. PLoS ONE, 6(5), 2011. DOI: 10.1371/journal.pone.0020181

John D Lafferty, Andrew McCallum, Fernando Pereira. Conditional random fields: Probabilistic models for segmenting and labeling sequence data. In Proceedings of the Eighteenth International Conference on Machine Learning. ICML '01, San Francisco, CA, USA, Morgan Kaufmann Publishers Inc. (2001) 282–289

Yaoyong Li, Kalina Bontcheva, Hamish Cunningham SVM-based learning system for information extraction. In Proceedings of the First international conference on Deterministic and Statistical Methods in Machine Learning, pp. 319–339, 2005.

Hiroshi Nakagawa and Tatsunori Mori: Automatic term recognition based on statistics of compound nouns and their components, In Terminology, Vol. 9, No. 2, pp. 201-219, 2003

rb tagger: available online at http://rbtagger.rubyforge.org/

Karl Ruping and Woody Sherman. Nanoinformatics: Emerging computational tools in nanoscale research. In Technical Proceedings of the 2004 NSTI Nanotechnology Conference and Trade Show, Volume 3, pp. 525–528, 2004

Anabel Usié, Joaquim Cruz, Jorge Comas, Francesc Solsona, Rui Alves. A tool for the identification of chemical entities (CheNER-BioC). Proceedings of the Fourth BioCreative Challenge Evaluation Workshop vol. 2 ,66-69 (2013)

YamCha : available on line at http://chasen.org/ taku/software/yamcha/.

Masaharu Yoshioka, Katsuhiro Tomioka, Shinjiroh Hara, and Takahashi Fukui. Knowledge exploratory project for nanodevice design and manuacturing. In iiWAS '10 Proceedings of the 12th International Conference on Information Integration and Web-based Application & Services, pp. 869-872, 2010.

Evaluating Term Extraction Methods for Interpreters

Ran Xu, Serge Sharoff
Centre for Translation Studies
School of Modern Languages and Cultures
University of Leeds, UK,
{sml3rx,s.sharoff}leeds.ac.uk

Abstract

The study investigates term extraction methods using comparable corpora for interpreters. Simultaneous interpreting requires efficient use of highly specialised domain-specific terminology in the working languages of an interpreter with limited time to prepare for new topics. We evaluate several terminology extraction methods for Chinese and English using settings which replicate real-life scenarios, concerning the task difficulty, the range of terms and the amount of materials available, etc. We also investigate interpreters' perception on the usefulness of automatic termlists. The results show the accuracy of the terminology extraction pipelines is not perfect, as their precision ranges from 27% on short texts to 83% on longer corpora for English, 24% to 31% on Chinese. Nevertheless, the use of even small corpora for specialised topics greatly facilitates interpreters in their preparation.

1 Introduction

The study investigates term extraction methods using comparable corpora for interpreters. Simultaneous interpreting requires efficient use of highly specialised domain-specific terminology in the working languages of the interpreter. By necessity, interpreters often work in a wide range of domains and have limited time to prepare for new topics. To ensure the best possible simultaneous interpreting of specialised conferences where a great number of domain-specific terms are used, interpreters need preparation, usually under considerable time pressure. They need to familiarise themselves with concepts, technical terms, and proper names in the interpreters' working languages.

However, there is little research into the use of modern terminology extraction tools and pipelines for the task of simultaneous interpretation. At the start of computer-assisted termbank development, Moser-Mercer (1992) overviewed the needs and workflow of practicing interpreters with respect to terminology and offered some guidelines for developing term management tools specifically for the interpreters. That study did review the functionalities of some termbanks and term management systems, yet there was no mention of corpus collection (a fairly new idea at the time) or automatic term extraction.

A few previous studies mentioned the application of corpora as potential electronic tools for the interpreters. Fantinuoli (2006) and Gorjanc (2009) discussed the functions of specific online crawling tools and explored ways to extract specialised terminology from disposable web corpora for interpreters. Our work is most closely connected to Fantinuoli's work on evaluation of termlists obtained from Web-derived corpora. However, that study relied on a single method of corpus collection and term extraction, and did not include an investigation into integration of corpus research into practice of interpreter training.

Rütten (2003) suggested a conceptual software model for interpreters' terminology management, in which termlists are expected to be extracted (semi-)automatically and then to be revised by their users, the interpreters, who can concentrate on those terms which are relevant and important to remember. However the study neither tested the functions of the term extraction tools nor further discussed interpreters' perception on the usefulness of the automatically lists in their preparation for interpreting tasks.

Proceedings of the 4th International Workshop on Computational Terminology, pages 86–93,
Dublin, Ireland, August 23 2014.

	FR0		FR1		FR2		SM1		SM2	
	En	Zh	En	Zh	En	Zh	En	Zh	En	Zh
Texts	1	1	9	9	81	86	9	12	74	84
Size	774	1,641	42,006	30,174	206,197	129,350	20,533	40,545	166,499	116,235

Table 1: Corpora used in this study (the size is in words for En, in characters for Zh)

Based on Rütten model, this paper will further test the functions of several term extraction tools for English and Chinese, and will discuss the interpreters' perception on the usefulness of the automatically-generated lists in their preparation for interpreting tasks.

In the remainder of this paper we will describe the pipelines for corpus collection and terminology extraction (Section 2), present the results of their numeric evaluation (Section 3), and discuss options for future research, including the challenges for the term extraction pipelines in this setting (Section 4).

2 Corpus collection and term extraction

In this section we describe pipelines for interpreters' terminology preparation with the use of term extraction tools. We compare several approaches to corpus compilation and processing for specialised texts as well as several pipelines for terminology extraction.

2.1 Description of the procedure

Two specialized topics In this study MA student interpreters were invited to prepare for simultaneous interpreting tasks on two specialised topics: fast reactors (FR) and Seabed minerals (SM). They were provided with two monolingual specialised corpora in both English and Chinese for their advance preparation on each of the topics (FR & SM).

Three term extractors The students started with the FR topic, and were asked to manually generate their own lists from the provided corpora (FR1 En & Zh) before their simultaneous interpreting exercise on the topic in both directions (English→Chinese and Chinese→English). After their interpreting tasks, they were then asked to evaluate the relevance of two monolingual lists (En & Zh) which were automatically generated by one of the three tools (TTC TermSuite, Syllabs Tools and TeaBoat). The purpose here is to see which tool could extract more relevant terms for the needs of trainee interpreters.

We collected and compared the annotation results from the students to select a single tool with comparatively better performance. We then invited the students to prepare for the other topic (SM) by using automatically-generated lists in the simultaneous interpreting preparation.

2.2 Corpus compilation

There are two types of sources where comparable corpora are from:

1. Conference documents and relevant background documents provided by the conference organisers
2. Specialised corpora collected from the internet using WebBootCat (Baroni and Bernardini, 2004)

Table 1 presents all the corpora we use in this study. FR0/SM0 has been created from a single relevant document, representing the speech that the trainee interpreters were asked to interpret from in this experiment. We also ran term extraction from this "corpus" since often a text of this length is the only source of information given to the interpreters in advance. We tried to balance the terminological difficulty for both languages, even if this was not always possible. After manual term selection, we found that FR0-Zh contains 147 terms per 591 seconds of delivery (15 terms per minute), FR0-En: 86 terms per 566 seconds (9 t/min), SM0-Zh: 157 terms per 604 seconds (16 t/min), SM0-En: 169 terms per 750 seconds (14/min).[1]

[1]Counting the term density per unit of text is not straightforward, because of very different tokenisation rules in Chinese and English.

Seeds (En)	Seeds (Zh)
fast breeder reactor	快中子增殖反应堆
fission	裂变
decay heat	余热
uranium	铀
plutonium	钚
core damage	堆芯损坏
Fukushima accident	福岛事故
nuclear waste	核废料
fuel cycle	燃料循环
coolant	冷却剂

Table 2: Parallel keyword seeds on Fast Reactors for FR2

FR1 (En & Zh) and SM1 (En & Zh) are comparable corpora, which represent conference documents and relevant background documents passed from the conference organisers, including speech outlines, research papers from experts and research institutes, reports from national and international authorities, as well as popular science articles, Wikipedia articles, specialised journal articles and interviews, etc.

FR2 (En & Zh) and SM2 (En & Zh) are corpora collected by Web crawling using Bootcat(Baroni and Bernardini, 2004). For instance, to produce FR2 we started with a set of ten relevant keywords in English and Chinese as shown in Table 2, then used BootCat to retrieve online resources and generate two corpora (FR2 En & Zh). All the keyword seeds are from the English speech-FR0 that the students were going to interpret from, and are therefore considered very relevant and important terms. The Chinese keywords are the translations of the English ones.

Preprocessing included webpage cleaning (Baroni et al., 2008), as well as basic linguistic processing. Lemmatisation and tagging for English was done using TreeTagger (Schmid, 1994), while for Chinese we used "Segmenter", an automatic tokenisation tool (Liang et al., 2010) followed by TreeTagger for POS tagging. Lemmatisation is needed because the keywords in a glossary are expected to be in their dictionary form. Lemmatisation also helps in reducing the nearly identical forms, e.g., *sulphide deposit(s)*. However, lemmatisation also leads to imperfect terms, e.g., *recognise type of marine resource*, while the plurals and participles should be expected in a dictionary form (*recognised type of marine resources*).

2.3 Automatic term extraction

TTC TermSuite (Daille, 2012) is based on lexical patterns defined in terms of Part-of-Speech (POS) tags with frequency comparison against a reference corpus using specificity index (Ahmad et al., 1994), which extracts both single (SWT) and multi-word terms (MWT) outputs their lemmas, part of speech, lexical pattern, term variants (if any), etc. The most important feature of the TTC TermSuite is the fact that term candidates can be output with their corresponding term variants. Syllabs Tools (Blancafort et al., 2013) is a knowledge-poor tool, which is based on unsupervised detection of POS tags, following the procedure of (Clark, 2003), and on the Conditional Random Field framework for term extraction (Lafferty et al., 2001). Teaboat (Sharoff, 2012) does term extraction by detecting noun phrases using simple POS patterns in IMS Corpus Workbench (Christ, 1994) and by applying log-likelihood statistics (Rayson and Garside, 2000) to rank terms by their relevance to the corpus in question against the Internet reference corpora for English and Chinese (Sharoff, 2006).

3 Term extraction evaluation

Fantinuoli (2006) used five categories to find the level of specialisation and well-formedness of the automatically-generated candidate termlist:

1. specialised terms that were manually extracted by the terminologist (and are contained in the reference term list);

FR-TTC		FR-Teaboat		FR-Syllabs		SM-Syllabs	
EN	ZH	EN	ZH	EN	ZH	EN	ZH
0.541	0.500	0.166	0.435	0.181	0.662	0.117	0.221

Table 3: Krippendorff's α for different term lists

2. highly specialised terms that were not detected by the terminologist;
3. non-specialised terms that are commonly used in the field of his study (medicine);
4. general terms that are not specific to the medical field;
5. ill-formed, incomplete expressions and fragments.

Our annotation system extends Fantinuoli's study because the purpose of annotation in this project is to give the interpreters possibility to extract relevant terms from all the candidate terms regardless of their levels of specialisation. Our premise is that interpreters may need relevant terms, both highly specialised and less specialised, in order to prepare themselves for a conference. The annotators are the end users of the list, i.e. the trainee interpreters who participated in this research. Since the interpreters are tasked with translating speeches in the domain, they need themselves to decide what is likely to be relevant instead of relying on the terminologists who describe the overall structure of the domain. The following is the five-category annotation system that we used in this research:

- R relevant terms (terms closely relevant to the topic), eg. *breed ratio, uranium-238, decay heat removal system*;
- P potentially relevant terms (a category between "I" and "R": they are terms; but annotators are not sure whether they are closely relevant to the topic of their assignment), eg. *daughter nuclide, neutron poison, Western reactor*;
- I irrelevant terms (terms not relevant to the topic), eg. *schematic diagram, milk crate*;
- G general words (rather than terms), eg. *technical option, monthly donation, Google tag, discussion forum*;
- IL ill-formed constructions (parts of terms or chunks of words), eg. *var, loss of cooling, separate sample container, first baseline data, control ranging*.

It only took several minutes to generate a termlist after uploading the designated corpus onto TTC TermSuite, Syllabs Tools and TeaBoat. Each of them automatically generated corresponding monolingual termlists sorted by their term specificity scores. For all the tools we set the threshold of obtaining 500 terms (if possible), as a practical limit for all evaluation experiments.

The trainee interpreters were asked to annotate the list by using the above annotation system. Each of them reported that it took them about 60 minutes to annotate both lists (in EN & ZH) on each of the topics (FR & SM). All the annotators were briefed about what counts as terms and the annotation system before they started their evaluation of term lists. We aim for consistency, yet inter-annotator disagreement does exist and there is a certain degree of subjectivity in annotation. To measure the level of agreement we used Krippendorff's α over the other measures, such as Fleiss' κ, because Krippendorff's α offers an extension of such measures as Fleiss' κ and Scott's π by introducing a distance metric for the pairwise disagreements, thus making it possible to work with interval-scale ratings, e.g., considering disagreement between **R** and **P** as less severe than between **R** and **I** (Krippendorff, 2004).

The values of Krippendorff's α (see Table 3) are relatively low. The most common cases of disagreement are between **R** and **P** (the boundary between them often depends on the amount of knowledge on the side of the annotator), but also quite surprisingly between **R** and **IL**, when some annotators interpret ill-formed sequences as a contribution to useful terms.

With the disagreement taken into consideration, our evaluation on the number of relevant terms was judged by the agreement between at least two annotators among four to six annotators for the topic of FR. This established the gold standard lists reported in Table 4.

The annotation results from Table 4 for English show that Syllabs generated more relevant terms than the other two tools from both FR0 and FR1. Both Syllabs and Teaboat generated good numbers of

English:

Tool	FR0	FR1	FR2	SM1
Syllabs	85/104(82%)	309/500 (62%)	400/500 (80%)	441/500 (88%)
Teaboat	44/56(79%)	232/376 (62%)	413/499 (83%)	
TTC	NA	136/500 (27%)	287/500 (57%)	

Chinese:

Tool	FR1	SM1
Syllabs	156/500(31%)	130/500 (26%)
Teaboat	141/450(31%)	
TTC	119/500(24%)	

Table 4: Number of relevant (R) terms against candidate terms

relevant terms from FR2. In addition, Syllabs' and TeaBoat's English lists contain more specialised terms in the domain of FR, such as *defence-in-depth, once-through fuel cycle, suppression chamber of the containment*, etc. These specialised terms with relatively low frequency are not included in the TTC's list. The terms included in TTC's list are more general terms, such as *steam, energy, liquid, heat, leak*, etc., which are likely to be already known by the trainee interpreters.

The English termlists from all the tools contain a number of repetitions in the form of term variants, following Daille's definition as "an utterance which is semantically and conceptually related to an original term" (Daille, 2005). The automatically generated termlists contain the following types of term variations, which are counted as individual term candidates scattered in the termlists:

Morphological variation: *bathymetry* vs *bathymetric* (not different when translated into Chinese)

Anaphoric variation: *pollymetallic sulphide deposit* vs *deposit*

Pattern switching: *meltdown of the core* vs *core meltdown*; *level of gamma radiation* vs *gamma radiation level*

Synonymy in variation: *deep sea mining* vs *deep seabed mining*, *seabed* vs *seafloor*, *ferromanganese crust* vs *iron-manganese crust*

One the one hand, these variations provide useful lexical information about the term, preparing the interpreters for what is possible in their assignment; on the other hand, the term variants need to be explicitly linked, which is possible only in the TTC TermSuite tool.

The annotation results from Table 4 for Chinese show, both Syllabs' and Teaboat's lists offer obviously less relevant terms from FR1 compared with the English lists. When we further investigate the distribution of the term classes in annotations in Table 5, Syllabs' Chinese list on FR1 contains a large number of ill-formed constructions, including incomplete terms, eg. 水堆 'water reactor', 里岛核电站 'Mile Island nuclear plant' and longer chunks, eg. 最大程度上保证了钠, 可用压水堆后处理得到的钚作为核燃料. Teaboat's list contains a number of general words, eg. 开发 'development', 生产 'production' or 工程 'project'. Both categories (G and IL) are frequent in the TTC's Chinese list.

On the basis of these results, we selected a single tool (Syllabs) with comparatively better performance in both languages to generate termlists on SM1 (En & Zh) and asked 12 annotators to select the relevant terms and learn the terms during their interpreting preparation. Among the 500 candidate terms for English, 441 terms were agreed as relevant by at least two annotators, 266 terms were agreed by five annotators. Precision rates are 88.2% and 53.2% respectively. On the other hand, only 130 terms were agreed as relevant by two annotators from the 500 Chinese candidate terms. The precision rate for the Chinese list is 26%. The results basically replicate the previous findings on FR1.

The other pattern we observe from the current data is that the larger the corpus is, the more relevant terms the tools can generate. If the corpus is of very limited size (eg. FR0-en has only 774 words), the TTC TermSuite fails to generate any list for a 'corpus' of only 774 words, while the Syllabs and Teaboat tools produce shorter lists of 104 or 56 terms respectively. The situation is similar to other studies which used small (single-document) corpora, e.g., (Matsuo and Ishizuka, 2004).

	FR1-en	FR2-en	FR1-zh
Syllabs	500	500	500
R	309	400	156
P	90	53	73
I	15	10	5
G	56	16	46
IL	30	21	220
Teaboat	376	499	450
R	232	413	141
P	33	20	61
I	19	5	7
G	73	29	191
IL	19	32	50
TTC	500	500	500
R	136	287	119
P	48	1	32
I	3	1	4
G	310	205	209
IL	3	6	136

Table 5: Distribution of term annotation classes

4 Conclusions and future work

Reliability of the three term extractors The results show the accuracy of the terminology extraction pipelines is not perfect, as its precision ranges from 27% on short texts to 83% on longer corpora for English, 24% to 31% for Chinese. Among the three term extractors (TTC TermSuite, Syllabs Tools and Teaboat), Syllabs is more reliable in generating more relevant terms in English. All the three tools perform less satisfactory in generating relevant terms in Chinese. We hypothesise that at least three factors play an important role here:

1. Chinese is written without explicit word boundaries, while term extraction starts with already tokenised texts. Errors of the tokenisation process lead to difficulties in obtaining proper terms, e.g., 一回路 'primary loop' becomes 一回 'once' 路 'road', also 和非能动安全性 'and passive security' becomes 和非 'and not' 能动 'active' 安全性 'security', which reduces the chances of detecting 非能动安全性 'passive security' as a term.
2. Word ambiguity in Chinese is high. This leads to POS tagging errors, for example, when nouns are treated as verbs, and this breaks the POS patterns for term extraction, e.g., 示范堆 'demonstration reactor' is treated as 示范/vn 堆/v.
3. Chinese exhibits more patterns than captured by the three term extraction tools we tested. For example, 并网发电 'connect to the grid' is potentially a useful term, which is correctly POS-tagged as 并网/v 发电/vn, but not captured by the patterns in all the tools.

Two of the three causes of the results in Chinese concern text pre-processing. . Further investigation might be helpful in finding out how the pre-processing steps affect the performance of the term extractors and which terms are affected by each source of errors.

Manual selection Vs Automatic extraction of terms For the interpreters, manually selecting terms from a single document of limited size (eg. FR0-en=774 words) is possible. However, when conference documents amount to the size of FR1 (FR1-en=42,006 words), it took the trainee interpreters 9 hours on average to extract terms manually and to produce initial termlists, since they had to spend the majority of their time on reading through fairly complex documents, copying the terms from the texts onto their own termlists and searching for unfamiliar terms.

With the use of automatically-generated termlists on the same preparation task, students in the experiment group spent an average of 4 hours producing their initial bilingual termlists. Therefore half of the time spent on reading could be saved for the interpreters to get familiar with the concepts relevant to the terms and further activate the terms for their simultaneous interpreting tasks.

Furthermore, if interpreters are given limited time for preparation, they would not be able to read through larger corpora of the size of FR2 (FR2-en=206,197 words) and to produce termlists from them manually. That is probably when such tools we discussed in this article may have obvious advantage over the manual terms extraction by the interpreters. Moreover, in other studies we also demonstrated that in addition to providing an automatically-extracted termlist, it is also beneficial to link the terms to their uses in the concordance lines of the corpus they have been extracted from. This is expected to give the interpreters an easy access to the context of the terms to see how they are used and get more background knowledge about the domain.

Feedback from students After doing annotation, the students offered their written feedback on the termlists generated by the three term extractors. They also commented on the usefulness of the Syllabs' lists for their interpreting preparation.

They generally reported that the termlists provided many relevant terms on the two topics, and the use of the lists saved their precious preparation time. Some of them found the lists 'unexpectedly accurate and complete', and the presence of irrelevant words in the lists and the repetitions in the lists 'tolerable' (even taking into account the 24% to 31% precision rate for Chinese).

The students told us they used the lists as an important indicator for the content of the conference documents and relevant background documents. The lists helped them prioritise their preparation on the most relevant terms and concepts. Most of them expressed the opinion that if they are given very limited time, they would prefer to use the automatically-generated lists for their preparation. On the other hand, students reported that the termlists in Chinese offered much less relevant terms and contained quite a number of ill-formed constructions compared with the lists in English; therefore they felt the lists in Chinese were less useful and less reliable.

Extraction of proper names Proper names (including names of organisations, names of places, names and titles of people) are equally if not more important than terms for interpreters, yet many of them are not included in the automatically-generated lists by the three term extractors (TTC, Syllabs and Teaboat). Therefore, named entity extraction tools in addition to term extraction are needed to generate more complete lists for interpreters' use. This would be further explored in our future research.

File formats, plain text, encodings All the tools we tested can only process plain text (including UTF-8). Nevertheless, all the meeting documents are normally in one of the word processing formats (.pdf, .doc, .xls or .ppt) other than .txt. Interpreters need to take some time to convert all the files they obtain from their customers into plain text before they can possibly use any tool mentioned above.

References

Ahmad, K., Davies, A., Fulford, H., and Rogers, M. (1994). What is a term? The semi-automatic extraction of terms from text. In Hornby, M. S., Pöchhacker, F., and Kaindl, K., editors, *Translation studies: an interdiscipline*, pages 267–278. Amsterdam: John Benjamins Publishing Company.

Baroni, M. and Bernardini, S. (2004). Bootcat: Bootstrapping corpora and terms from the web. In *Proc. of LREC2004*, Lisbon.

Baroni, M., Chantree, F., Kilgarriff, A., and Sharoff, S. (2008). Cleaneval: a competition for cleaning web pages. In *Proc. of the Sixth Language Resources and Evaluation Conference, LREC 2008*, Marrakech.

Blancafort, H., Bouvier, F., Daille, B., Heid, U., Ramm, A., et al. (2013). TTC Web platform: from corpus compilation to bilingual terminologies for MT and CAT tools. In *Proceedings, Conference'Futures in technologies for translation (TRALOGY II)'*.

Christ, O. (1994). A modular and flexible architecture for an integrated corpus query system. In *COMPLEX'94*, Budapest.

Clark, A. (2003). Combining distributional and morphological information for part of speech induction. In *Proceedings of EACL*, pages 59–66.

Daille, B. (2005). Variations and application-oriented terminology engineering. *Terminology*, 11(1):181–197.

Daille, B. (2012). Building bilingual terminologies from comparable corpora: The TTC TermSuite. In *5th Workshop on Building and Using Comparable Corpora at LREC 2012*.

Fantinuoli, C. (2006). Specialized corpora from the web and term extraction for simultaneous interpreters. In Baroni, M. and Bernardini, S., editors, *WaCky! Working papers on the Web as Corpus*, pages 173–190. Gedit, Bologna. http://wackybook.sslmit.unibo.it.

Gorjanc, V. (2009). Terminology resources and terminological data management for medical interpreters. In Andres, D. and Pöllabauer, S., editors, *Spürst Du, wie der Bauch rauf-runter? Fachdolmetschen im Gesundheitsbereich*. `http://www.uni-graz.at/06gorjanc.pdf`.

Krippendorff, K. (2004). Reliability in content analysis: Some common misconceptions and recommendations. *Human Communication Research*, 30(3).

Lafferty, J., McCallum, A., and Pereira, F. C. (2001). Conditional random fields: Probabilistic models for segmenting and labeling sequence data. In *Proceedings of ICML-01*.

Liang, M., Li, W., and Xu, J. (2010). *Using corpora: a practical coursebook*. Foreign Langue Teaching and Research Press, Beijing.

Matsuo, Y. and Ishizuka, M. (2004). Keyword extraction from a single document using word co-occurrence statistical information. *International Journal on Artificial Intelligence Tools*, 13(01):157–169.

Moser-Mercer, B. (1992). Banking on terminology conference interpreters in the electronic age. *Meta: Translators' Journal*, 37(3):507–522.

Rayson, P. and Garside, R. (2000). Comparing corpora using frequency profiling. In *Proc. of the Comparing Corpora Workshop at ACL 2000*, pages 1–6, Hong Kong.

Rütten, A. (2003). Computer-based information management for conference interpreters-or how will i make my computer act like an infallible information butler? In *Proc. Translating and the computer*, pages 14–14.

Schmid, H. (1994). Probabilistic part-of-speech tagging using decision trees. In *International Conference on New Methods in Language Processing*, Manchester.

Sharoff, S. (2006). Open-source corpora: using the net to fish for linguistic data. *International Journal of Corpus Linguistics*, 11(4):435–462.

Sharoff, S. (2012). Beyond Translation Memories: Finding similar documents in comparable corpora. In *Proc. Translating and the Computer Conference*, London.

Unsupervised method for the acquisition of general language paraphrases for medical compounds

Natalia Grabar
CNRS UMR 8163 STL
Université Lille 3
59653 Villeneuve d'Ascq, France
natalia.grabar@univ-lille3.fr

Thierry Hamon
LIMSI-CNRS, BP133, Orsay
Université Paris 13
Sorbonne Paris Cité, France
hamon@limsi.fr

Abstract

Medical information is widespread in modern society (*e.g.* scientific research, medical blogs, clinical documents, TV and radio broadcast, novels). Moreover, everybody's life may be concerned with medical problems. However, the medical field conveys very specific and often opaque notions (*e.g.*, *myocardial infarction, cholecystectomy, abdominal strangulated hernia, galactose urine*), that are difficult to understand by lay people. We propose an automatic method based on the morphological analysis of terms and on text mining for finding the paraphrases of technical terms. Analysis of the results and their evaluation indicate that we can find correct paraphrases for 343 terms. Depending on the semantics of the terms, error rate of the extractions ranges between 0 and 59%. This kind of resources is useful for several Natural Language Processing applications (*i.e.*, information extraction, text simplification, question and answering).

1 Background

Medical and health information is widespread in the modern society in light of pressing health concerns and of maintaining of healthy lifestyles. Besides, it is also available through modern media: scientific research, articles, medical blogs and fora, clinical documents, TV and radio broadcast, novels, discussion fora, epidemiological alerts, etc. Still, availability of medical and health information does not guarantee its easy and correct understanding by lay people. The medical field conveys indeed very technical notions, such as in example (1).

(1) *myocardial infarction, cholecystectomy, erythredema polyneuropathy, acromegaly, galactosemia*

Although technical, these notions are nevertheless important for patients (AMA, 1999; McCray, 2005; Eysenbach, 2007; Oregon Evidence-based Practice Center, 2008). It has been shown that in several situations such notions cannot be correctly understood by patients: the steps needed for the medication preparing and use (Patel et al., 2002); the instructions on drugs from patient package inserts, and the information delivered in informed consensus and health brochures: it appears that among the 2,600 patients recruited in two hospitals, 26% to 60% cannot manage information available in these sources (Williams et al., 1995); health information in different languages (English, Spanish, French) provided in websites created for patients require high reading level (Berland et al., 2001; Hargrave et al., 2003; Kusec, 2004) and remains difficult to manage by patients, which can be negative for the communication between patients and medical professionals, and the healthcare process (Tran et al., 2009). This situation sets the context of our work. Our objective is to propose method for the automatic acquisition of paraphrases for technical medical notions. More particularly, we propose to concentrate on terms and their words that show neoclassical compounding word formation (Booij, 2010; Iacobini, 1997; Amiot and Dal, 2005), such as in the example (1). Such words often involve Latin and Greek roots or bases, which makes them more difficult to understand, as such words must be decomposed first (see examples (2) and (3)). To our knowledge, this kind of approach has not been applied for the acquisition of laymen paraphrases.

Proceedings of the 4th International Workshop on Computational Terminology, pages 94–103,
Dublin, Ireland, August 23 2014.

(2) *myocardial* is formed with Latin *myo (muscle)* and Greek *cardia (heart)*

(3) *cholecystectomy* is formed with Greek *chole (bile)*, Latin *cystis (bladder)*, and Greek *ectomy (surgical removal)*

Our work is related to the following research topics:

- *Readability*. The readability studies the ease in which text can be understood. Two kinds of readability measures are distinguished: classical and computational (François, 2011). Classical measures are usually based on number of characters and/or syllables in words, sentences or documents and on linear regression models (Flesch, 1948; Gunning, 1973; Dubay, 2004). Computational measures, that are more recent, can involve vectorial models and a great variety of descriptors. These descriptors, usually specific to the texts processed, are for instance: combination of classical measures with medical terminologies (Kokkinakis and Toporowska Gronostaj, 2006); n-grams of characters (Poprat et al., 2006); discursive descriptors (Goeuriot et al., 2007); lexicon (Miller et al., 2007); morphological descriptors (Chmielik and Grabar, 2011); combination of various descriptors (Wang, 2006; Zeng-Treiler et al., 2007; Leroy et al., 2008; François and Fairon, 2013).

- *Lexical simplification*. The lexical simplification helps to make text easier to understand. Lexical simplification of texts in English has been addressed during the *SemEval* 2012 challenge[a]. Given a short input text and a target word in English, and given several English substitutes for the target word that fit the context, the goal was to rank these substitutes according to how simple they are (Specia et al., 2012). Several clues have been applied: lexicon extracted from oral corpus and Wikipedia, Google n-grams, WordNet (Sinha, 2012); word length, number of syllables, mutual information and frequency of words (Jauhar and Specia, 2012); frequency in Wikipedia, word length, n-grams of characters and of words, syntactic complexity of documents (Johannsen et al., 2012); n-grams, frequency in Wikipedia, n-Google grams (Ligozat et al., 2012); WordNet and word frequency (Amoia and Romanelli, 2012).

- *Dedicated resources*. The building of resources suitable for performing the simplification is another related research topics. Such resources are mainly two-fold lexica in which specialized and non-specialized vocabularies are aligned (in examples (4) to (6), the technical terms are followed by their non-technical equivalents). The first initiative of the kind appeared with the collaborative effort Consumer Health Vocabulary (Zeng and Tse, 2006) (examples in (4)). One of the methods was applied to the most frequently occurring medical queries aligned to the UMLS (Unified Medical Language System) concepts (Lindberg et al., 1993). Another work exploited a small corpus and several statistical association measures for building aligned lexicon with technical terms from the UMLS and their lay equivalents (Elhadad and Sutaria, 2007). Similar work in other languages followed. In French, researchers proposed methods for the acquisition of syntactic variation (Deléger and Zweigenbaum, 2008; Cartoni and Deléger, 2011) from comparable specialized and non-specialized corpora, that led to the detection of verb/noun variations (examples in (5)) and a larger set of syntactic variations (examples in (6)). Besides, research on the acquisition of terminological variation (Hahn et al., 2001), synonymy (Fernández-Silva et al., 2011) and paraphrasing (Max et al., 2012) is also relevant to outline the topics.

(4) {*myocardial infarction, heart attack*}, {*abortion, termination of pregnancy*}, {*acrodynia, pink disease*}

(5) {*consommation régulière, consommer de façon régulière*} *(regular use)*, {*gêne à la lecture, empêche de lire*} *(reading difficulty)*, {*évolution de l'affection, la maladie évolue*} *(evolution of the condition)*

(6) {*retard de cicatrisation, retarder la cicatrisation*} *(delay the healing)*, {*apports caloriques, apport en calories*} *(calorie supply)*, {*calculer les doses, doses sont calculées*} *(calculate the dose)*, {*efficacité est renforcée, renforcer son efficacité*} *(improve the efficiency)*

[a]http://www.cs.york.ac.uk/semeval-2012/

Our work is closely related to the building of resources dedicated to the lexical simplification. Our objective is to propose method for paraphrasing the technical medical terms (*i.e.* medical compounds) in expressions that are easier to understand by lay people. This aspect is seldom addressed: we can observe that only some examples in (4) are concerned with the paraphrasing of technical and compound terms (*myocardial infarction*, *acrodynia*). We work with the French data. Contrary to previous work, we do not use comparable corpora with technical and non-technical texts. Instead, we exploit terms from an existing medical terminology and corpora built from social media sources. We assume that this kind of corpora may provide lay people equivalents for technical terms. We also rely on the morphological analysis of technical terms. The expected result is to obtain pairs like {*myocardial*, *heart muscle*} or {*cholecystectomy*, *removal of gall bladder*}. In the following, we start with the presentation of the resources used (section 2), we present then the steps of the methodology (section 3). We describe and discuss the obtained results (section 4) and conclude with some directions for future work (section 5).

2 Resources

2.1 Medical terms

The material processed is issued from the French part of the UMLS. It provides syntactically simple terms that contain one word only (*acrodynia*), and syntactically complex terms that contain more than one word (*myocardial infarction*). Syntactically complex terms are segmented in words. Each term is associated to semantic types. When a given word receives more than one semantic type, a manual post-processing allows to disambiguate it: each word is assigned to one semantic type only. Among the semantic types available, we consider the three most common in the medical practice to which the lay people are the most exposed: Anatomy (616 words): describe human body anatomy (*e.g. abdominopelvic*); Disorders (2,283 words): describe medical problems and their signs (*e.g. infarction, diabetes*); Procedures (1,271 words): describe procedures which may be performed by medical staff to detect or cure disorders (*e.g. cholecystectomy*). In what follows, *word* and *term* can be exchangeable and mean either the graphical unit provided by the segmentation, or the medical notion.

2.2 Corpora

	Wiki	*LesDiab*	*DiabDoct*	*HT*	*Dos*
Number of pages/threads	17,525	6,939	387,435	67,652	8,319
Number of articles/messages	17,525	1,438	22,431	12,588	1,124
Number of words	4,326,880	624,571	35,059,868	6,788,361	836,520

Table 1: Size of the corpora exploited.

We use several corpora collected from the social media sources (their sizes are indicated in Table 1):

1. *Wiki* contains French Wikipedia articles downloaded in February 2014, of which we keep those that are categorized under the medical category *Portail de la médecine*;
2. *LesDiab* is collected from the discussion forum *Les diabétiques*[b] posted between June and July 2013. It is dedicated to diabetes;
3. *DiabDoct* is collected in June 2011 from the discussion forum *Diabète* of Doctissimo[c]
4. *HT* is collected in May 2013 from the discussion forum *Hypertension* of Doctissimo[d]
5. *Dos* is collected in May 2013 from the discussion forum *Douleurs de dos* (backache) of Doctissimo[e]

[b] *http://www.lesdiabetiques.com/modules.php?name=Forums*
[c] *http://forum.doctissimo.fr/sante/diabete/liste_sujet-1.htm*
[d] *http://forum.doctissimo.fr/sante/hypertension-problemes-cardiaques/liste_sujet-1.htm*
[e] *http://forum.doctissimo.fr/sante/douleur-dos/liste_sujet-1.htm*

The *Wiki* corpus contains encyclopaedic information on several medical notions from Wikipedia. Thanks to the collaborative writing of the articles, these contain mostly correct information about the topics concerned. Other corpora are collected from the dedicated fora (*e.g.* diabetes or backache). We assume that people involved in these discussions may show low, middle or high degree of knowledge about the disorders and related notions. We expect that all our corpora are written in a simple style and that they contain paraphrases of technical terms. From Table 1, we can observe that the corpora vary in size.

3 Methodology for the automatic acquisition of paraphrases for medical compounds

The methodology is designed for analyzing the neoclassical medical compounds and for searching their non-technical paraphrases in corpora. In our approach, the paraphrases may occur alone, such as *heart muscle*, without being accompanied by their technical compounds (*myocarde*). In this case, we need first to acquire the knowledge needed for their automatic detection. We propose to rely on the morphological analysis of terms. The method is composed of four main steps: the processing of terms, the processing of corpora, the extraction of layman paraphrases for technical terms, and the evaluation of the extractions.

3.1 The processing of medical terms

To reach the morphological information on terms we apply three specific processing:

1. *Morpho-syntactic tagging and lemmatization of terms.* The terms are morpho-syntactically tagged and lemmatized with `TreeTagger` for French (Schmid, 1994). The morpho-syntactic tagging is done in context of the terms. If a given word receives more than one tag, the most frequent one is kept. At this step, we obtain term lemmas with their part-of-speech tags, such as in example (7).

   (7) *myocardique/A* *(myocardial/A)*, *cholécystectomie/N* *(cholecystectomy/N)*, *polyneuropathie/N* *(polyneuropathy/N)*, *acromégalie/N* *(acromegaly/N)*, *galactosémie/N* *(galactosemia/N)*

2. *Morphological analysis.* The lemmas are then morphologically analyzed with `DériF` (Namer, 2009). This tool performs the analysis of lemmas in order to detect their morphological structure, to decompose them into their components (bases and affixes), and to semantically analyze their structure. We give some examples of the morphological analysis in (8).

   (8) *myocardique/A*: *[[[myo N*] [carde N*] NOM] ique ADJ]*
   cholécystectomie/N: *[[cholécysto N*] [ectomie N*] NOM]*
   polyneuropathie/N: *[poly [[neur N*] [pathie N*] NOM] NOM]*
   acromégalie/N: *[[acr N*] [mégal N*] ie NOM]*
   galactosémie/N: *[[galactose NOM] [ém N*] ie NOM]*

   The computed bases and affixes are associated with syntactic categories (*NOM, ADJ, V*). When a given base is suppletive (does not exist in modern French but was borrowed from Latin or Greek languages), `DériF` assigns the most probable category (*e.g.* *N** for nouns, *A** for adjectives). For instance, the analysis of *myocardique/A* indicates that this word contains the suppletive noun bases *myo N* (muscle)* and *carde N* (heart)*, and the affix *-ique/ADJ*. We can observe that some bases can be decomposed further (*e.g.* *galactose* in *galact (milk)* and *ose (sugars)*, *cholecystectomy* in *chole (bile)* and *cystis (bladder)*). The words that contain more than one base are considered to be compounds and are processed in the further steps of the method.

3. *Association of morphological components with French words.* The bases are "translated" with words from modern French. We use for this resource built in previous work (Zweigenbaum and Grabar, 2003; Namer, 2003) (see some examples in (9)).

   (9) *myocardique/A*: *myo=muscle (muscle)*, *carde=coeur (heart)*
   cholécystectomie/N: *cholécysto=vésicule biliaire (gall bladder)*, *ectomie=ablation (removal)*

polyneuropathie/N: *poly=nombreux (several)*, *neuro=nerf (nerve)*, *pathie=maladie (disorder)*
acromégalie/N: *acr=extrémité (extremity)*, *mégal=grandeur (size)*
galactosémie/N: *galactose=galactose (galactose)*, *ém=sang (blood)*

Some words can remain technical (*e.g.*, *galactose*, *vésicule biliaire*), while other components totally lose their technical meaning (*e.g. mégal=grandeur (size)*, *poly=nombreux (several)*).

3.2 The processing of corpora

The corpora are first segmented in words and sentences. Then, we also perform morpho-syntactic tagging and lemmatization with `TreeTagger` for French.

3.3 The extraction of layman paraphrases corresponding to technical terms

French words corresponding to the morphological decomposition of terms (examples in (9)) are projected on corpora in order to extract sentences and their segments which can provide the layman paraphrases for the corresponding technical terms. Sentences that contain the translated French words are extracted as candidates for proposing the paraphrases. Additionally, the segments delimited by these words are also extracted. We consider the co-occurrence of the words issued from the morphological decomposition in a sliding graphical window of n words. In the experiments presented, the window size n is fixed to 10 words. Smaller or larger windows show less performance.

(10) *Les causes de tachycardie ventriculaire sont superposables à celles des extrasystoles ventriculaires: infarctus du myocarde, insuffisance cardiaque, hypertrophie du muscle du coeur et prolapsus de la valve mitrale.*

The sentence in (10) contains words *muscle* and *coeur*, underlined in the example, that correspond to the morphological components of *myocardique* (see examples in (9)). For this reason, this sentence is extracted, as well as the segment delimited by these two words *muscle du coeur (heart muscle)*.

3.4 The evaluation

The objective of the evaluation is to assess whether the proposed method is valid for the acquisition of paraphrases for technical medical terms. The obtained results are evaluated manually by a computer scientist with no training in biomedicine, but with background in computational linguistics and morphology. We analyze the candidates for paraphrases from several points of view: Are the French words corresponding to the components extracted correctly? Do these French words provide valid candidates for paraphrases? How easy are these paraphrases to be understood by laymen or by non-experts in medicine? During the evaluation related to the second point (*Do these French words provide valid candidates for paraphrases?*), we distinguish four situations:

1. the extraction is correct: *e.g. myocardique* paraphrased in *muscle du coeur (heart muscle)*;
2. the extraction suffers from the incorrect morphological decomposition or from the wrong "translation" in French: *e.g. périanal* is "translated" in *autour (around)* and *an (meaning year as it is)*. The "translation" of this last word *an* is not correct and should be *anus (anus)* instead. Because of the wrong "translation", we collect a lot of incorrect segments like *autour de 30 ans (around 30 years)*;
3. the extraction should be post-processed but contains the correct paraphrase: *e.g. spondylarthrose*, "translated" in *vertèbre (vertebra)* and *arthrose (arthrosis)*, is paraphrased in *arthrose que l'on ne voyait pas sur la vertèbre (arthrosis that was not seen on the vertebra)*, while the correct paraphrase from this segment should be *arthrose sur la vertèbre (arthrosis on the vertebra)*;
4. the extraction is wrong and can provide no useful information.

This evaluation allows to estimate precision of the results in three versions: strong precision P_{strong} (only the correct extractions are considered (extractions from 1)); weak precision P_{weak} (correct extractions and extractions that need post-processing are considered (extractions from 1 and 3)); rate of incorrect extractions $\%_{incorrect}$ (the percentage of the incorrect extractions is computed (extractions from 4)).

4 Results and Discussion

4.1 The morphological analysis of terms

We generate the morphological analysis for 218 single words from the anatomy semantic type, 1,789 disorder words and 1,023 procedure words: over 70% of words are morphologically analyzed. Among these words, we observe compounds (*myocardique*) and words formed with affixes (*e.g. réadaptation* derived from *adaptation*, derived in its turn from *adapter*). The remaining words may be simple (*e.g. abcès* (abscess), *lèpre* (leprosy), *cicatrice* (scar)) or contain bases and affixes that are not managed by `Dérif` (*e.g. pneumostrongylose* (pneumostrongylosis), *lagophtalmie* (lagophthalmos), *nécatorose* (necatorosis)). Among the generated decompositions by `Dérif`, we can find some cases with ambiguous decomposition that occur when medical terms can be decomposed in several possible ways, among which only one is semantically correct. For instance, *posturographie* (posturography) is decomposed into: *[post [[uro N*] [graphie N*] NOM] NOM]*, which may be glossed as *control during the period which follows the therapy done on the urinary system*. From the formal point of view, such decomposition is very possible, although it is weak semantically. For the term *posturographie*, the right decomposition is: *[[posturo N*] [graphie N*] NOM]*, which is related to the *definition of the optimal body position when walking or sitting*. As indicated above, some terms (*e.g. périanal*) can be incorrectly "translated" in French.

4.2 The preprocessing of corpora

Our main difficulty at this step is related to the processing of forum messages and to their segmentation into sentences. In addition to possible and frequent spelling and grammatical errors, forum messages have also a very specific punctuation, which may be missing or convey personal feelings and emotions. This seriously impedes the possibility to provide the correct segmentation in sentences, and means that, because of the missing punctuation, the mapping of decomposed terms with corpora may be done with bigger text segments in which the semantic relations between the mapped components may be weak or non-existent, and provide incorrect extractions. We plan to combine the current method with the syntactic analysis in order to ensure that stronger syntactic and semantic relations exist between the components.

4.3 The extraction of paraphrases and their evaluation

We present the results on extraction of sentences and paraphrases from the corpora processed. In Table 2, for the three semantic types of terms (anatomy *ana.*, disorders *dis.*, and procedures *pro.*) from each corpus, we indicate the following information: the number of different sentences extracted (*sentences*), yje number of different terms (*uniq. terms*), the number of correct paraphrases (*correct*), the number of paraphrases that are possibly correct (*pos. correct*), the number of paraphrases which morphological analysis and "translation" should be improved (*morph. ana.*), and the number of incorrect paraphrases (*incorrect*). The last three lines indicate the precision values: strong precision (P_{strong}), weak precision (P_{weak}) and incorrect extractions ($\%_{incorrect}$).

Number of	*Wiki*			*LesDiab*			*DiabDoct*			*HT*			*Dos*		
	ana	*dis*	*pro*	*ana*	*dis*	*pro*	*ana*	*dis*	*pro*	*ana*	*dis*	*pro*	*ana*	*dis*	*pro*
sentences	1238	4003	999	15	71	10	721	2901	564	246	1233	678	42	708	30
uniq. terms	93	382	154	7	30	5	35	204	48	29	133	42	13	44	13
correct	469	1571	364	3	32	4	227	1189	67	114	637	38	12	466	13
pos. correct	270	868	93	3	7	-	40	332	5	10	85	9	3	98	2
morph. ana.	41	155	323	1	2	6	100	3	394	22	-	591	2	1	12
incorrect	462	1424	220	8	30	-	354	1	98	100	511	40	25	135	3
P_{strong}	38	39	36	20	45	40	32	40	12	46	52	6	29	66	43
P_{weak}	60	61	46	40	55	40	37	52	13	50	59	7	36	80	50
$\%_{incorrect}$	40	39	54	53	42	0	49	47	17	41	41	41	59	20	10

Table 2: Results on the paraphrases extracted and evaluated.

From the data presented in Table 2, we can propose several observations: (1) the *Wiki* corpus, that is not the largest in our dataset, provides the largest number of extractions (sentences and unique terms); (2) among the three semantic types (anatomy, disorders and procedures), the number of paraphrases extracted for disorders is the largest in all corpora; (3) the largest set of paraphrases, that suffer from the incorrect morphological decomposition or "translation", is obtained for the procedure terms. According to these observations, P_{strong} ranges between 20 to 46% for anatomy, 39 and 66% for disorders, and 6 to 43 for procedures. The P_{weak} values, that takes into account the paraphrases that need post-processing, show the increase by 0 to 28% by comparison with the P_{strong} values. The $\%_{incorrect}$ values indicate that anatomy terms show the largest rate (40 to 59%) of incorrect paraphrases: it is possible that the anatomy terms present the lowest rate of compositionality. The incorrect paraphrases are between 20 and 47 among the disorder terms, and between 0 to 54 among the procedure terms. The syntactic analysis may help to improve the current results. On the whole, the proposed method allows to extract the paraphrases for 722 different terms from the corpora processed. Within the evaluated set of extractions, these paraphrases are correct for 273 terms; while 343 terms are provided with correct paraphrases and paraphrases that need to be post-processed. Most of the extracted paraphrases are noun phrases, and, at a lesser extent, verb phrases. We present some examples of the correct paraphrases extracted:

- *dorsalgie* (*dorsalgia*): *douleur dans le dos* (*pain in the back*)
- *myélocyte* (*myelocyte*): *cellules dans la moelle osseuse* (*cells of the bone marrow*)
- *lombalgie* (*lombalgia*): *douleurs dans les reins* (*pain in kidney*)
- *gastralgie* (*gastralgia*): *douleurs à l'estomac* (*stomach pain*)
- *desmorrhexie* (*desmorrhexia*): *rupture des ligaments* (*ligamentous rupture*)
- *hépatite* (*hepatitis*): *inflammation du foie* (*liver inflammation*)

We can find several types of paraphrases that suffer from incorrect decomposition or "translation":

- *syringomyélie* (*syringomyelia*) is currently "translated" in *moelle* (*marrow or spinal cord*) and *canal* (*canal*). This term means a disorder in which a cyst or cavity forms within the spinal cord. We assume that a more correct "translation" of this term should be: *moelle* (*marrow or spinal cord*) and *cavité* (*cavity*);

- *sous-dural* is "translated" in *sous* (*sub*) and *dur* (*hard*). The term is related to specific space in brain that can be opened by the separation of the arachnoid mater from the dura mater. Concerning its "translation", we assume that *dure-mère* (*dura mater*) should be used instead of *dur* (*hard*). Besides, the names of anatomical locations often remains difficult to understand. We assume that even when terms are decomposed and "translated" correctly, the paraphrases for such terms may be not suitable for laymen: other types of explanations (*e.g.* schemes or pictures) should be used instead;

- *hyperémie* (*hyperaemia*) is "translated" in *hyper* and *sang* (*blood*). The term means the increase of blood flow to different tissues in the body. This term is not fully compositional because the notion of tissues is absent, while necessary for its understanding. The proposed extractions for this term mainly come from corpora related to diabetes, in which *hyper* and *hypo* are often used in relation with the *hyperglycemia* or *hypoglycemia*. This means that *hyper* should be "translated" with other words, such as *increase* or *elevated*;

- *hétérotopie* is translated in *autre* (*another*) and *endroit* (*place*). The term means the displacement of an organ from its normal position and that [an organ] is found in another place than the one expected. This term brings no correct candidates for paraphrases because: it is not fully compositional and its "translation" provides very common words widely used in the corpora.

Among the incorrect extractions we can find: (1) more terms with non-compositional semantics (such as *ostéodermie* (*osteoderm*), *causalgie* (*causalgia*), *adénoïde* (*adenoid*), or *xanthochromie* (*xanthochromia*)) for which the extracted paraphrases capture only part of the meaning; and (2) extractions that must be controled by the syntactic analysis (*e.g. petite boule de peau qui a sortie entre l'ongle et...* (*small skinball that appeared between the nail and...*) for *micronychie* (*micronychia*)) to make them more grammatical. Paraphrases extracted from the *Wiki* corpus cover larger range of medical terms, while those extracted from fora dedicated to a given medical topics are redundant. On the whole, we can consider that the currently proposed method allows extracting interesting candidates as the paraphrases of technical terms, that are indeed much easier to understand than the technical terms by themselves.

If we compare the obtained results with those presented in previous work, we can observe that:

- we extract paraphrases for larger number of terms: 343 terms with correct and possibly correct paraphrases (722 terms with paraphrases in total) in our work against a total of 65 and 82 in (Deléger and Zweigenbaum, 2008), 109 in (Cartoni and Deléger, 2011), and 152 in (Elhadad and Sutaria, 2007). In our work, the terms may receive more than one paraphrase;
- the precision values we obtain are comparable with those indicated in previous work: 67% and 60% in (Deléger and Zweigenbaum, 2008), 66% in (Cartoni and Deléger, 2011), and 58% in (Elhadad and Sutaria, 2007);
- in the cited work, the content of the corpora is explored but no reference is done to the set of terms expected to be found. Because we work with a termset, we can compute the recall. If we consider the terms that can be analyzed morphologically (3,030 terms), and for which we can find the paraphrases with the proposed method, the recall value is close to 10% with the correct paraphrases (299 terms), and to 24% with all the paraphrases extracted (722 terms). Yet, it is not sure that all of the terms, that have been analyzed morphologically, can be provided with paraphrases in the corpora processed.

Besides, we should not forget that the nature of compounds and the decomposition of terms into components also mean that specific semantic relations exist between these components (Namer and Zweigenbaum, 2004; Booij, 2010). These are inherent to the syntactic constructions extracted. The characteristics of these relations will be described and modeled in future work.

5 Conclusions and Future work

We propose to exploit social media texts in order to detect paraphrases for technical medical terms, concentrating particularly on neoclassical compounds (*e.g., myocardial, cholecystectomy, galactose, acromegaly*). The work is done in French. The method relies on the morphological analysis of terms, on the "translation" of the components of terms in modern French words (*e.g.* {*card*, *heart*}), and on the projection of these words on corpora. The method allows extracting correct and possibly correct paraphrases for up to 343 technical terms. For covering larger set of terms, additional corpora must be treated. The extracted paraphrases are easier to understand than the original technical terms. Moreover, the semantic relations among the components, although non explicated, are conveyed by the paraphrases. We can consider that the method proves to be efficient and promising for the creation of lexicon suitable for the simplification of medical texts. Besides, the purpose of the method is to cover neoclassical compound terms that are usually non treated with automatic approaches, as they do not present clear formal similarity with their paraphrases. One of the difficulties we have currently is related to the lack of constrains on the extracted segments. In future work, we plan to apply the syntactic analysis for parsing the extracted sentences. Another possibility is to compute the probability for a given paraphrase to be correct, which can rely for instance on frequency of the extracted paraphrases, on their syntactic structure, etc. In order to make the extraction of paraphrases more exhaustive, we will apply the method to other corpora and we will use additional resources (synonyms, associative resources) for performing the approximate mapping of paraphrases. In future work, we will take into account syntactically complex terms and not only simple words. The very objective of our work is to exploit and test the resource created for the simplification of medical texts.

Acknowledgments

The authors acknowledge the support of the Université Paris 13 (project BQR Bonus Quality Research, 2011), the support of the MESHS Lille projet Émergent CoMeTe, and the support of the French Agence Nationale de la Recherche (ANR) and the DGA, under the Tecsan grant ANR-11-TECS-012.

References

AMA. 1999. Health literacy: report of the council on scientific affairs. Ad hoc committee on health literacy for the council on scientific affairs, American Medical Association. *JAMA*, 281(6):552–7.

D Amiot and G Dal. 2005. Integrating combining forms into a lexeme-based morphology. In *Mediterranean Morphology Meeting (MMM5)*, pages 323–336.

M Amoia and M Romanelli. 2012. Sb: mmsystem - using decompositional semantics for lexical simplification. In **SEM 2012*, pages 482–486, Montréal, Canada, 7-8 June. Association for Computational Linguistics.

GK Berland, MN Elliott, LS Morales, JI Algazy, RL Kravitz, MS Broder, DE Kanouse, JA Munoz, JA Puyol, M Lara, KE Watkins, H Yang, and EA McGlynn. 2001. Health information on the internet. accessibility, quality, and readability in english ans spanish. *JAMA*, 285(20):2612–2621.

Geert Booij. 2010. *Construction Morphology*. Oxford University Press, Oxford.

B Cartoni and L Deléger. 2011. Dcouverte de patrons paraphrastiques en corpus comparable: une approche base sur les n-grammes. In *TALN*.

J Chmielik and N Grabar. 2011. Détection de la spécialisation scientifique et technique des documents biomédicaux grâce aux informations morphologiques. *TAL*, 51(2):151–179.

L Deléger and P Zweigenbaum. 2008. Paraphrase acquisition from comparable medical corpora of specialized and lay texts. In *AMIA 2008*, pages 146–50.

William H. Dubay. 2004. The principles of readability. *Impact Information*. Available at *http://almacenplantillasweb.es/wp-content/uploads/2009/11/The-Principles-of-Readability.pdf*.

N Elhadad and K Sutaria. 2007. Mining a lexicon of technical terms and lay equivalents. In *BioNLP*, pages 49–56.

Gunther Eysenbach. 2007. Poverty, human development, and the role of ehealth. *J Med Internet Res*, 9(4):e34.

S Fernández-Silva, J Freixa, and MT Cabré. 2011. A proposed method for analysing the dynamics of cognition through term variation. *Terminology*, 17(1):49–73.

R Flesch. 1948. A new readability yardstick. *Journal of Applied Psychology*, 23:221–233.

T François and C Fairon. 2013. Les apports du TAL à la lisibilité du français langue étrangère. *TAL*, 54(1):171–202.

T François. 2011. *Les apports du traitements automatique du langage la lisibilit du franais langue trangre*. Phd thesis, Universit Catholique de Louvain, Louvain.

L Goeuriot, N Grabar, and B Daille. 2007. Caractérisation des discours scientifique et vulgarisé en français, japonais et russe. In *TALN*, pages 93–102.

R Gunning. 1973. *The art of clear writing*. McGraw Hill, New York, NY.

Udo Hahn, Martin Honeck, Michael Piotrowsky, and Stefan Schulz. 2001. Subword segmentation - leveling out morphological variations for medical document retrieval. In *AMIA*, 229-33.

Darren Hargrave, Ute Bartels, Loretta Lau, Carlos Esquembre, and Éric Bouffet. 2003. évaluation de la qualité de l'information médicale francophone accessible au public sur internet : application aux tumeurs cérébrales de l'enfant. *Bulletin du Cancer*, 90(7):650–5.

C Iacobini. 1997. Distinguishing derivational prefixes from initial combining forms. In *First mediterranean conference of morphology*, Mytilene, Island of Lesbos, Greece, septembre.

SK Jauhar and L Specia. 2012. Uow-shef: Simplex – lexical simplicity ranking based on contextual and psycholinguistic features. In **SEM 2012*, pages 477–481, Montréal, Canada, 7-8 June. Association for Computational Linguistics.

A Johannsen, H Martínez, S Klerke, and A Søgaard. 2012. Emnlp@cph: Is frequency all there is to simplicity? In **SEM 2012*, pages 408–412, Montréal, Canada, 7-8 June. Association for Computational Linguistics.

D Kokkinakis and M Toporowska Gronostaj. 2006. Comparing lay and professional language in cardiovascular disorders corpora. In Australia Pham T., James Cook University, editor, *WSEAS Transactions on BIOLOGY and BIOMEDICINE*, pages 429–437.

Sanja Kusec. 2004. Les sites web relatifs au diabète, sont-ils lisibles ? *Dibète et société*, 49(3):46–48.

G Leroy, S Helmreich, J Cowie, T Miller, and W Zheng. 2008. Evaluating online health information: Beyond readability formulas. In *AMIA 2008*, pages 394–8.

AL Ligozat, C Grouin, A Garcia-Fernandez, and D Bernhard. 2012. Annlor: A naïve notation-system for lexical outputs ranking. In **SEM 2012*, pages 487–492.

DA Lindberg, BL Humphreys, and AT McCray. 1993. The unified medical language system. *Methods Inf Med*, 32(4):281–291.

Aurélien Max, Houda Bouamor, and Anne Vilnat. 2012. Generalizing sub-sentential paraphrase acquisition across original signal type of text pairs. In *EMNLP*, pages 721–31.

A McCray. 2005. Promoting health literacy. *J of Am Med Infor Ass*, 12:152–163.

T Miller, G Leroy, S Chatterjee, J Fan, and B Thoms. 2007. A classifier to evaluate language specificity of medical documents. In *HICSS*, pages 134–140.

Fiammetta Namer and Pierre Zweigenbaum. 2004. Acquiring meaning for French medical terminology: contribution of morphosemantics. In *Annual Symposium of the American Medical Informatics Association (AMIA)*, San-Francisco.

F Namer. 2003. Automatiser l'analyse morpho-sémantique non affixale: le système DériF. *Cahiers de Grammaire*, 28:31–48.

F Namer. 2009. *Morphologie, Lexique et TAL : l'analyseur DériF. TIC et Sciences cognitives*. Hermes Sciences Publishing, London.

Oregon Evidence-based Practice Center. 2008. Barriers and drivers of health information technology use for the elderly, chronically ill, and underserved. Technical report, Agency for healthcare research and quality.

V Patel, T Branch, and J Arocha. 2002. Errors in interpreting quantities as procedures : The case of pharmaceutical labels. *International journal of medical informatics*, 65(3):193–211.

M Poprat, K Markó, and U Hahn. 2006. A language classifier that automatically divides medical documents for experts and health care consumers. In *MIE 2006 - Proceedings of the XX International Congress of the European Federation for Medical Informatics*, pages 503–508, Maastricht.

H Schmid. 1994. Probabilistic part-of-speech tagging using decision trees. In *ICNMLP*, pages 44–49, Manchester, UK.

R Sinha. 2012. Unt-simprank: Systems for lexical simplification ranking. In **SEM 2012*, pages 493–496, Montréal, Canada, 7-8 June. Association for Computational Linguistics.

L Specia, SK Jauhar, and R Mihalcea. 2012. Semeval-2012 task 1: English lexical simplification. In **SEM 2012*, pages 347–355.

TM Tran, H Chekroud, P Thiery, and A Julienne. 2009. Internet et soins : un tiers invisible dans la relation médecine/patient ? *Ethica Clinica*, 53:34–43.

Y Wang. 2006. Automatic recognition of text difficulty from consumers health information. In IEEE, editor, *Computer-Based Medical Systems*, pages 131–136.

MV Williams, RM Parker, DW Baker, NS Parikh, K Pitkin, WC Coates, and JR Nurss. 1995. Inadequate functional health literacy among patients at two public hospitals. *JAMA*, 274(21):1677–82.

QT Zeng and T Tse. 2006. Exploring and developing consumer health vocabularies. *JAMIA*, 13:24–29.

Q Zeng-Treiler, H Kim, S Goryachev, A Keselman, L Slaugther, and CA Smith. 2007. Text characteristics of clinical reports and their implications for the readability of personal health records. In *MEDINFO*, pages 1117–1121, Brisbane, Australia.

Pierre Zweigenbaum and Natalia Grabar. 2003. Corpus-based associations provide additional morphological variants to medical terminologies. In *AMIA*.

Identifying Portuguese Multiword Expressions using Different Classification Algorithms - A Comparative Analysis

Alexsandro Fonseca
University of Quebec in Montreal
201 President Kennedy, Montreal, QC, Canada
affonseca@gmail.com

Fatiha Sadat
University of Quebec in Montreal
201 President Kennedy, Montreal, QC, Canada
sadat.fatiha@uqam.ca

Alexandre Blondin Massé
University of Quebec in Chicoutimi
555, boul. de l'Univ. Chicoutimi, QC, G7H 2B1
alexandre.blondin.masse@gmail.com

Abstract

This paper presents a comparative analysis based on different classification algorithms and tools for the identification of Portuguese multiword expressions. Our focus is on two-word expressions formed by nouns, adjectives and verbs. The candidates are selected on the basis of the frequency of the bigrams; then on the basis of the grammatical class of each bigram's constituent words. This analysis compares the performance of three different multi-layer perceptron training functions in the task of extracting different patterns of multiword expressions, using and comparing nine different classification algorithms, including decision trees, multilayer perceptron and SVM. Moreover, this analysis compares two different tools, Text-NSP and Termostat for the identification of multiword expressions using different association measures.

1 Introduction

The exact definition of a multiword expression (MWE) is a challenging task and it varies from author to author. For example, Moon (1998) says: "… there is no unified phenomenon to describe but rather a complex of features that interact in various, often untidy, ways and represent a broad continuum between non-compositional (or idiomatic) and compositional groups of words." Moreover, this phenomenon receives different names in the literature (Proost, 2005): phraseological units, fixed expressions, word combinations, phrasemes, etc.

In this study, we consider MWE in a similar way Mel'čuk (1998) defines a phraseme: a phrase which is not free, i.e. the expression's signifier and/or signified are not unrestrictedly and regularly constructed.

A phrase P is unrestrictedly constructed when the rules applied to construct P are not mandatory. For example, instead of the phrase: "doing a research" it is possible to say "performing a research", "executing a research" i.e., this expression is not fixed. However, in a sign like "No smoking", it is not common to see variants like "Smoking prohibited" or "Do not smoke", although those are grammatically correct variants which express the same meaning. Then, "No smoking" is a phraseme (MWE), because it is not unrestrictedly constructed.

A phrase P is regularly constructed when the words forming it are combined following the general rules of the grammar and its sense can be derived exclusively from the sense of its constituent words. The phrase: "he died yesterday", is regularly constructed because it follows the rules of the grammar and its sense follows from the sense the words forming it. However, the expression "kicked the bucket" is not regularly constructed, in relation to its meaning (the combination of words follows the rules of the grammar), because its sense, "died", cannot be derived from the sense of its constituent

Proceedings of the 4th International Workshop on Computational Terminology, pages 104–113,
Dublin, Ireland, August 23 2014.

words. On the other hand, the expression "passing by" is not regularly constructed because it does not follow the general rules of the grammar.

According to Mel'čuk (1998), it is possible to divide the phrasemes (MWEs) in two groups: pragmatemes and semantic phrasemes. As pragmatemes, we can have:

- Expressions in which both the signified and the signifier are not unrestrictedly constructed (although they are regularly constructed), e.g. "all you can eat", or
- Expressions in which only the signified is not unrestrictedly constructed. For example, in a library it is possible to have signs like "Please be quiet", "No talking please", etc. In this case, the signifier (the form, the words forming the expression) is more or less free; however, the sense is always the same.

In semantic phrasemes, the signified is free (it is constructed unrestrictedly; however, it is not constructed regularly) and the signifier is not free. We can have three types of semantic phrasemes:

- Idioms: the sense of the expression goes beyond the sense of its constituent words, and does not include their senses. Examples: "of course", "(to) pull (someone's) leg", "(to) spill the beans";
- Collocations: the sense of the expression includes the sense of one of its constituent words, say, w1. The other word is freely chosen and w1 is chosen contingent to it. Collocations can be (Manning and Schütze, 1999): light verbs constructions (e.g. make a call, take a decision), verb particle constructions (e.g. to switch on, to pass by), proper names (e.g. San Francisco, Bill Gates) and terminological expressions, i.e., multiword terms (e.g. gross domestic product, light year).
- Quasi-phrasemes or quasi-idioms: the signified of the expression contains the signified of its constituent words; however, it also contains a signified that goes beyond the signified of the isolated words (e.g. (to) start a family, bed and breakfast).

For a more complete explanation about pragmatemes and semantic phrasemes, refer to (Mel'čuk, 1998) or to (Morgan, 1978). For a more detailed linguistic description on the properties of MWEs, see (Baldwin and Kim, 2010).

In this paper, we assume as MWE any kind of phraseme. However, we are interested in the study of Portuguese two-word expressions formed mostly by nouns, adjectives and verbs. For this reason, since most of pragmatemes and idioms are formed by more than two words, basically our focus is on quasi-phrasemes and collocations (mostly light verbs constructions, proper names and multiword terms (MWT)).

The literature on MWE extraction describes different methods for the identification or extraction of MWEs. Many of them rely on association measures, such as Dice's coefficient (Smadja, 1996) or mutual information (Church and Hanks, 1990). A complete explanation on the use of this association measures on the task of extraction MWEs from text can be found in (Manning and Schütze, 1999). The main idea behind such measures is that the higher the association among the words that appear together in a text, the higher the probability that they constitute a single semantic unit.

There are other methods, which use linguistic information or hybrid approaches that combine statistical measures with the linguistic information, such as the grammatical class of each word, the sense of the expression or the syntactic regularities. Yet others are based on classification algorithms, popular in machine learning systems.

In this study we performed two types of comparison. In the first one, we compared the performance of nine different classification algorithms in the task of identifying MWEs. In the second, we compared two different tools, Text-NSP and Termostat, using different association measures, in the task of extracting MWEs from text. Although our focus is in general MWE, the current study could also be applied to corpus in a specific area for the extraction of multiword terms (MWT).

2 Related Work

Baptista (1994) presents a linguistic study about the nominal expressions formed by more than two words in Portuguese. From a set of 10,000 expressions, he created a typology of nominal MWEs. He found that 70% of the nominal MWEs follow only five different patterns (A = adjective, N = noun, V = verb and P = preposition): A-N, N-A, N-P-N, N-N and V-N. He analyses the syntactic proprieties of each of these groups, focusing his attention on the patterns N-A and N-P-N, which he considers less rigid and more difficult to treat automatically. Finally, he integrates the MWEs' morphological information to an electronic dictionary.

Antunes and Mendes (2013) propose the creation of a MWE typology that includes its semantic, syntactic and pragmatic properties, aiming the annotation of a MWE lexicon using this typology information. They divide the MWEs in three groups, from a semantic standpoint: expressions with compositional meaning, e.g. "banana bread", expression with partial idiomatic meaning, e.g. "vontade de ferro" (iron will) and expressions with total idiomatical meaning (or with no compositionality), e.g. "spill the beans". Within each of these three groups, the expressions are subdivided according to their grammatical categories and lexical and syntactical fixedness.

After a survey and a comparison on different association measures, algorithms and tools used on the identification of MWEs, Portela (2011) presents a study on the identification of Portuguese MWEs following two patterns, N-A and N-P-N, using different association measures. After the extraction of candidates, syntactic criteria are applied to them, to verify their fixedness and determine if a candidate is a MWE. Examples of syntactic criteria applied to bigrams following the pattern N-A and N-P-N:

- Loss of adjective's predicative characteristic: when the adjective comes after the noun and it can be paraphrased by a copulative verb (e.g. verb "to be") + the same adjective, keeping the same sense, the adjective has a predicative function. For example, in the expression: "homem cansado" (tired man, lit. man tired), it is possible to substitute "cansado" for "que estava cansado" (that was tired), and the adjective's predicative characteristic is maintained. However, in the expression "sorriso amarelo" (false, not natural smile, lit. smile yellow), if we substitute the expression for "sorriso que é amarelo", (smile that is yellow), the predicative characteristic is not maintained, because the original sense is lost. This loss of predicative characteristic shows that the expression is fixed, and it is evidence that the expression is a MWE.
- Insertion of elements in the expression (N-P-N): consider the expression "livro de bolso" (pocket book, lit. book of pocket). It is not possible to freely insert a modifier, for example "*livro do Paulo de bolso" (lit. book of Paulo of Pocket). In this example, the modifier can be inserted only at the end of the expression: "livro de bolso do Paulo". This kind of fixedness is evidence that the expression is a MWE.

3 Methodology

We restricted the present study on the extraction of two-word MWEs. For their data, for example, Piao et al. (2003) found that 81.88% of the recognized MWEs were bigrams.

The current study uses CETENFolha (Corpus de Extractos de Textos Electrónicos/NILC Folha de São Paulo) as a Brazilian Portuguese corpus, available on the Linguateca Portuguesa website, which is part of a project on the automatic processing of the Portuguese language (Kinoshita et al., 2006). CETENFolha is composed by excerpts from the Brazilian newspaper "Folha de São Paulo", and contains over 24 million words. At the current stage, we use a small fraction of the corpus, comprising 3,409 excerpts of text (about 250,000 words). Each excerpt corresponds to individual news covering different areas. The number 3,409 represents 1% of the number of excerpts composing the corpus.

We performed different types of evaluation. First, we generated a reference file containing the most frequent MWEs in the corpus and we compared nine different classification algorithms against this reference in the task of identifying Portuguese MWEs. Second, we tested a multilayer perceptron using three different training functions in the task of classifying MWEs in different patterns. We also extracted automatically the 2,000 most frequent bigrams from the entire corpus and we identified, by hand, which ones are MWEs, and we classified them in patterns. Finally, we used two different tools for the identification of MWEs: Text-NSP (Banerjee and Pedersen, 2003) and Termostat (Drouin, 2003). For these tools, we are interested in two types of evaluation. In the first evaluation, we used our reference list to automatically compare the best candidates obtained by each tool against this reference. In the second evaluation, we manually counted the number of MWEs, among a list of the 500-best candidates ranked by one of the association measures, log-likelihood, and we calculated the precision for each tool.

3.1 Reference File Creation

Before the indexation, some pre-processing methods on the corpus were performed, such as lemmatization and elimination of stop words (articles, prepositions, conjunctions). In this study, we are mostly interested in analyzing MWEs formed by nouns, adjectives and verbs. And since those stop words are very common in Portuguese, their elimination reduces considerably the number of MWE candidates that would not be relevant to this study. In this case, some common Portuguese MWEs are not considered, especially the ones following the pattern noun-preposition-noun, e.g. "teia de aranha" (cobweb), or the pattern preposition-noun, e.g. "às vezes" (sometimes).

We obtained 49,589 bigrams and we established a frequency of 3 as a threshold. We selected 1,170 bigrams that appeared more than 3 times in our corpus' excerpts as our MWE candidates, and by hand we recognized 447 of them as Portuguese MWEs, and we considered those 447 MWEs as our reference file.

It is important to note that our reference file does not contain all the two-word MWEs in the corpus' excerpt, since we generated more than 49,000 bigrams, and we could not evaluate all of them by hand. Furthermore, the corpus is formed by newspaper texts, treating different subjects, thus it is more difficult to create a closed set of all possible two-word MWEs. Therefore, our evaluation in the present study is based on a comparison of how many of the most frequent two-word MWEs in our corpus are ranked as *n*-best candidates by some of the association measures implemented by each tool.

3.2 Comparison of Different Classification Algorithms

First, we computed the frequency of each of those 1,170 bigrams and the frequency of its constituent words. Then, we classified by hand each of the words according to their grammatical class: 1 for nouns, 2 for adjectives, 3 for verbs, 4 for other classes (adverbs, pronouns and numbers) and 5 for proper names. We decided not to use a POS-tagger to guarantee the correct grammatical class assignment to each word. This gave us 25 patterns of bigrams: N-N (noun-noun), N-A (noun-adjective), N-V (noun-verb), V-N, PN-PN (proper name-proper name), etc.

Second, we created a matrix of 1,170 lines and five columns. For each line, the first column represents the frequency of a bigram in the excerpt of text, the second column represents the frequency of the first bigram's word, the third column represents the frequency of the second bigram's word, the fourth column represents the grammatical class of the first bigram's word and the fifth column represents the grammatical class of the second bigram's word. This matrix was used to evaluate the precision and recall of nine different classification algorithms: decision tree, random forest, ada boost (using decision stamp as classifier), bagging (using fast decision tree learner as classifier), KNN (K nearest neighbors), SVM, multilayer perceptron, naïve Bayesian net and Bayesian net.

3.3 Bigrams Pattern Classification

We chose one of the algorithms with the best performance (multi-layer perceptron) and we evaluated it using three different training functions, Bayesian regulation back propagation (br), Levenberg-Marquardt (lm) and scaled conjugate gradient (scg), and we compared their performance in the classification of different patterns of bigrams as MWE. The data used for the classification is formatted in the same way as in the Subsection 3.2. However, for this comparison, we used only the patterns that gave 10 or more samples of MWE, for example, the patterns: N-A, N-N and N-PN.

3.4 The Text-NSP Tool

Text-NSP is a tool used in the task of MWE extraction from texts (Banerjee and Pedersen, 2003). In order to use Text-NSP tool, we do not provide a file containing the POS patterns of the bigrams that we would like to extract as MWE candidates. Therefore, before applying this tool, the only pre-processing task we performed with the source corpus, was removing the XML tags they contained. The next step was to define a stop words list file, since we were interested in finding MWEs following the bigram's patterns formed only by nouns, adjectives, verbs and others classes (adverbs, pronouns and numbers), e.g. N-N, N-A, N-V, O-N.

We ran the program using the "count.pl" script, giving the stop words file and the corpus files as parameters, and 2 as n-gram value, which refers to our aim to generate only bigrams.

The output file is a list of all bigrams in the corpus, and each line contains a bigram, the frequency of the bigram, and the frequency of each of the two words forming the bigram.

Using the output file and the "statistics.pl" script, we generated the candidates' files ranked by four different association measures: Dice's coefficient (dice), log-likelihood (ll), pointwise mutual information (pmi) and Student's t-test (t). Then we transformed each of the candidate files to the XML format used by MWEtoolkit (Ramisch, 2012) and used MWEtoolkit's scripts to create files with the *n*-best candidates (*n* = 50, 100, 500, 1000 and 3000) and compare each candidate file against the reference file.

3.5 The Termostat Tool

Termostat (Drouin, 2003) is a tool developed for an automatic extraction of terms. It can be currently used with five different languages: English, French, Italian, Portuguese and Spanish. It generates statistics for simple and complex expressions. Since in this study we are interested in MWE, we extracted only the complex expressions.

As for Text-NSP, Termostat requires the elimination of the XML tags the corpus contained; which was the only pre-processing step of the corpus.

After the analysis of the corpus, the system generated the lists of expressions ranked by four association measures: log-likelihood (ll), chi-squared (χ^2), log-odds ratio (lor) and the "spécificité" measure (Lafon, 1980) (sp).

Then we proceeded as for Text-NSP: we created files with the *n*-best candidates, ranked by the four association measures and compared each candidate file against the reference file.

3.6 Comparison between the 500-best Candidates of each Tool

Using the association measure that is implemented by both tools, the log-likelihood, we analyzed the 500-best candidates ranked by this association measure using each tool. We selected by hand the MWEs among those candidates and we calculated the precision of each tool, for the *n*-best first candidates (*n* = 50, 100, 150…500).

4 Evaluations

4.1 Comparison of Different Classification Algorithms

First, we had to proceed to an indirect estimative of the recall. We found 49,589 bigrams in the selected excerpts of texts, and the manual evaluation of each one, in order to decide which one is a MWE, would take too much time. So, we estimated the amount of MWEs for the total 49,589 bigrams as in (Piao et al., 2003). Using 100 excerpts of text we generated all the bigrams, with all frequencies. We obtained 1,715 bigrams.

Then, we found by hand 136 MWEs, which tells us that about 7.93% of the bigrams are MWEs. Considering that the corpus is homogeneous, we can extrapolate and say that about 7.93% of the 49,589 bigrams in our total excerpts are MWEs, which gives 3,932 MWEs. Since we found 447 MWEs after applying the filter of frequency (> 3), our base recall is 11.37% (447/3,932). We used this base recall as a multiplying factor for the recall given by each classification algorithm.

We used our generated data to test nine different classification algorithms: decision tree, random forest, ada boost, bagging, KNN (K nearest neighbors), SVM, multilayer perceptron, naïve Bayesian net and Bayesian net. The main parameters used with each algorithm are listed below.

Decision tree: C4.5 algorithm (Quinlan, 1993) with confidence factor = 0.25.

Random Forest (Breiman, 2001): number of trees = 10; max depth = 0; seed = 1.

Ada Boost (Freund and Schapire, 1996): classifier = decision stamp; weight threshold = 100; iterations = 10; seed = 1.

Bagging (Breiman, 1996): classifier = fast decision tree learner (min. number = 2; min. variance = 0.001; number of folds = 3; seed = 1; max. depth = -1); bag size percent = 100; seed = 1; number of execution slots = 1; iterations = 10.

KNN (Aha and Kibler, 1991): K = 3; window size = 0; search algorithm = linear NN search (distance function = Euclidian distance).

SVM (Chang and Lin, 2001): cache size = 40; cost = 1; degree = 3; eps = 0.001; loss = 0.1; kernel type = radial basis function; nu = 0.5; seed = 1.

Multilayer perceptron: learning rate = 0.3; momentum = 0.2; training time = 500; validation threshold = 500; seed = 0;

Bayesian net: search algorithm = k2 (Cooper and Herskovits, 1992); estimator = simple estimator (alpha = 0.5).

The results are summarized in Table 1, where Recall-1 is the recall given by each algorithm based on the 447 MWEs found among the MWE candidates and Recall-2 is Recall-1 multiplied by 0.1137 (base recall, as previously calculated), which gives an estimative of the recall for the entire corpus.

As we see in Table 1, the values of precision are very similar for all the algorithms, varying between 0.830 (random forest) and 0.857 (bagging), with the exception of SVM, which gave a precision of 0.738. The recall-1values were between 0.831 and 0.857 (0.655 for SVM) and the recall-2 between 9.4% and 9.7% (7.4% for SVM).

We observe that we obtained good precision and weak recall. This is due, as observed by Piao et al. (2003), to the fact that the extraction of the MWE candidates is based only on the frequency of the bigrams, and only after the extraction of these candidates we applied the linguistic information (classification in grammatical classes).

However, we must consider that, although we extracted only about 11% of the MWEs, these 11% are the most frequent and they represent about 46% of all the MWEs in the corpus, if we sum up the frequency of each MWE. Together, the 447 MWEs found appear 4,824 times in our corpus' excerpt, while the remaining 3,485 (from a predicted 3,932 MWEs in the corpus' excerpt) appear 5,576 times. In absolute terms we have: 4,824 / (4,824+5,576) = 0.46.

Algorithm	**TP Rate**	**FP Rate**	**Precision**	**Recall**	**Recall-2**
Decision tree	0.853	0.158	0.854	0.853	0.097
Random forest	0.831	0.194	0.830	0.831	0.094
Ada boost	0.837	0.196	0.836	0.837	0.095
Bagging	0.857	0.163	0.857	0.857	0.097
KNN – k = 3	0.846	0.171	0.846	0.846	0.096
SVM	0.655	0.553	0.738	0.655	0.074
M. perceptron	0.852	0.174	0.851	0.852	0.097
Naïve B. net	0.836	0.170	0.839	0.836	0.095
Bayesian net	0.842	0.170	0.843	0.842	0.096
Base recall	**0.1137**				

Table 1: True-positive rate, false-positive rate, precision and recall for nine classification algorithms.

4.2 Bigrams Patterns Classification

We obtained eight patterns that together represent 59% of the candidate bigrams (689/1,170) and 94% of the MWEs that appear three or more times in the corpus (420/447). The rest of the bigrams' patterns (41%) rarely formed MWE (only 6% of the total MWEs). Table 2 shows the results. "N" stands for "Noun", "A" for adjective, "O" for other classes (adverbs, pronouns and numbers) and "PN" for "proper names".

Analyzing the table, we had best results with the patterns N-A (e.g. "comissão técnica", "banco central", "imposto único") and PN-PN ("Fidel Castro", "José Sarney", "Max Mosley"). The function lm gave the best value for the F1 measure (0.912) for the pattern N-A, and the function scg gave the best value for the pattern PN-PN (0.931).

In general, we had the weakest results with the patterns O-N, e.g. "terceiro mundo", (third world) and A-PN, e.g. "Nova York", "Santa Catarina". Using the training functions "lm" and "scg", none of the 10 MWEs belonging to the pattern O-O, e.g. "até agora" (until now), "além disso" (moreover, lit. beyond this) was recognized, and none of the 46 MWEs belonging to the pattern O-N was recognized, when using the training function "scg".

The last line of each table presents the total values for the eight patterns, for the three learning functions. We had the best precision and recall using the "lm" function.

			br			lm			scg		
Pattern	**Bigrams**	**MWE**	**Prec.**	**Rec.**	**F1**	**Prec.**	**Rec.**	**F1**	**Prec.**	**Rec.**	**F1**
N-A	229	193	0.867	0.912	0.889	0.845	0.990	0.912	0.850	0.969	0.906
O-N	164	46	0.378	0.304	0.337	0.647	0.239	0.349	0.720	0.000	0.000
PN-PN	117	101	0.862	0.931	0.895	0.863	1.000	0.927	0.871	1.000	0.931
A-N	53	21	0.813	0.619	0.703	0.810	0.810	0.810	0.630	0.810	0.708
O-O	46	10	0.357	0.500	0.417	0.000	0.000	0.000	0.783	0.000	0.000
N-PN	34	16	0.438	0.438	0.438	0.688	0.688	0.688	0.222	0.125	0.160
N-N	31	20	0.647	0.550	0.595	0.696	0.800	0.744	0.692	0.900	0.783
A-PN	15	13	0.750	0.231	0.353	0.500	0.154	0.235	0.667	0.154	0.250
All Pat.	689	420	0.776	0.769	0.773	0.819	0.831	0.825	0.815	0.779	0.797

Table 2: Multi-layer perceptron precision, recall and F-measure in the classification of the most common bigram's patterns using different training functions: Bayesian regulation back-propagation (br), Levenberg-Marquardt (lm) and scaled conjugate gradient (scg).

Using Text-NSP tool, we extracted from the entire corpus all the bigrams (including the ones formed by stop words) and we analyzed by hand the 2,000 most frequent bigrams. We found 165 two-word MWEs formed by nouns, adjectives, verbs and other classes (adverbs, pronouns and numerals) and we classified them according to their pattern. Table 3 shows the number of MWEs and their total frequency in the corpus, classified by patterns. The words belonging to the classes of adverb, pronoun and numeral were classified as "O" (other classes).

The much smaller proportion of bigrams recognized as MWEs (165/2000) in comparison to the previous analysis (447/1,170) is explained by the fact that in the previous analysis we had eliminated the stop words before generating the bigrams, and now all the bigrams were generated. This created many bigrams composed by prepositions or conjunctions that do not form MWE, for example: "de um", "de uma", "de São", "que os", "diz que", "do que", "em que".

We note that the five most common patterns are the same as found before, in the small excerpt of text, with the pattern N-A giving the greatest number of expressions, e.g. "ano passado" (last year, lit. year last), "Banco Central" (Central Bank, lit. bank central), "norte americano" (north American), "seleção brasileira" (Brazilian team, lit. selection Brazilian), "equipe econômica" (economic team, lit. team economic). In terms of frequency, the MWEs following the pattern N-A represent about 38% of the most frequent two-word MWEs found in the corpus.

It is important to observe that, although we are not differentiating Brazilian and Portuguese MWEs in this study, the recognized MWEs follow the Brazilian orthography (e.g. "equipe econômica" vs "equipa econômica", "seleção brasileira" vs "selecção brasileira"), since we used a Brazilian Portuguese corpus.

Pattern	**MWE**	**Frequency**
N-A	58	101,442
O-N	27	29,697
PN-PN	24	39,270
O-O	23	13,923
A-N	13	51,460
N-N	12	21,559
A-O	2	1,975
A-PN	2	2,115
V-N	2	2,263
N-PN	1	2,589
N-V	1	1,423
Total	165	267,716

Table 3: Frequency of the most common MWEs patterns extracted from the entire corpus

4.3 Text-NSP

Before applying this tool, the only pre-processing performed in the corpus was to remove the XML tags. The next step was to define a stop words list file like in Subsections 4.1 and 4.2.

We ran the program using the script "count.pl", giving as parameter the stop word file and the corpus file, and 2 as n-gram value, meaning that we wanted to generate only bigrams.

The exit file is a list of all bigrams in the corpus' excerpt, and each line contains a bigram, the frequency of the bigram, and the frequency of each of the two words forming the bigram.

Using the output file and the script "statistics.pl" we generated the candidates' files ranked by the four association measures listed in Subsection 3.4. Then we transformed each of the candidates' files to the XML format used by the MWEtoolkit and we used the MWEtoolkit's scripts to create files with the n-best candidates and to evaluate each of the files against our reference file. Table 4a shows the results of this evaluation.

The results show that for values of n = 50, 100 and 500 we had the best results using the log-likelihood measure and for n = 1000 and 3000, Student's t-test gave the best results.

Table 4b shows the precision, recall and F-measure that we obtained using the log-likelihood measure. We had very good values of precision using the Text-NSP using this measure. For example, from the 50 best ranked candidates by this measure, 31 were MWEs present in our reference list.

4.4 Termostat

Termostat generated n-grams following eleven POS patterns, all of them are nominal ones: N-N, N-A, N-P-N, N-N-N, N-P-N-A, N-N-N-N, N-V-N, N-N-N-N-N, N-A-A, N-N-A and N-A-N. In total, 4,284 n-grams were generated, and we selected only the bigrams (N-N and N-A), which gave 3,458 bigrams (81% of all n-grams). The last five patterns listed above produced less than ten candidates each one and the patterns N-P-N-A, N-N-N-N produced less than 30 candidates each one.

Those 3,458 candidates were ranked according to the four association measures listed in Subsection 3.5. Then we compared the n-best candidates against our reference file. The results are in Table 5a. Table 5b shows the precision, recall and F-measure that we obtained using the log-likelihood measure.

Looking at Table 5a, we notice that we had best performance with χ^2 for the 50 and 100 best candidates and for the 500, 1000 and 3000 best candidates we had better results using the ll measure.

Comparing with Text-NSP, Termostat had best performance for the first 50 and 100 candidates. However, Text-NSP outperformed for n = 500, 1000 and 3000, when using the ll measure and Student's t-test.

	dice	ll	pmi	t
50	7	31	0	23
100	7	64	0	39
500	8	241	1	180
1000	11	314	4	331
3000	69	375	11	392

(a)

ll	TP	Prec.	Recall	F1
50	31	0.62	0.07	0.12
100	64	0.64	0.14	0.23
500	241	0.48	0.54	0.51
1000	314	0.31	0.70	0.43
3000	375	0.13	0.84	0.22

(b)

Table 4: Text-NSP: Number of MWEs among the first n-best candidates, ranked by four association measures (a) and precision, recall and F-measure for the log-likelihood measure (b).

	χ^2	ll	lor	sp
50	42	38	32	38
100	72	68	66	68
500	153	162	117	159
1000	181	197	127	192
3000	198	211	143	208

(a)

ll	TP	Prec.	Recall	F1
50	38	0.76	0.09	0.15
100	68	0.68	0.15	0.25
500	162	0.32	0.36	0.34
1000	197	0.20	0.44	0.27
3000	211	0.07	0.47	0.12

(b)

Table 5: Termostat: Number of MWEs among the first n-best candidates, ranked by four association measures (a) and precision, recall and F-measure for the log-likelihood measure (b).

4.5 Comparing the 500-best candidates of each tool

We analyzed by hand the 500-best candidates obtained using Text-NSP and Termostat, ranked by the log-likelihood association measure, to decide which ones are MWEs. Table 6 shows the precision given by each tool, for the first *n* candidates, $n = 50, 100, 150 \ldots 500$.

With Termostat, we had the best precision for all values of *n* candidates, going from 86% for the first 50 candidates to 82% for the first 500 candidates. Using Text-NSP, the precision starts with 82% for the first best 50 candidates and decreases to 72% for the first 500-best candidates.

As in the tests performed in Subsection 4.2, the most common patterns of MWE found by both tools were noun-adjective, e.g. "Congresso Nacional", "emenda constitucional", "deputado federal" and proper name-proper name, e.g. "Fernando Collor", "Getúlio Vargas", "Itamar Franco".

n first cand.	Text-NSP	Termostat
50	0.82	0.86
100	0.82	0.85
150	0.83	0.86
200	0.79	0.84
250	0.76	0.84
300	0.75	0.84
350	0.74	0.83
400	0.74	0.82
450	0.73	0.81
500	0.72	0.82

Table 6: Text-NSP and Termostat precision for the first *n* best candidates, using log likelihood association measure.

5 Conclusions and Future Work

In this paper, we presented a comparative study on different classification algorithms and tools for the identification of Portuguese multiword expressions, using information about the frequency, the grammatical classes of the words and bigrams and different association measures.

In what concerns the classification algorithms, bagging, decision trees and multi-layer perceptron had a slightly better precision. Using multi-layer perceptron with three different training functions, we identified the part-of-speech patterns that are best classified as two-word MWEs. Using the function Levenberg-Marquardt we had better results in classifying the pattern noun-adjective (the most common in our corpus) and we were more successful in classifying MWEs following the pattern "proper name-proper name" using the function scaled conjugate gradient.

With the objective of making an estimative on the part-of-speech patterns followed by the most frequent two-word MWEs in the corpus, we applied Text-NSP to the extraction of the 2,000 most frequent bigrams and we identified and classified the MWEs, according to their part-of-speech patterns. As a result, we found that the patterns "noun-adjective" and "proper name-proper name" are the most common two-word MWE patterns in the corpus. We also found that verbs do not form a great variety of two-word MWE in Portuguese.

The comparison between tools for the automatic identification of MWEs showed that Termostat had better precision than Text-NSP when applied to a small number of candidates (50 and 100). When the number of candidates increases, Text-NSP had better precision using log-likelihood measure and Student's t-test association measures.

As future work, we intend to apply the same tools, especially Termostat, to a specific domain corpus, in order to compare their performance in the identification of Portuguese multiword terms, not limiting the study to bigrams, but also analyzing n-grams in general.

References

Aha, D. and Kibler, D. (1991). Instance-based learning algorithms. *In: Machine Learning*. 6:37-66.

Antunes, S. and Mendes, A. (2013). MWE in Portuguese - Proposal for a Typology for Annotation in Running Text. *Proceedings of the 9th Workshop on Multiword Expressions (MWE 2013)*, pp. 87–92, Atlanta, Georgia.

Baldwin, T. and Kim, S. N. (2010). Multiword expressions. Nitin Indurkhya and Fred J. Damerau (eds.), *In: Handbook of Natural Language Processing, Second Ed.* Chapman & Hall/CRC, London, UK., pp. 267-292.

Banerjee, S and Pedersen, T. (2003). The Design, Implementation, and Use of the Ngram Statistic Package. *In: Proceedings of Fourth International Conference on Intelligent Text Processing and Computational Linguistics*, pp. 370-381, Mexico City. http://search.cpan.org/~tpederse/Text-NSP/

Baptista, J. (1994). Estabelecimento e Formalização de Classes de Nomes Compostos. Master Thesis. Faculdade de Letras, Universidade de Lisboa, 145 pp.

Breiman, L. (2001). Random Forests. *In: Machine Learning*. 45(1):5-32.

Breiman , L. (1996). Bagging predictors. *In: Machine Learning*. 24(2):123-140.

Chang, Chih-Chung and Lin, Chih-Jen (2001). LIBSVM - A Library for Support Vector Machines. http://www.csie.ntu.edu.tw/~cjlin/libsvm/.

Church, K. W. and Hanks, P (1990). Word Association Norms, Mutual Information and Lexicography. *In: Computational Linguistics*, 16(1):22–29.

Cooper, G. and Herskovits, E. (1992). A Bayesian Method for the Induction of Probabilistic Networks from Data. *In: Machine Learning*. 9(4):309-347.

Drouin, P. (2003). Term Extraction Using Non-technical Corpora as a Point of Leverage, *In: Terminology*, 9(1): 99-117. - http://termostat.ling.umontreal.ca/

Freund, Y. and Schapire, R. E (1996). Experiments with a new boosting algorithm. *In: Thirteenth International Conference on Machine Learning, San Francisco*, pp. 148-156.

Kinoshita, J., Nascimento Salvador, L.D., Dantas de Menezes, C., E. (2006). CoGrOO: a Brazilian-Portuguese Grammar Checker based on the CETENFOLHA Corpus. *In: Proceedings of Fifth International Conference on Language Resources and Evaluation*, pp. 2190-2193.

Lafon, P. (1980). Sur la Variabilité de la Fréquence des Formes dans un Corpus. *In: MOTS*, no 1, pp. 128-165.

Manning, C. D. and Schütze, H. (1999). Foundations of Statistical Natural Language Processing. Cambridge, MA: The MIT Press, 1999, 680 pp.

Mel'čuk, I. (1998). Collocations and Lexical Functions. *In: A.P. Cowie (ed.), Phraseology. Theory, Analysis, and Applications*, 1998, Oxford: Clarendon Press, pp. 23-53.

Moon, R. E. (1998). Fixed Expressions and Idioms in English: A Corpus Based Approach. Oxford: Clarendon Press, 356 pp.

Morgan, J. L. (1978). Two Types of Convention in Indirect Speech acts. *In: P. Cole (ed.), Syntax and Semantics, v.9. Pragmatics* (New York etc.: Academic Press), pp. 261-80.

Piao, S., Rayson, P., Archer, D., Wilson, A., and McEnery, T. (2003). Extracting Multiword Expressions with a Semantic Tagger. *In: Workshop on Multiword Expressions: Analysis, Acquisition and Treatment*, at *ACL 2003, 41st Annual Meeting of the Association for Computational Linguistics*, pp. 49-56, Sapporo, Japan.

Portela, R. J. R. (2011). Identificação Automática de Nomes Compostos. Instituto Superior Técnico, Universidade Técnica de Lisboa. Master Thesis. November 2011, Lisbon, Portugal, 104 pp.

Proost, K. (2007). Conceptual Structure in Lexical Items: The Lexicalisation of Communication Concepts in English, German and Dutch. John Benjamins Pub. Co, 304 pp.

Quinlan, J. R. (1993). C4.5: Programs for Machine Learning. Morgan Kaufmann Publishers, 303 pp.

Ramisch, C. (2012). A Generic and Open Framework for MWE Treatment – From Acquisition to Applications - Ph.D. Thesis, Universidade Federal do Rio Grande do Sul - UFRGS, Brazil, 248 pp. http://mwetoolkit.sourceforge.net/PHITE.php?sitesig=MWE

Smadja, F. A. (1996). Translating Collocations for Bilingual Lexicons: A Statistical Approach. *Association for Computational Linguistics*, 22 (1):1-38.

Towards Automatic Distinction between Specialized and Non-Specialized Occurrences of Verbs in Medical Corpora

Ornella Wandji Tchami, Natalia Grabar
CNRS UMR 8163 STL
Université Lille 3
59653 Villeneuve d'Ascq, France
ornwandji@yahoo.fr, natalia.grabar@univ-lille3.fr

Abstract

The medical field gathers people of different social statuses, such as students, pharmacists, managers, biologists, nurses and mainly medical doctors and patients, who represent the main actors. Despite their different levels of expertise, these actors need to interact and understand each other but the communication is not always easy and effective. This paper describes a method for a contrastive automatic analysis of verbs in medical corpora, based on the semantic annotation of the verbs nominal co-occurents. The corpora used are specialized in cardiology and distinguished according to their levels of expertise (high and low). The semantic annotation of these corpora is performed by using an existing medical terminology. The results indicate that the same verbs occurring in the two corpora show different specialization levels, which are indicated by the words (nouns and adjectives derived from medical terms) they occur with.

1 Introduction

The medical field gathers people of different social statuses, such as medical doctors, students, pharmacists, managers, biologists, nurses, imaging experts and of course patients. These actors have different levels of expertise ranging from low (typically, the patients) up to high (*e.g.*, medical doctors, pharmacists, medical students). Despite their different levels of expertise, these actors need to interact. But their mutual understanding might not always be completely successful. This situation specifically applies to patients and medical doctors who are the two main actors within the medical field (McCray, 2005; Zeng-Treiler et al., 2007). Beyond the medical field, this situation can also apply to other domains (*e.g.*, law, economics, biology). The research question is closely linked to the readability studies (Dubay, 2004), whose purpose is to address the ease with which a document can be read and understood by people, and also the ease with which the corresponding information can be exploited by the people later. As noticed, one source of difficulty may be due to the specific and specialized notions that are used : for instance, *abdominoplasty, hymenorrhaphy, escharotomy* in medical documents, *affidavit, allegation, adjudication* in legal documents, etc. This difficulty occurs at the lexical and conceptual level. Another difficulty may come from complex syntactic structures (*e.g.*, coordinated or subordinated phrases) that can occur in such documents. Hence, this difficulty is of syntactic nature. With very simple features, reduced to the length of words and sentences, the classical readability scores address these two aspects (Flesch, 1948; Dale and Chall, 1948; Bormuth, 1966; Kincaid et al., 1975). Typically, such scores do not account for the semantics of the documents. In recent readability approaches, the semantics is being taken into account through several features, such as: medical terminologies (Kokkinakis and Toporowska Gronostaj, 2006); stylistics of documents (Grabar et al., 2007; Goeuriot et al., 2007); lexicon used (Miller et al., 2007); morphological information (Chmielik and Grabar, 2011); and combination of various features (Wang, 2006; Zeng-Treiler et al., 2007; Leroy et al., 2008; François and Fairon, 2013).

We propose to continue studying the readability level of specialized documents through the semantic features. More precisely, we propose to perform a comparative analysis of verbs observed in medical corpora written in French. These corpora are differentiated according to their levels of expertise and

Proceedings of the 4th International Workshop on Computational Terminology, pages 114–124,
Dublin, Ireland, August 23 2014.

thereby they represent the patients and the medical doctors' languages. Our study focuses on verbs and their co-occurents (nouns and adjectives deriving from medical terms), and aims to investigate on the verb semantics, according to the types of constructions and to the words with which the verb occurs in the corpora. In order to achieve this, we pay a particular attention to the syntactic and semantic features of the verbs' co-occurents in the studied texts.

Our method is based on the hypothesis according to which the meaning of a verb can be influenced or determined by its context of appearance (L'Homme, 2012) and by its arguments. Indeed, various studies on specialized languages have shown that the verb is not specialized by itself (L'Homme, 1998; Lerat, 2002). Rather, being a predicative unit that involves participants called arguments, the verb can be specialized or not, depending on its argumental structure and the nature of these arguments.

In our study, the description of verbs is similar to the one performed in Frame Semantics (FS) (Fillmore, 1982), since we provide semantic information about the verbs co-occurents. The Frame Semantics framework is increasingly used for the description of lexical units in different languages (Atkins et al., 2003; Padó and Pitel, 2007; Burchardt et al., 2009; Borin et al., 2010; Koeva, 2010) and specialized fields (Dolbey et al., 2006; Schmidt, 2009; Pimentel, 2011). Among other things, Frame Semantics provides for a full description of the semantic and syntactic properties of lexical units. FS puts forward the notion of "frames", which are defined as conceptual scenarios that underlie lexical realizations in language. A frame comprises a frame evoking lexical units (ULs) and the Frame Elements (FEs), which represent the participants to the verbal process. For instance, in FrameNet (Ruppenhofer et al., 2006), the frame CURE is described as a situation that involves some specific Frame Elements, (such as HEALER, AFFLICTION, PATIENT, TREATMENT), and includes a lexical unit such as *cure, alleviate, heal, incurable, treat.*[1] In our approach, an FS-like modeling should allow us to describe the semantic properties of verbs. Using this framework, we will be able to highlight the differences between the studied verbs usages through their various frames and, by doing so, uncover the linguistic differences observed in corpora of different levels of expertise. However, the FS framework will be adapted in order to fit our own objectives. Indeed, the automatic annotation of the verbs co-occurents into frames will rely on the use of a terminology (Côté, 1996) which provides a semantic category for each recorded term. These categories (*e.g.*, anatomy, disorders, procedures, chemical products) typically apply to the verb co-occurents and should be evocative of the semantics of these co-occurents and the semantic properties of verbs: we consider that the semantic categories represent the frame elements which are lexically realized by the terms, while the verbs represent the frame evoking lexical units.

In a previous study, we have looked at the behavior of four verbs (*observer* (*observe*), *détecter* (*detect*), *développer* (*develop*), and *activer* (*activate*)) in medical corpora written by medical doctors by contrast to texts written by patients (Wandji Tchami et al., 2013). The results showed that in the corpus written by doctors some verbs tend to have specific meanings, according to the type of arguments that surround them. In the current work, we try to go further by enhancing our method (improved semantic annotation, automated analysis of verbs) and by distinguishing specialized and non-specialized occurrences of verbs.

In the next sections, we present the material used (section 2), the method designed (section 3). We then introduce the results and discuss them (section 4), and conclude with future work (section 5).

2 Material

We use several kinds of material: the corpora to be processed (section 2.1), the semantic resources (section 2.2), a resource with verbal forms and lemmas (section 2.3) and a list of stopwords (section 2.4).

2.1 Corpora

We study two medical corpora dealing with the specific field of cardiology (heart disorders and treatments). These corpora are distinguished according to their levels of expertise and their discursive specificities (Pearson, 1998): *Expert* corpus contains expert documents written by medical experts for medical experts. This corpus typically contains scientific publications, and show a high level of expertise. The

[1] *https://framenet.icsi.berkeley.edu/fndrupal*

corpus is collected through the CISMeF portal[2], which indexes French language medical documents and assigns them categories according to the topic they deal with (*e.g.*, cardiology, intensive care) and to their levels of expertise (*i.e.*, for medical experts, medical students or patients). *Forum* corpus contains non-expert documents written by patients for patients. This corpus contains messages from the Doctissimo forum *Hypertension Problemes Cardiaques*[3]. It shows low level of expertise, although technical terms may also be used. The size of corpora in terms of occurrences of words is indicated in Table 1. We can see that, in number of occurrences, these two corpora are comparable as for their sizes.

Corpus	Size (occ of words)
Expert	1,285,665
Forum	1,588,697

Table 1: Size of the two corpora studied.

2.2 Semantic resources

The semantic annotation of corpora is performed using the Snomed International terminology (Côté, 1996). This resource provides terms which use is suitable for the NLP processing of documents, as these are expressions close to those used in real documents. It is structured into several semantic axes:

$\mathcal{T}$: TOPOGRAPHY or ANATOMICAL LOCATIONS (*e.g.*, *coeur (heart), cardiaque (cardiac), digestif (digestive), vaisseau (vessel)*);

$\mathcal{S}$: SOCIAL STATUS (*e.g.*, *mari (husband), soeur (sister), mère (mother), ancien fumeur (former smoker), donneur (donnor)*);

$\mathcal{P}$: PROCEDURES (*e.g.*, *césarienne (caesarean), transducteur à ultrasons (ultrasound transducer), télé-expertise (tele-expertise)*);

$\mathcal{L}$: LIVING ORGANISMS, such as bacteries and viruses (*e.g.*, *Bacillus, Enterobacter, Klebsiella, Salmonella*), but also human subjects (*e.g.*, *patients (patients), traumatisés (wounded), tu (you)*);

$\mathcal{J}$: PROFESSIONAL OCCUPATIONS (*e.g.*, *équipe de SAMU (ambulance team), anesthésiste (anesthesiologist), assureur (insurer), magasinier (storekeeper)*);

$\mathcal{F}$: FUNCTIONS of the organism (*e.g.*, *pression artérielle (arterial pressure), métabolique (metabolic), protéinurie (proteinuria), détresse (distress), insuffisance (deficiency)*);

$\mathcal{D}$: DISORDERS and pathologies (*e.g.*, *obésité (obesity), hypertension artérielle (arterial hypertension), cancer (cancer), maladie (disease)*);

$\mathcal{C}$: CHEMICAL PRODUCTS (*e.g.*, *médicament (medication), sodium, héparine (heparin), bleu de méthylène (methylene blue)*);

$\mathcal{A}$: PHYSICAL AGENTS (*e.g.*, *prothèses (prosthesis), tube (tube), accident (accident), cathéter (catheter)*).

Further to our previous work (Wandji Tchami et al., 2013), we have added another semantic axis $\mathcal{E}$ STUDIES, that groups terms related to the scientific work and experiments (*e.g.*, *méthode (method), hypothèse (hypothesis)*...). Such notions are quite frequent in the corpora, while they are missing in the terminology used. The only semantic category of Snomed that we ignore in this analysis contains modifiers (*e.g.*, *aigu (acute), droit (right), antérieur (anterior)*), which are meaningful only in combination with other terms. Besides, such descriptors can occur within medical and non-medical contexts.

As stated above, we expect these semantic categories to be indicative of frame elements (FEs), while the individual terms should correspond to lexical realizations of those FEs, as in Framenet. For instance,

[2] *http://www.cismef.org/*

[3] *http://forum.doctissimo.fr/sante/hypertension-problemes-cardiaques/liste_sujet-1.htm*

the Snomed category DISORDERS should allow us to discover and group under a single label terms that denote the same notion (*e.g.*, *hypertension* (*hypertension*), *obésité* (*obesity*)) related to the FE DISORDER.

The existing terminologies may not provide the entire coverage of the domain notions (Chute et al., 1996; Humphreys et al., 1997; Hole and Srinivasan, 2000; Penz et al., 2004). For this reason, we attempted to complete the coverage of the Snomed International terminology in relation with the corpora used. We addressed this question in two ways:

- We computed the plural forms for simple terms that contain one word only. The motivation for this processing is that the terminologies often record terms in singular forms, while the documents may contain singular and plural forms of these terms.
- We tried to detect the misspellings of the terms using the string edit distance (Levenshtein, 1966). This measure considers three operations: deletion, addition and substitution of characters. Each operations cost is set to 1. For instance, the Levenshtein distance between *ambolie* and *embolie* is 1, that corresponds to the substitution of *a* by *e*. The minimal length of the processed words should not be lesser than six characters, because with shorter words the propositions contain too much of errors. The motivation for this kind of processing is that it is possible and frequent to find misspelled words in real documents, especially in the forum discussions (Balahur, 2013).

In both cases, the computed forms inherit the semantic type of the terms from the terminology. For instance, *ambolie* inherits the $\mathcal{D}$ DISORDER semantic type of *embolie*. Besides, we also added the medication names from the Thériaque resource[4]. These are assigned to the $\mathcal{C}$ CHEMICAL PRODUCTS semantic type. The whole resource contains 158,298 entries.

2.3 Resource with verbal forms

We have built a resource with inflected forms of verbs: 177,468 forms for 1,964 verbs. The resource is built from the information available online[5]. The resource contains simple (*consulte, consultes, consultons* (*consult*)) and complex (*ai consulté, avons consulté* (*have consulted*)) verbal forms. This resource is required for the lemmatization of verbs (section 3.3).

2.4 List of stopwords

The list of stopwords contains grammatical units, such as prepositions, determinants, pronouns and conjunctions. It provides 263 entries.

3 Method

We first perform the description of verbs in a way similar to FS and then compare the observations made in the two corpora processed. The proposed method comprises three steps: corpora pre-processing (section 3.1), semantic annotation (section 3.2), and contrastive analysis of verbs (section 3.3). The method relies on some existing tools and on specifically designed Perl scripts.

3.1 Corpora pre-processing

The corpora are collected online from the websites indicated above and properly formatted. The corpora are then analyzed syntactically using the Bonsai parser (Candito et al., 2010). Its output contains sentences segmented into syntactic chunks (*e.g.*, NP, PP, VP) in which words are assigned parts of speech, as shown in the example that follows:

> *Le traitement repose sur les dérivés thiazidiques, plus accessibles, disponibles sous forme de médicaments génériques.*
> (*The treatment is based on thiazidic derivates, more easily accessible, and available as generic drugs.*)
> *((SENT (NP (DET Le) (NC traitement)) (VN (V repose)) (PP (P sur) (NP (DET les) (NC*

[4] *http://www.theriaque.org/*
[5] *http://leconjugueur.lefigaro.fr/frlistedeverbe.php*

dérivés) (AP (ADJ thiazidiques) (COORD (PONCT ,) (NP (DET les) (ADV plus) (ADJ accessibles)) (PONCT ,) (AP (ADJ disponibles)))) (PP (P sous_forme_de) (NP (NC médicaments) (AP (ADJ génériques)))))))))

The syntactic parsing was performed in order to identify the syntactic chunks, nominal and verbal, to prepare the recognition and annotation of the terms they contain and to better the recognition of verbs. The Bonsai parser was chosen: it is adapted for french texts and it provides several hierarchical syntactic levels within the sentences and phrases. For instance, the phrase *médicaments génériques* (*generic drugs*) is syntactically analyzed as NP: *(NP (NC médicaments) (AP (ADJ génériques))))* that contains one NP *médicaments* and two APs *génériques* and the final dot. The VP of the sentence contains the verb *repose* (*is based*). As we can observe, the output of the Bonsai parser neither provides the lemmas of the forms nor the syntactic dependencies between the constituents. So our study concentrates on the verbs co-occurences with nouns, noun phrases and some relationnal adjectives. The further analysis of the corpora is based on this output.

3.2 Semantic annotation

The Bonsai format is first converted into the XML format: we work on the XML-tree structure. The semantic annotation of the corpora is done automatically. For this task, the Snomed International terminology was chosen because it is suitable for french and it offers a better outreach of the french medical language. We perform the projection of terms from the terminology on the syntactically parsed texts :

- All the chunks (NPs, PPs, APs and VPs) are processed from the largest to the smallest chunks, within which we try to recognize the terminology entries which co-occur with the verbs in the corpora. Indeed, at this stage, since our chunker does not provide dependency relations, we can only work on nouns and noun phrases that co-occur with the verbs. For instance, the largest chunk *(NP (NC médicaments) (AP (ADJ génériques))))* gives *médicaments génériques*, (*generic drugs*) that is not known in the terminology. We then test *médicaments* (*drugs*) and *génériques* (*generic*), of which *médicaments* (*drugs*) is found in the terminology and tagged with the $\mathcal{C}$ CHEMICAL PRODUCTS semantic type.
- Those VPs in which no terms have been identified are considered to be verbal forms or verbs.

Examples of corpora enriched with the semantic information are shown in Figures 1 (expert corpus) and 2 (forum corpus). In these Figures, verbs are in bold characters, semantic labels for the verbs co-occurents are represented by different colors: DISORDERS in red, FUNCTIONS in purple, ANATOMY in clear blue. These semantic categories, provided by the terminological resource, label the words that are likely to correspond to FEs.

Figure 1: Examples of annotations in expert corpus

We can see that in the two corpora, there are both short and long sentences. Besides, the terms recognized are often atomic. For instance, we do not recognize complex terms *embolie pulmonaire* and *thrombose du tronc*, but their simple atomic components *embolie, pulmonaire, thrombose* and *tronc*. Also, some terms match none of the terminology's entries because they are part of VPs, such as *cathéter* in Figure 1.

Ayant **été** victime d' une thrombose$_{NC}$ du tronc$_{NC}$ basilaire par ischémie$_{NC}$, **je recherche** d'_autres femmes$_{NC}$ dans mon cas , en_particulier celles qui **ont pris** un contraceptif$_{NC}$ oral$_{ADJ}$ durant les périodes antérieures$_{VPP}$ à leur AVC$_{NC}$ ..

Avez -vous gardé comme moi des séquelles$_{NC}$ notables et quels traitements$_{NC}$ (médicamenteux$_{ADJ}$ ou rééducatifs) vous **ont -ils été** indiqués ?

Figure 2: Examples of annotations in forum corpus.

3.3 Automatic analysis of verbs

For the analysis of the verbs, we extract information related to verbs and to the words with which they occur. Currently, only sentences with one VP are processed 8 842 sentences for the expert corpus and 10 563 for the forum corpus.

- *Lemmatization of verbs.* As we noticed, the syntactic parser's output does not provide the lemmas. For the lemmatization of the verbs, we use the verbal resource described in section 2.3. Hence, the content of the verbal chunk is analyzed:
  - it may contain a simple or complex verbal form that exists in the resource, in which case we record the corresponding lemma;
  - if the whole chunk doesnot appear in the resource, we check out its atomic components: if all or some of these components are known, we record the corresponding lemmas. This case may apply to passive structures (*a été conseillé* (*has been advised*)), insertions (*est souvent conseillé is often advised*) or negations (*n'est pas conseillé* (*is not advised*)): in these cases, the lemmas are *avoir être conseiller*, *être conseiller* and *être conseiller*. These lemmas will be normalized in the further step: the head verb will be chosen automatically and considered as the main lemma within the verbal phrase;
  - finally, the VPs may consist of words that are not known in the verb resource. These may be morphologically contructed verbs (*réévaluer* (*reevaluate*)) or, words from other parts of speech, errouneously considered as verbs (*e.g., télédéclaration, artérielle, stroke*). This is unfortunately a very frequent case.
- *Extraction of information related to the verb co-occurents.* For the extraction of these information, we consider all the verbs appearing in sentences with one VP. For each verb, we distinguish between:
  - semantically annotated co-occurents, that are considered to be specialized;
  - and the remaining content of the sentence (except the words that are part of the stoplist), more precisely noun phrases, is considered to contain non specialized co-occurents.

  In both cases, for each verb, we compute the number and the percentage of words in each of the above mentionned categories of co-occurents.

Finally, we provide a general analysis of the corpora. For each verb, we compute: the number of occurrences in each corpus, the total, minimal, maximal and average numbers of co-occurents, both specialized and non-specialized. On the basis of this information, we analyse the differences and similarities which may exist between the use of verbs in the two corpora studied. The purpose is to provide information about the specialized and non-specialized occurrences of verbs.

4 Results and Discussion

4.1 Corpora pre-processing

The parsing, done with the Bonsai parser, provided the syntactic annotation of corpora into syntactic constituents. We have noticed some limitations:

- The Bonsai parser does not perform the lemmatization of lexical units whereas we needed to extract the verbs lemmas. The use of external resources made it possible to overcome this limitation;

- The verbal chunks do not always contain verbal constituents, but can contain other parts of speech (*e.g.*, *télédéclaration, artérielle, stroke*) and even punctuation. This is an important limitation for our work, mainly because we focus on verbs. Therefore, if we cannot extract the verbs properly, this can obviously have a negative impact on the final results. These limitations, resulting from the Bonsai parser, highlight some of the issues that characterize the state of arts as far as the syntatic analysis for French is concerned. For the future work, we are planning to try other syntactic parsers for French.

4.2 Semantic annotation

Concerning the semantic annotation we have made several observations:

- Some annotations are missing, such as *site d'insertion* (*insertion site*) that can be labeled as TOPOGRAPHY or *risque* (*risk*) as FUNCTION. This limitation is also related to the annotation of the forum corpus, that often contains misspellings or non-specialized equivalents of the terms. This limitation must be addressed in future work in order to detect new terms or the variations of the existing terms to make the annotation more exhaustive;

- Other annotations are erroneous, such as *or* (*ou*) in French annotated as CHEMICALS (*gold*)) in English-language sentences. In future, the sentences in English will be forehand filtered out at the processing stage;

- The terminological variation and the syntactic parsing provided by Bonsai make the recognition of several complex terms difficult. As we noticed previously, we mainly recognize simple atomic terms. For the current purpose, this is not a real limitation: the main objective is to detect the specialized and non-specialized words that co-occur with the verbs. Still, the number and semantic types of these words co-occuring with verbs can become biased. For instance, instead of one DISORDER term *embolie pulmonaire* (*air embolism*), we obtain one DISORDER term *embolie* (*embolism*) and one ANATOMY term *pulmonaire* (*air*).

4.3 Automatic analysis of verbs

The contrastive analysis of the words, co-occuring with verbs, provides the main results of the proposed study.

Corpus	$Total_V$	$Total_{coocc}$	$Total_{sp-coocc}$	$Total_{\neg sp-coocc}$	$A_{sp-coocc}/V$	$A_{\neg sp-coocc}/V$
Expert Ex	545	17632	8354	9272	15	17
Forum Fo	592	10852	5545	5307	9	8

Table 2: General information related to the verbs and their co-occurent words: total and average numbers of co-occurents

In Table 2, we compute the total number of verbs ($Total_V$), the total number of words co-occuring with verbs per corpus ($Total_{coocc}$), the total number of non specialized co-occurents per corpus ($N_{sp-coocc}$), the average number of specialized co-occurents per verb ($A_{sp-coocc}/V$), the average number of non specialized per verb ($A_{\neg sp-coocc}/V$). We can notice that the forum corpus provides slightly more verbs than the expert corpus. This observation might be considered to be obvious, since the forum corpus is a bit larger than the expert corpus. But if we combine this with the fact that the numbers and average numbers of co-occurents (specialized and non-specialized) are higher in the expert corpus, then the observation start making sense, since these results can be related to the confirmation by (Condamines and Bourigault, 1999) of the fact that nominal forms tend to be more frequent in specialized texts, whereas verbal forms tend to be more frequent in non-specialized texts. However, it is important to notice that some candidates in the list of non-specialized co-occurents have to be filtered out, such as adverbs (*conformément, régulièrement, précocément, partiellement*) and non relationnal adjectives (*variables, inconscients, différents*). The abundance of adverbs in the expert corpus (Table 4) by contrast to the forum corpus, where their presence seems to be less important, is consistent with the previous work, which show that non-specialized documents tend to have simpler syntactic and semantic structures (Wandji Tchami et al., 2013) and less adverbs (Brouwers et al., 2012).

Verbs	N_{occ}		N_{coocc}		$N_{sp-coocc}$		$\%_{sp-coocc}$		$N_{\neg sp-coocc}$		$\%_{\neg sp-coocc}$		$A_{sp-coocc}$		$A_{\neg sp-coocc}$	
	Ex	Fo	Ex	Fo	Ex	Fo	Ex	Fo	Ex	Fo	Ex	Fo	Ex	Fo	Ex	Fo
augmenter	21	14	122	52	62	26	51.5	56.2	60	26	48.4	43.7	2.9	1.8	2.8	1.8
causer	5	7	26	27	17	19	72	68.2	9	8	28	31.72	3.4	2.7	1.8	1.1
favoriser	10	6	56	22	38	17	70.5	77.3	18	5	29.4	22.6	3.8	2.8	1.8	0.8
prescrire	6	29	30	108	16	71	58.9	69.7	14	37	41	30.2	2.6	2.4	2.3	1.2
provoquer	7	15	60	64	32	37	57	70.2	28	27	42.9	29.7	4.5	2.4	4	1.8
risquer	7	7	18	13	12	11	1.7	1.5	6	2	0.8	0.2	78.5	90	21.42	10
signaler	12	4	73	14	32	7	46.9	48.3	41	7	53	51.6	2.6	1.7	3.4	1.7
subir	4	24	20	98	15	54	76.1	63	5	44	23.8	36.9	3.7	2.5	1.2	1.8
traiter	24	17	107	67	66	34	65	60.2	41	33	34.9	39.7	2.7	2	1.7	1.9

Table 3: Information on some verbs that occur in Expert Ex and Forum Fo corpora

In Table 3, we give similar information but for with individual verbs. For each verb, in every corpus, we compute the number of occurence (N_{occ}), the number of words (N_{coocc}) occuring with the verb, the number of specialized co-occurents ($N_{sp-coocc}$), the percentage of specialized co-occurents ($\%_{sp-coocc}$), the number of non specialized co-occurents ($N_{\neg sp-coocc}$), the percentage of non specialized co-occurents ($\%_{\neg sp-coocc}$), the average number of specialized co-occurents ($A_{sp-coocc}$) and the average number of non specialized co-occurents ($A_{\neg sp-coocc}$). These verbs are chosen because they occur in the two corpora studied and because they are sufficiently frequent as compared to others. In our opinion, these verbs may receive specialized and non-specialized meanings according to their usage. Indeed, Table 3 shows that these verbs behave differently according to the corpus. On the one hand, there are verbs (*e.g.*, *augmenter, favoriser, signaler, traiter, risquer*) that occur with an important number of specialized co-occurents in the Experts Ex corpus while they have lower numbers of specialized co-occurents in the Forum Fo corpus. On the other hand, there are verbs (*e.g.*, *causer, subir, prescrire*) that have more specialized co-occurents in the Forum corpus than in the Expert corpus. If we consider the number of occurrences of these verbs, we can definitely notice that some of them (*e.g.* *causer* and *subir*) regularly occur with more specialized co-occurents in the Expert corpus (although with lower number of specialized co-occurents) than in the Forum corpus. This means that their frames involve different numbers of specialized co-occurents, that are higher in the Expert corpus.

In table 4, we show the frequent co-occurents for five verbs. We can propose two main observations:

- Some verbs involve an important number of specialized co-occurents, that have different semantic types in the Expert and Forum corpora. For instance, the verb *augmenter* provides a total of 88 specialized co-occurents that belong to nine semantic types ($\mathcal{D}$, $\mathcal{P}$, $\mathcal{S}$, $\mathcal{J}$, $\mathcal{C}$, $\mathcal{F}$, $\mathcal{T}$, $\mathcal{L}$ and $\mathcal{A}$). The most frequent among them are $\mathcal{F}$ (27), $\mathcal{D}$ (18), $\mathcal{T}$ (15), and $\mathcal{P}$ (9), and occur mostly in the Expert corpus. These might be more general verbs, with weaker specific selectional restrictions.

- Other verbs frequently occur with specialized terms that belong to a specific semantic type. This most frequent label can be specific to one corpus only or simultaneously to the two. For instance, for the verb *prescrire*, the most frequent labels are the same in the two corpora: $\mathcal{C}$, $\mathcal{J}$, $\mathcal{P}$ and $\mathcal{T}$ terms. *Traiter* frequently occurs, in the two corpora, with $\mathcal{C}$ and $\mathcal{D}$ terms.

The general observation is that, for a given verb, the Expert corpus shows more sophisticated syntactic structures with higher number of specialized co-occurents. Besides, some verbs may show similar or different behavior in the two corpora studied. According to the objectives of the proposed work, we consider that an important presence of specialized terms in a sentence or corpus indicates a very specialized use and meaning of the verbs. Quantitative and qualitative analysis of the data support this first study and results.

	$sp - coocc$		$\neg sp - coocc$	
verbs	*Expert*	*Forum*	*Expert*	*Forum*
augmenter	thrombolyses/$\mathcal{F}$, gliomes/$\mathcal{D}$, O2/$\mathcal{C}$, rétinopathie/$\mathcal{D}$, Glasgow/$\mathcal{P}$, myocardique/$\mathcal{T}$	BNP/$\mathcal{P}$, infarctus/$\mathcal{D}$, lasilix/$\mathcal{C}$, mouvements/$\mathcal{A}$, tabac/$\mathcal{L}$	inférieur, égal, score, groupe, inconscients, précocément	heures, légèrement
prescrire	protocole/$\mathcal{P}$, anticoagulant/$\mathcal{C}$, BNP/$\mathcal{P}$	comprimé/$\mathcal{C}$, diurétique/$\mathcal{C}$, médecin/$\mathcal{J}$	ministre, publication, régulièrement	jour, matin, variables
produire	pression/$\mathcal{F}$, contraction/$\mathcal{D}$	spasmes/$\mathcal{F}$, coronnaires/$\mathcal{T}$, stenosees/$\mathcal{D}$	gauche, grande, onde, antérograde, différents	général, déja
traiter	hypoglycémies/$\mathcal{D}$, prévention/$\mathcal{P}$	insuffisance/$\mathcal{F}$, cardiaque/$\mathcal{T}$, anévrismes/$\mathcal{D}$	réccurentes, cas, partiellement	succès, près de, suite
provoquer	fibrose/$\mathcal{D}$, tissus/$\mathcal{A}$, nerveux/$\mathcal{T}$, Vibrio/$\mathcal{L}$, vomissements/$\mathcal{F}$	extrasystoles/T, AVC/$\mathcal{D}$, père/$\mathcal{S}$, malaise/$\mathcal{F}$, mouvement/$\mathcal{A}$	secondaires, volontairement, insatisfaisantes, relativement, peu, alimentaire, striés	différent, beaucoup, génant, angoissant, mini, gros, longue, petite, soirée
subir	patient/$\mathcal{J}$, arthroplastie/$\mathcal{P}$	pose/$\mathcal{P}$, fibrillation/$\mathcal{F}$, AVC/$\mathcal{D}$	raison,fixateur, externe	fuite, grade

Table 4: Description of the verbs co-occurents

5 Conclusion

We have proposed an automatic method to distinguish between specialized and non-specialized occurrences of verbs in medical corpora. This work is intended to enhance the previous study (Wandji-2013). Indeed, the method used has changed from semi-automatic to completely automatic; and a new task is performed in order to enhance the annotation process : the syntactic parsing of the corpora. Also, some new materials are used namely the Bonsai parser, the resource of verbal forms, the stoplist. There is an increase in the quantity of data analyzed; all the verbs of the various corpora were considered in this study. The annotation is based on an approach similar to Frame Semantics, considering the fact that semantic information related to the verbs co-occurents are provided through the use of a medical terminology. Though our method is still under development, it has helped to notice that some verbs regularly co-occur with specialized terms in a given context or corpus while in another, the same verbs mostly occurs with general language words. This observation takes us back to the issue of text readability, described in the introduction. Indeed, the verbs whose occurences are characterized by the predominance of specialized terms, can be considered as sources of reading difficulties for non experts in medecine.

6 Future work

We plan to extend this study in different ways. The recognition of the verb neighbors must be improved with the main objective to make the annotations more exhaustive. In this study, we have portrayed the verbs behaviors and their relations with the words with which they occur in the corpora. However, our aim is to automatically identify the verbs arguments, among his co-occurents. We also plan to peform an automatic distinction between : the syntactic functions (subject, object, etc.) of the verbs arguments and the core and non-core elements. We also plan to compute the dependency relations within sentences, either by using another chunker or by integrating to our treatment chain a tool that can perform this task. In addition, we will concentrate on the description of semantic frames of the medical verbs and on the identification of other eventual reading difficulties that might be related to the verbs usages in the corpora. As indicated above, we processed sentences that have only one verbal phrase (8 842 for the Forum corpus and 10 563 for the Expert corpus). In the future, we will process other sentences, coordinated or subordinated, which will be segmented into simple propositions before the processing. Another point is related to the exploitation of these findings for the simplification of medical documents at two levels: syntactic and lexical. Finally, working at a fine-grained verbal semantics, we can distinguish the uses of verbs according to whether their semantics and frames remain close or indicate different meanings.

Acknowledgements

The authors acknowledge the support of the French Agence Nationale de la Recherche (ANR) and the DGA, under the Tecsan grant ANR-11-TECS-012.

References

S Atkins, M Rundell, and H Sato. 2003. The contribution of framenet to practical lexicography. *International Journal of Lexicography*, 16(3):333–357.

A Balahur. 2013. Sentiment analysis in social media texts. In *Computational Approaches to Subjectivity, Sentiment and Social Media Analysis*, pages 120–128.

L Borin, D Dannélls, M Forsberg, M Toporowska Gronostaj, and D Kokkinakis. 2010. The past meets the present in the swedish framenet++. In *14th EURALEX International Congress*, pages 269–281.

J Bormuth. 1966. Readability: A new approach. *Reading research quarterly*, 1(3):79–132.

Laetitia Brouwers, Delphine Bernhard, Anne-Laure Ligozat, and Thomas François. 2012. Simplification syntaxique de phrases pour le français. In *TALN*, pages 211–224.

A Burchardt, K Erk, A Frank, A Kowalski, S Padó, and M Pinkal, 2009. *Using FrameNet for the semantic analysis of German: Annotation, representation, and automation*, pages 209–244.

M Candito, J Nivre, P Denis, and E Anguiano. 2010. Benchmarking of statistical dependency parsers for french. In *International Conference on Computational Linguistics*, pages 108–116.

J Chmielik and N Grabar. 2011. Détection de la spécialisation scientifique et technique des documents biomédicaux grâce aux informations morphologiques. *TAL*, 51(2):151–179.

CG Chute, SP Cohn, KE Campbell, DE Oliver, and JR Campbell. 1996. The content coverage of clinical classifications. for the computer-based patient record institute's work group on codes & structures. *J Am Med Inform Assoc*, 3(3):224–33.

Anne Condamines and Didier Bourigault. 1999. Alternance nom/verbe : explorations en corpus spécialisés. In *Cahiers de l'Elsap*, pages 41–48, Caen, France.

RA Côté, 1996. *Répertoire d'anatomopathologie de la SNOMED internationale, v3.4*. Université de Sherbrooke, Sherbrooke, Québec.

E Dale and JS Chall. 1948. A formula for predicting readability. *Educational research bulletin*, 27:11–20.

AM Dolbey, M Ellsworth, and J Scheffczyk. 2006. BioFrameNet: A domain-specific FrameNet extension with links to biomedical ontologies. In *KR-MED*. 87-94.

William H. Dubay. 2004. The principles of readability. *Impact Information*. Available at *http://almacenplantillasweb.es/wp-content/uploads/2009/11/The-Principles-of-Readability.pdf*.

C Fillmore, 1982. *Frame Semantics*, pages 111–137.

R Flesch. 1948. A new readability yardstick. *Journal of Applied Psychology*, 23:221–233.

T François and C Fairon. 2013. Les apports du TAL à la lisibilité du français langue étrangère. *TAL*, 54(1):171–202.

L Goeuriot, N Grabar, and B Daille. 2007. Caractérisation des discours scientifique et vulgarisé en français, japonais et russe. In *TALN*, pages 93–102.

N Grabar, S Krivine, and MC Jaulent. 2007. Classification of health webpages as expert and non expert with a reduced set of cross-language features. In *AMIA*, pages 284–288.

WT Hole and S Srinivasan. 2000. Discovering missed synonymy in a large concept-oriented metathesaurus. In *AMIA 2000*, pages 354–8.

BL Humphreys, AT McCray, and ML Cheh. 1997. Evaluating the coverage of controlled health data terminologies: report on the results of the NLM/AHCPR large scale vocabulary test. *J Am Med Inform Assoc*, 4(6):484–500.

JP Kincaid, RP Jr Fishburne, RL Rogers, and BS Chissom. 1975. Derivation of new readability formulas (automated readability index, fog count and flesch reading ease formula) for navy enlisted personnel. Technical report, Naval Technical Training, U. S. Naval Air Station, Memphis, TN.

S Koeva. 2010. Lexicon and grammar in bulgarian framenet. In *LREC'10*.

D Kokkinakis and M Toporowska Gronostaj. 2006. Comparing lay and professional language in cardiovascular disorders corpora. In Australia Pham T., James Cook University, editor, *WSEAS Transactions on BIOLOGY and BIOMEDICINE*, pages 429–437.

P Lerat. 2002. Qu'est-ce que le verbe spécialisé? le cas du droit. *Cahiers de Lexicologie*, 80:201–211.

G Leroy, S Helmreich, J Cowie, T Miller, and W Zheng. 2008. Evaluating online health information: Beyond readability formulas. In *AMIA 2008*, pages 394–8.

V. I. Levenshtein. 1966. Binary codes capable of correcting deletions, insertions and reversals. *Soviet physics. Doklady*, 707(10).

MC L'Homme. 1998. Le statut du verbe en langue de spécialité et sa description lexicographique. *Cahiers de lexicologie*, 73(2):61–84.

Marie-Claude L'Homme. 2012. Le verbe terminologique: un portrait des travaux récents. In *CMLF 2012*, pages 93–107.

A McCray. 2005. Promoting health literacy. *J of Am Med Infor Ass*, 12:152–163.

T Miller, G Leroy, S Chatterjee, J Fan, and B Thoms. 2007. A classifier to evaluate language specificity of medical documents. In *HICSS*, pages 134–140.

S Padó and G Pitel. 2007. Annotation précise du francais en sémantique de rôles par projection cross-linguistique. In *TALN 2007*.

J Pearson. 1998. *Terms in Context*, volume 1 of *Studies in Corpus Linguistics*. John Benjamins, Amsterdam/Philadelphia.

JF Penz, SH Brown, JS Carter, PL Elkin, VN Nguyen, SA Sims, and MJ Lincoln. 2004. Evaluation of snomed coverage of veterans health administration terms. In *Medinfo*, pages 540–4.

J Pimentel. 2011. Description de verbes juridiques au moyen de la sémantique des cadres. In *TOTH*.

J Ruppenhofer, M Ellsworth, MRL Petruck, C R. Johnson, and J Scheffczyk. 2006. Framenet ii: Extended theory and practice. Technical report, FrameNet. Available online http://framenet.icsi.berkeley.edu.

T Schmidt, 2009. *The Kicktionary – A Multilingual Lexical Resource of Football Language*, pages 101–134.

O Wandji Tchami, MC L'Homme, and N Grabar. 2013. Discovering semantic frames for a contrastive study of verbs in medical corpora. In *Terminologie et intelligence artificielle (TIA)*, Villetaneuse.

Y Wang. 2006. Automatic recognition of text difficulty from consumers health information. In IEEE, editor, *Computer-Based Medical Systems*, pages 131–136.

Q Zeng-Treiler, H Kim, S Goryachev, A Keselman, L Slaugther, and CA Smith. 2007. Text characteristics of clinical reports and their implications for the readability of personal health records. In *MEDINFO*, pages 1117–1121, Brisbane, Australia.

Author Index